Palgrave Studies in Prisons and Penology

Series editors
Ben Crewe
Institute of Criminology
University of Cambridge
Cambridge, United Kingdom

Yvonne Jewkes
School of Applied Social Science
University of Brighton
Brighton, United Kingdom

Thomas Ugelvik
Criminology and Sociology of Law
Faculty of Law, University of Oslo
Oslo, Norway

This is a unique and innovative series, the first of its kind dedicated entirely to prison scholarship. At a historical point in which the prison population has reached an all-time high, the series seeks to analyse the form, nature and consequences of incarceration and related forms of punishment. Palgrave Studies in Prisons and Penology provides an important forum for burgeoning prison research across the world. Series Advisory Board: Anna Eriksson (Monash University), Andrew M. Jefferson (DIGNITY - Danish Institute Against Torture), Shadd Maruna (Rutgers University), Jonathon Simon (Berkeley Law, University of California) and Michael Welch (Rutgers University).

More information about this series at
http://www.palgrave.com/gp/series/14596

Dario Melossi • Massimo Pavarini

The Prison and the Factory (40th Anniversary Edition)

Origins of the Penitentiary System

palgrave
macmillan

Dario Melossi
University of Bologna
Bologna, Italy

Massimo Pavarini
University of Bologna
Bologna, Italy

1981 Sections translated by Glynis Cousin

Palgrave Studies in Prisons and Penology
ISBN 978-1-137-56589-1   ISBN 978-1-137-56590-7   (eBook)
DOI 10.1057/978-1-137-56590-7

Library of Congress Control Number: 2017954182

Cover illustration: The cover illustration shows a team of raspers at work in the Amsterdam Rasphuys in the late sixteenth century

Printed on acid-free paper

This Palgrave Macmillan imprint is published by Springer Nature
The registered company is Macmillan Publishers Ltd.
The registered company address is: The Campus, 4 Crinan Street, London, N1 9XW, United Kingdom

IN MEMORY OF MASSIMO PAVARINI (1947–2015)

Preface (2017): Melossi and Pavarini's The Prison and the Factory

Today the study of punishment and society, global patterns and genealogies of penal practices is one of the most lively subfields in the social sciences and humanities, generating scores of articles, edited volumes and monographs every year. Little wonder, you might say, the great pillars of social theory—Emile Durkheim, Max Weber and Karl Marx—had offered important analyses of the role of penal practices in modern society, making it one of the best examples of the modernisation process and its discontents. Moreover, the emergence of mass incarceration in the USA during the last decades of the twentieth century, and the punitive turn underway in many recently industrialised societies around the globe has made it obvious that forms of punitive exclusion are core features of power and social order.

It is true that Durkheim and Weber made important analyses of penal practices (especially Durkheim) and that Marxist social theorists of the twentieth century, particularly Frankfurt School member Georg Rusche explored the role of penality in the regulation of the capitalist economic system. And yet, the field of punishment and society today is not really an extension or a synthesis of any of these classical social theories. Moreover, the crucial works that launched this subfield began a decade before anyone observed mass incarceration and indeed in quite different conjunctural circumstances.

It is, in fact, in the late 1970s and very early 1980s that the intellectual elements of contemporary punishment and society research emerge. Two books, researched in the mid-1970s and published in their original languages in 1975 and 1977 by authors working completely independently, brought classical social theory on punishment into striking dialog with critical observations on the central struggles over penal power going on at the time. The first, Michel Foucault's *Discipline and Punishment: the Birth of the Prison* (published in English in 1977), remains among the best known books on punishment and in contemporary critical analysis generally. The second, *The Prison and the Factory: Origins of the Penitentiary System* (published in English in 1981) remains largely unknown outside radical criminology and punishment and society studies and read by too few even in those fields today. That is misfortune that this timely new edition can remedy. For not only are all the crucial innovations in the analysis of penal practices attributed to Foucault brilliantly at work in *The Prison and the Factory*, they are presented without the often dazzling but frequently confounding efforts of Foucault to lay the foundations of his uncompleted project for a genealogy of the modern soul (as he put it). Melossi and Pavarini's study of the political-economic context of the invention of the penitentiary is the proper starting point for the study of punishment and society.

Remarkably both books developed an approach to examining the social work of punishment that built on, while revising considerably, the classic social theorists, especially Durkheim and Marx, who had given punishment more or less prominent roles in largely structuralist theories of social practices. Rather than focus on the 'function of punishment' (whether expressing social solidarity or directing coercive power in the interest of elite control), both studies offered a way of treating punishment as part of a larger political technology of the body, to use Foucault's productive metaphor. For both books this meant tracing the transformation in the penal field to developments in the availability of various schemas for coordinating and controlling assembled groups of people. Both studies placed political economy and the forms of inequality and conflict necessitated by economic production at the start of their analysis, but then look beyond traditional linkages between economic base and legal and political superstructure to trace the effects of penal mechanisms on subjects and their bodies. Important changes in political-economic structure can force dramatic changes in penal forms, but rarely direct an alternative.

As their subtitles hinted, both studies were historical, but also intensely interested in the present. The past in both instances was the early nineteenth century, when the prison, or penitentiary as it is called by some of its exponents, emerges in Europe and North America as a leading candidate to take up the slack created by a shrinking use of capital and corporal punishment (especially for property crimes) and the growth of crime and commercial society. The present, framed by significant radical political organising and related protests in and around prisons in both Europe and the USA, was an intense debate in the 1970s over the future of the prison in the late twentieth century. Then carceral populations, including both prisons and asylums, were shrinking, and the direction of state social control appeared to be moving towards community-based supervision with treatment. Few experts or critics expected mass incarceration and its desertion of disciplinary mechanisms of power in favour of exclusion, segregation and abandonment.

The rise of mass incarceration may render the focus on the origins of the penitentiary strange at first. The vision of the prison as a mechanism of both punishment and productive investment in the bodies of prisoners may seem unfamiliar to contemporary observers well aware that overcrowded prisons have long eschewed rehabilitation or even labour, in favour of punitive forms of exclusion, not just in the USA but also around the globe. The place of the prison as mediating framework in between the emerging capitalist economy and the disciplining of everyday metropolitan life may seem irrelevant to a globalised capitalist economy that regularly bypasses domestic workers in favour of more desperate bodies in the developing world.

Yet this is a particularly excellent time to republish and reread these works and especially *The Prison and the Factory*. First, the analytic research strategy of thinking about penal forms in terms of political technologies of the body can be used very productively to examine penal practices comparatively and historically far beyond the point of application of the original study. The proliferation of new penal practices associated with the current crisis of mass incarceration awaits examination.

Second, the penitentiary project, which is the subject of this study, is far from exhausted in our time and may be in the midst of yet another reinvention. As the wages of warehousing overwhelming numbers of citizens, many with chronic illness, in poorly designed prisons, is coming home, there is increasing interest in using more rehabilitation in prisons and replacing prison with forms of supervised release that promise to do more good and cost less. Policy entrepreneurs are competing to reinvent the American carceral state as a kinder and gentler model of punishment in terms that echo the promoters of the original penitentiaries.

Of course the contemporary politics of prison that we now bring to a reading of *The Prison and the Factory* is quite different than in the early 1980s, but the value of the analysis remains enduring. Then it was the vicissitudes of penal welfarism and the role of prisons in the increasing crisis of capitalist hegemony in an era of global revolutionary possibility. Today it is the crisis of neoliberalism and the place of the penitentiary project in an era of exclusion and segregation. In both times, it is Melossi and Pavarini's analysis of discipline as an emergent technology of power in the early nineteenth century, animating penal transformation towards the penitentiary, that can provide a critical point of interrogation for the present.

At both conjunctures, the post-1968 political crisis of the post-War regime of managerial capitalism and the crisis of the Neoliberalism today, this history confronts us with the question of whether that disciplinary imperative is one that contemporary law should continue to legitimate as a crucial means for democratic social order. The epoch of mass incarceration in between, with its shift away from disciplinary forms of knowledge power and towards exclusion, segregation and aggregate risk management, suggests that this time the answer from a broader public may be no. The scandalous conditions of neoliberal penality, coexisting as they do with historically crime rates and high levels of social order on other measures, suggests that discipline has long ceased to be relevant and that efforts to reinvent and extend the carceral state into the life world of the poor along disciplinary lines in a repeat of the 1970s would be pointless and very likely destructive.

This revised edition of *The Prison and the Factory* comes at a time when both capitalism and the prison have achieved global hegemonic standing.

It is imperative that students of punishment and society look beyond the national framework and in particular the much studied case of the USA. Melossi and Pavarini's examination of the beginning of that process remains not only a crucial historical baseline for contemporary studies but an introduction to the central analytic tools critical to exploring its most recent consequences.

Adrian A. Kragen Professor of Law   Jonathan Simon
University of California
Berkeley

Acknowledgements (1981)

We would like to thank the following:

Professors A. Baratta and F. Bricola, scientific directors of CNR research, in whose institute this work was carried out. We are particularly indebted to them for the opportunity made available to us to carry out valuable research abroad.

Our special thanks to Professor G. Neppi Modona, who followed our work from the beginning. Also thanks to Professor M. Sbriccoli, who made useful suggestions, criticisms and improvements to our work.

Finally, thanks to our British colleagues at the Universities of Edinburgh, Sheffield, Cambridge and London.

We would like to extend particular thanks to Richard Kinsey, John Lea, Victoria Greenwood and Jock Young for the preparation of this English edition—and to Glynis Cousin for the translation.

This book is the result of work carried out under the auspices of CNR on the principle of Social Defence in Italy from pre-unification codification to today, under the scientific direction of Professors A. Baratta and F. Bricola.

Contents

Translator's Note (1981)

Carcere e fabbrica was first published in 1977; in 1979 a new edition was published with some alterations, which are incorporated into this translation. Additionally, the authors have made minor additions and amendments to this English edition.

Glynis Cousin

Editors' Introduction (1981)

This is the first appearance in English of an Italian work which has become one of the seminal books in its field and which has been influential in shaping recent Marxist studies of social discipline and control. *The Prison and the Factory*, like Rusche and Kirchheimer's *Punishment and Social Structure*, has become a much cited but largely unavailable text for those working in the field of deviance and social control. Because of the attention which *The Prison and the Factory* has attracted, we believe it to be important to provide a translation for English-speaking audiences. A second reason for publishing this work is to extend more widely the interest that has been generated by more recent work by Dario Melossi which has become available in English.[1]

The Prison and the Factory is where Melossi and Pavarini established their fundamental arguments concerning the inter-relationship between the development of capitalist accumulation and forms of punishment and discipline. These arguments have become a basis for increasing exploration and debate in this area, which has merged a variety of different academic starting points: in law, sociology and history. This focus of interest has been manifested in recent work in Britain, in organisations such as the National Deviancy Conference and the Conference of Socialist Economists; in the USA, particularly through *Crime and Social Justice*; as well as in other European countries through the European

Group for the Study of Deviance and Social Control, and *La Questione Criminale*.

In more general terms, the work of Melossi and Pavarini coincides with a major expansion of interest in historical criminology: for example, in the work of Hay, Linebaugh and Thompson. As Melossi and Pavarini themselves point out in their Introduction, one particularly sharp focus of this move to historical analysis has been the relationship between the crisis of prison systems and the attempt to unearth the social and historical origins of those institutions. It has become increasingly apparent that in all Western societies, the penal system, no matter what its specific national form, is failing in its self-proclaimed tasks of rehabilitation and deterrence. One of the responses to this 'crisis' has been the attempt to excavate the real nature of the connection between prisons and social structures. As such, the prison has emerged as one of the key sites for analysing the relation between social regimes and forms of discipline and regulation.[2]

Melossi and Pavarini's entry to this debate follows the direction established in Rusche and Kirchheimer's pioneering work, *Punishment and Social Structure*. *The Prison and the Factory* reconsiders and develops the work of Rusche and Kirchheimer in examining the relation between modes of production and modes of punishment. The specific form of this project in *The Prison and the Factory* is the analysis of the connection between the genealogy of capitalism and the genealogy of the penal institution. The prison as a specific form of punishment is located within the emergence of capitalist social relations and the development of generalised labour. It is this development which they argue produces a regime of punishment based on the deprivation of liberty.

Within this analysis, Melossi and Pavarini provide a synoptic tracing of the shifts and developments in penal regimes in relation to changes in the process of capital accumulation and the problems of the regulation of labour associated with that process. This work deals with the early stages of capitalist development through the specific national forms which this development took in a number of European states and in North America. *The Prison and the Factory* thus lays the foundation for major investigations of the relationship between capitalist modes of production and their apparatuses of social discipline and control.

John Clarke
Mike Fitzgerald
Victoria Greenwood
Jock Young

Notes

1. D. Melossi, 'The Penal Question in *Capital*', *Crime and Social Justice*, no. 5 (1976) pp. 26–33; D. Melossi, 'Review article: Rusche and Kirchheimer, *Punishment and Social Structure*', *Crime and Social Justice*, no. 9 (1978) pp. 73–85; D. Melossi, 'Institutions of Social Control and the Capitalist Organization of Work' in NDC/CSE (eds), *Capitalism and the Rule of Law* (London: Hutchinson, 1979) pp. 90–9; D. Melossi, 'Strategies of Social Control in Capitalism: a Comment on Recent Work', *Contemporary Crises*, 4 (1980) pp. 381–402.
2. M. Foucault, *Discipline and Punish* (London: Allen Lane, 1977); M. Ignatieff, *A Just Measure of Pain* (London: Macmillan, 1978); A. Scull, *Decarceration* (New York: Prentice-Hall, 1977).

Introduction (1981)

Dario Melossi and Massimo Pavarini

Our initial interest in the history of prison was aroused during the late 1960s at a time when this institution in Italy (and elsewhere) was thrown into a deep crisis.

As always happens at times like these, we were obliged to pose some basic questions concerning the very phenomenon of prison. In so doing, we were surprised to discover—and this discovery affected the way of thinking to which we had subscribed until then—that despite the existence of a great number of studies within various political approaches, no one had clearly posed a question which began to appear increasingly central to us: *why prison?* Why is it that in every industrial society, this institution has become the dominant punitive instrument to such an extent that prison and punishment are commonly regarded as almost synonymous?

Moreover, we raised this question because it seemed to us that both the theoretical terms of the debate on prison and the legislative formulae proposed in regard to prison reform were far from being capable of responding to the radicalism of the problem, a radicalism which, before being political, was intimately connected with the very *raison d'être* of the institution.

We also realised that we were by no means the first to attempt a redefinition of the 'penal question' within a Marxist framework. Most notably, we were following in the footsteps of Georg Rusche and Otto Kirchheimer.[1]

This book then seeks to establish the connection between the rise of the capitalist mode of production and the origins of the modern prison[2]: such (and that is all!) is the theme of the following two essays. This has led to a rather precise temporal (and spatial) definition of our theme. Its spatio-temporal dimensions coincided with those of the formation of a determinate social structure. What we had to deal with was an architectural detail of this whole structure. However, it is necessary to preface our discussion with a twofold warning relating to the *ante* and the *post* of our theme.

In pre-capitalist societies prison as a form of punishment did not exist. This can be seen to be the case historically so long as we bear in mind that it was not so much the prison institution that was unknown to pre-capitalist society but the penalty of confinement as a deprivation of liberty. Looking at feudalism, for example, one can correctly speak of preventive and debtors' prisons within this system but it would be quite wrong to state that the simple privation of liberty, prolonged for a determinate period and unaccompanied by some further form of suffering, was recognised and provided for as an autonomous and common form of punishment. This position—which tends to highlight the essentially custodial nature of the medieval prison—has gained almost universal acceptance amongst historians of penology. Even those that dissent from this view—such as Pugh[3]—are in any event compelled to acknowledge that the first historically traceable instance of prison punishment in Britain was around the end of the fourteenth century, that is, at a time when feudalism was already showing marked signs of disintegration.

Without going into the historiographic debate on the nature of certain atypical punishments (*pro-correctione* prisons, prisons for prostitutes and 'sodomites', etc.), and given that these are introductory remarks, one may reasonably advance a hypothesis capable of explaining, if only in general terms, the significant absence of prison punishment from feudal society.

A correct approach to this problem would be to look at the definition of the ethical-juridical category of the *lex-talionis* (retributive punishment, the law of an eye for an eye and a tooth for a tooth) in the feudal conception of punishment. One can see equivalents here as being originally nothing but the sublimation of a vendetta and thus as something which is based on an almost privatised claim of the victim of a crime.

'Felony', to cite the famous thesis of Pashukanis, 'can be seen as a par-ticular variant of circulation, in which the exchange relation, that is the contractual relation, is determined retrospectively, after arbitrary action by one of the parties … punishment emerged as an equivalent which compensates the damage sustained by the injured party'.[4]

The transition from private vendetta to retributive punishment, that is, the transition from an almost 'biological' phenomenon to a juridical cat-egory, requires as a necessary precondition the cultural dominance of the concept of equivalents based on exchange value.

Medieval punishment certainly maintained an equivalent nature even if the idea of retribution ceased to be directly connected to an injury sus-tained by the victim of a crime and came to be connected to an offence against God, thereby rendering punishment more and more a matter of *espiatio*, of divine chastisement.

The rather hybrid nature of penal sanctions in the age of feudalism—*retributio* and *espiatio*—could not by definition be realised through prison, that is to say, through the privation of a *quantum* of liberty. In fact, as far as the law of equivalents is concerned, 'for it to be possible for the idea to emerge that one could make recompense for an offence with a piece of abstract freedom determined in advance, it was necessary for all concrete forms of social wealth to be reduced to the most abstract and simple form, to human labour measured in time'.[5] Thus, under a socio-economic system such as feudalism—in which the historic development of 'human labour measured in time' (read: wage labour) was still incom-plete—retributive punishment, determined by an exchange value, was not in a position to find in the privation of time the equivalent of the crime. Instead, the equivalent of the injury produced by the crime was realised in the privation of assets socially valued at that time: life, physical wholeness, money and loss of status.

On the other hand, it is in the nature of *espiatio* (vendetta, divine chas-tisement) that the punishment could not but reap satisfactory results. Here, punishment removed the collective fear of contagion originally called forth by the violation of a commandment. In this event, defence against crime and the criminal was not so much a question of protecting the concrete interests threatened by the illicit act as of countering the possible, but not foreseeable and hence socially uncontrollable, negative effects of that first stimulus. What followed from this was the need to repress the transgressor. Only thus could the possible future calamity hanging over the community be avoided. Moreover, fear aroused by this impending threat meant that chastisement had to be spectacular and cruel in order to inhibit onlookers from committing a similar offence.

If, then, divine judgement was to be the model for these sanctions, if suffering was accepted as an effective means of expiation and spiritual catharsis, as religion taught, punishments would carry no limitations. In fact, translated into practical terms, this meant the imposition of a degree of suffering which strove to anticipate and match the impossible goal—eternal punishment. Clearly, in this context, prison punishment as such was inappropriate.

There was one context, however, for certain alternative aspects of feudal punishment, in which there was clearly a place for the penitentiary. We refer here to canon law.

The existence of such an alternative does not contradict the clearly theocratic character of the feudal state. Without doubt, in certain particular areas and at specific times, the canonical penal system assumed original and autonomous forms not encountered in the secular system. Due to the deep penetration of ecclesiastical power into medieval political life, these specific areas and periods are difficult to identify. The influence of canonical and juridical thought on the medieval punitive system varied in intensity according to the degree of competition between ecclesiastical and secular power.

The first embryonic forms of sanction were imposed by the Church upon erring clergy. It is extremely misleading to describe these 'errors' simply as crimes. Rather they seem to have been regarded as religious infractions which directly reflected on ecclesiastical authority or aroused alarm within the religious community. At least so far as the initial period was concerned, the necessarily hybrid nature of these sanctions adequately explains how this type of deviancy produced on the part of ecclesiastical power a reaction which retained a religious-sacramental character. It also explains the inspiration behind the ritual of confession and penance, although this is accompanied—due to the particular nature of this deviancy—by a further element, that is to say by a public form: the sanction of penance to be expiated in secret until repentance is achieved (*usque ad correctionem*) was thus born.

The therapeutic nature of this ecclesiastical punishment was later combined with and thus perverted by the acquisition of a new vindictive character which came to be socially felt as *satisfaction*; this superimposed goal, this enforced period of time *usque ad satisfactionem*, necessarily accentuated the public character of the punishment. It emerged from the private court (the soul, religious conscience) in order to assume the appearance of a social institution, its execution made public and exemplary in order to intimidate and deter. But something of its original intention survived—even if only on the level of value. At the moment when it was transformed into a penal sanction true and proper, penance still retained something of its corrective character. It was in fact transformed into *confinement in a monastery for a determinate period*. Absolute separation from the outside world, the closest contact with religious life and worship gave the wrongdoer the opportunity to expiate his guilt through meditation.

The canonical prison regime took diverse forms. Apart from the basic differentiation between simple confinement in monastery, cell or episcopal prison, there was also some variation in the sentences: privation of liberty accompanied by physical suffering, solitary confinement (*cella, carcer, ergastulum*) and above all, the rule of silence. The features of canonical prison emphasised here originated in monastic organisational forms, especially in those connected with the most extreme type of mysticism.

Monastic organisation had a special influence on prison; projection of the original sacramental rite of penance onto the field of public institutions found its true inspiration in the Eastern monastic tradition of contemplation and asceticism. In fact, it must be stressed, as a fundamental element in our evaluation, that labour as a possible form of punishment had no place in the canonical prison regime.

The absence of prison labour in canonical punishment clarifies the significance attributed by ecclesiastical organisation to the privation of liberty for a fixed period. It seems to us that in the case of canonical prison, its significance was that of the *quantum* of time necessary for purification according to the criteria of the sacrament of penance. It was thus not so much the privation of liberty per se which satisfied the punishment but the possibility held out by isolation from social life that constituted the ideal aim of the punishment: *repentance*. This aim had to be seen as reform, or the possibility of reform before God and not as the moral and social regeneration of the condemned sinner; in this sense punishment could only be retributive and based therefore on the parameter of the gravity of the offence rather than on the dangerousness of the offender.

The essentially penitential nature of canonical prison was borne out by its unsuitability to directly political ends. Its existence was seen and felt to be a religious exigency, comprehensible only within the confines of a rigid system of values geared towards the absolute and intransigent affirmation of God's presence in social life—*thus it was an essentially ideological aim*.

The second warning relates to what comes *after* this text; it is not a conclusion but the premise for a different area of research—it has more to do with the disintegration of the prison structure than its construction, which is our concern here—research which centres on competitive capitalism through to the last century. The period covering the last decades of the nineteenth century up to the middle of the twentieth century witnessed a series of gradual and profound changes in the basic socio-economic framework of the whole capitalist world,[6] changes affecting fundamental elements of our present order: the composition of capital, the organisation of labour, the emergence of an organised workers' movement, class composition, the role of the state and the whole complex relationship between the state and civil society.

The sphere of circulation and consumption were subjected to the direct rule of capital: decisions on prices, the organisation of the market and at the same time of a consensus, all became part of one and the same thing. Not only were the traditional instruments of social control strengthened—those areas of 'the sphere of production' outside the factory from capitalism's inception—but also new instruments were created. The new strategy was towards dispersion, towards the extension and pervasion of control. Individuals are no longer locked up; they are got at where they are *normally* locked up: outside the factory, in society as a whole. Propaganda, the mass media, a new and more efficient network of police and social assistance—these are the bearers of a new kind of social control.

Thus, if prison (in common with other ancillary institutions) arose at the same time as and in a particular relationship with the capitalist mode of production (which is the theme of this book), then the profound structural changes referred to above must have been accompanied by similarly radical alterations in the sphere of social control and of the reproduction of the labour force: the relationships between primary and secondary social control were shaken up as was the very administration of various forms of control.

Rusche and Kirchheimer demonstrate that from the end of the last century to the 1930s, the prison population fell significantly in Britain, France and Germany. This was unquestionably the case in Italy from 1880 to the present day with a slight exception during the fascist period. The reduction of the prison population was accompanied by the increasingly widespread adoption (outside Italy) of penal control 'in liberty' such as that of the probation system widely practised in the USA. Throughout the twentieth century, therefore, depending on the particular political-economic situation, strategies for reform assumed a typically bifurcated trend in terms of a relative diminution (on both an individual and mass level) of prison sentences on the one hand, and the growth of repression for certain categories of crimes and offenders (above all in moments of political crisis) on the other. As a result, the phases in which attempts were made to empty prisons and introduce soft, resocialising regimes increasingly clashed with those in which the reins were tightened and a harsh regime again became 'necessary' (the development of prison reform in Britain since the Second World War exemplifies this point).[7]

This became particularly evident with the crisis of the 1960s. Particularly in Italy at this time, the explosions in the prisons did not occur in isolation but were linked to a high level of working-class struggle and a deep social crisis which pervaded a number of institutions (schools, mental hospitals, military barracks and the very structure of the bourgeois family itself). We cannot dwell on this point, as it implies a general discussion far beyond the reaches of the subject we have set ourselves here. Suffice it to observe that since the whole system of control is modelled on the (historically determined) relations of production, and given that it was in the factories that the equilibrium was broken in the

1960s, it is only in the attempt to re-establish its own power in the relations of production that capital can try to play a new card in the game of social control in order to bring about—from its own point of view—a radical solution to the prison question. And so a fundamental element in research today—and on this point we hasten to our conclusion—should be the identification of changes in social control on the basis of the new pattern of capital-labour relationships which has emerged from the crisis (naturally, the first task is to clarify the latter).

In short, only an understanding of the close connection between the rise of capitalism and what is now called the 'genealogy' of prison has made clear to us that the contemporary social crisis, whether in the factory or in other 'ancillary' institutions, above all, prison, was not a matter of chance but historically determined. This was the result of our work. As always, it was only a beginning.

Notes

1. G. Rusche and O. Kirchheimer, *Punishment and Social Structure* (1939) (New York, 1968).
2. See D. Melossi, 'The Penal Question in *Capital*' Crime and Social Justice, no. 5 (1976) pp. 26–33.
3. R. B. Pugh, *Imprisonment in Medieval England* (Cambridge, 1970).
4. E. B. Pashukanis, *Law and Marxism: A General Theory*, ed. C. Arthur (London, 1978) pp. 168–9.
5. Ibid., p. 181.
6. The observations which follow are more widely developed in D. Melossi, 'Institutions of Social Control and Capitalist Organization of Work', in NDC/CSE (eds), *Capitalism & The Rule of Law* (London: Hutchinson, 1979) pp. 90–9, and especially in D. Melossi, 'Strategies of Social Control in Capitalism: a Comment on Recent Work', *Contemporary Crises*, 4 (1980) pp. 381–402.
7. See R. Kinsey, 'Risocializzazione e controllo nelle carceri inglesi', in *La questione criminale* (1976) nos 2–3.

"The Prison and the Factory" Revisited (2017): Penality and the Critique of Political Economy Between Marx and Foucault

Dario Melossi

In 1977 the manuscript of *Carcere e fabbrica: alle origini del sistema penitenziario* was published in Italian (Melossi and Pavarini 1977). We are therefore publishing this new edition in English[1] exactly 40 years since the original publication. Essentially the book consisted of a review of historical material about the origins of imprisonment, informed by a Marxist vision. This was also its claim to originality in the sense that, by applying a Marxist reading to prison history materials, it appeared clearly that the very origin, the very "invention" of the prison, is tightly linked to what Marx, in the first volume of *Capital*, calls "original" or "primitive" accumulation. Not

I thank my good friends Maximo Sozzo and José A. Brandariz-Garcia for all the feedback and exchanges that took place when I presented the main ideas for what follows, within lectures given at the Winter School in Criminology of the Faculty of Legal and Social Sciences, Universidad Nacional del Litoral, Santa Fe, Argentina (July 2014) and at two International Conferences organized at the University of A Coruna, Spain, in September 2014 and September 2016. I am particularly grateful to Maximo Sozzo and Alessandro De Giorgi for their comments on a previous version of this chapter (usual disclaimers apply). I also thank the Center for the Study of Law and Society of the University of California, Berkeley, for having provided me once more with the ideal physical and intellectual space during the completion of this work!

© The Author(s) 2018
D. Melossi, M. Pavarini, *The Prison and the Factory (40ᵗʰ Anniversary Edition)*,
Palgrave Studies in Prisons and Penology, DOI 10.1057/978-1-137-56590-7_1

only this but, in the centuries that followed, the very logic of primitive accumulation would be reproduced and expanded through the incessant conquest and colonization of pre-capitalist areas of society, not only, obviously, in its capitalist matrix, but also in the penal system, by virtue of the crucial requirement of "discipline" (I shall expand on this later on). Notwithstanding, the book has often been read as if it had been a story about the invention of the prison as some kind of "school" (a "professional training school" perhaps?) for an apprentice working class—confusing our thesis, I surmise, with penological visions on rehabilitation/resocialisation/ re-education (as Italians call it) by means of work. Hence, there were lots of instances in which critics were only too happy to show that this was not indeed the case. Even if, at times, prisons might indeed have looked a bit like such schools or vocational institutes, this is certainly not what we meant. Through the following very synthetic reconstruction of the genesis of the book, as well as of some of its aftermath, I will try to show why I have always been quite unhappy with such a (wrong) reading.

Genealogy

Franco Bricola, who held the Chair of Criminal Law at the University of Bologna, where both Massimo and I had earned our *Laurea*,[2] was at the head, together with Alessandro Baratta,[3] of a CNR[4] Research entitled (in translation) "The Principle of Social Defence in Italy from Pre-Unitary Codifications to Today". Within such much broader research endeavour, Massimo and I decided to write a piece on the history of penal institutions since the Italian Unity (1861). When we started discussing the matter, however, we realized that there was no way we could deal with the start of the prison system in the newly unified Italian State without asking the question about what was there before and, more generally, what were the roots of the prison institution, today one could say its "genealogy" (even if at the time we were not familiar with such use of the term). That the cultural and political climate surrounding us at the time might have been conducive to ask such questions was certainly a possibility, a consideration which will be entertained later in this chapter. What followed was a rather intense period of research, including a remarkable trip to the UK and Scotland—in the extremely cold (and poor) winter of

1974, the winter of the "oil energy crisis", of the miners' strike and of the limitations to the use of electricity, when the squalor and misery of some of the window shops in Edinburgh reminded me of those I had seen behind the Iron Curtain. During this trip we touched upon what, to our rather naive eyes, seemed to be the most important centres of a new "critical criminology"—those were the heydays of the National Deviancy Conference (NDC)[5]—from Edinburgh to Sheffield to Cambridge to London and got in touch with some of its best known proponents, such as Richard Kinsey, Ian Taylor and Jock Young.[6]

This resulted in a volume made up of two parts, mine on Europe and Italy, Massimo's on America, a rather ironic choice, thinking about the routes which each of us would then follow. In any case, the inspiration for my section went back to my 1971 Law *Laurea*, entitled (in translation) "Research for a Marxist Theory of Crime and Punishment". The essential of the first part of the thesis, dedicated to an analysis of Marx's various works on the topic, was then the basis of an article, published in Italian in 1975 (Melossi 1975a) in the second issue of the newly founded journal *La questione criminale*[7] and then in English in 1976 in the American *Crime and Social Justice*[8] and entitled "The Penal Question in Capital", where I reconstructed what seemed to me to be the basic notions of Marx on "the penal question" especially in those sections on "primitive accumulation" in the first volume of *Capital* that will then be at the roots of *The Prison and the Factory* (Melossi 1976).

If, however, we step back a little we realize that the discussion about the origin of prisons, in light of Marx's contributions, was but one way to deal with what our generation perceived as *the* problem, the problem of "ideology"—the problem that we would have later encountered under many guises, not least in the discussions in the early meetings of the "European Group for the Study of Deviance and Social Control", from Stuart Hall's emphasis on the concept of hegemony to discussion of Louis Althusser's "state ideological apparatuses"—both steeped in a reading of Gramsci, even if of a rather different nature. The main point, however, was—we seemed to think rather confusedly—that the question of ideology could not be reduced to that of "superstructure", as in Marx's ill-fated "Preface" of 1859 (Marx 1859). Of course the story would be quite long to tell but, to make it really short, both the domination of an "American" way of life—which would not yet appear at the time in all its grandiosity but that we were all too aware of helping to instantiate with our generational choices about culture, music, movies, lifestyles and the like—and the awful demise of what it was then called "Socialism" seemed unerringly linked to what we thought of as "ideology", the strength of ideology. More specifically, law seemed to us, young law students, the very avatar of ideology. Indeed, in a "self-managed seminar" in my first year in the Bologna Law School, which we "occupied" for the whole second semester, from March to May 1968, we came to conclusions that we proceeded to print in a stencilled document entitled (in translation) *Epistemological and Practical Conditioning Due to a Legal Specialization: Suggestions for a Reconstruction of Law as a Social Object.*[9]

Political Economy of Punishment

Coming back now, however, to when, with our degrees fresh in our pockets, we were approaching the issue of the origins of imprisonment, we soon seemed to have in front of us two possible venues of exploration. One we found mentioned in Maurice Dobb's *Studies in the Development of Capitalism* (1946: 23, 235) and we had then retrieved it from the British libraries during our tour briefly mentioned above: Georg Rusche and Otto Kirchheimer's *Punishment and Social Structure* (1939).[10] As I later happened to suggest (Melossi 2003), I found Rusche's emphasis on the importance of the labour market a good example of "economism" (then read as "Marxist", following a common vulgate) but not really of "Marxism", according to a concept of Marxism that I will try to at least hint at in the remainder of this chapter.

The other one was the one that we took (and in my opinion that Foucault took) and that was the importance of, and the emphasis on, the issue of *discipline*. Breathing very much the air of the times, that surrounded us and that we lived in, we located the site of class struggle in the factory, about the extraction of "surplus value". According to such a view, essentially to be found in the first volume of *Capital*, at the end of the day, the value of production has to be greater than the cost of the various factors of production. This very simple and rather banal statement is the heart of the idea of class struggle. The government of production is in fact in the hands of capital on one hand and of workers' resistance on the other. In terms of the history of imprisonment, one could not underestimate therefore the crucial importance of the institution of the "workhouse" (that I had discovered in the steps of Thorsten Sellin's *Pioneering in Penology* (1944), a picture taken from which would then grace the cover of the English edition of *The Prison and the Factory*). The workhouse, which early seventeenth-century Dutch people called the *Rasphuis*, would in fact be central as a link with the future penitentiary, through William Penn and the Quakers especially.[11] Central also as prefiguration of the new prison institution, because of the fame and notoriety of the *Rasphuis*. Central, especially, in the relationship between penality and capitalism. What other institution could better represent in fact the Weberian "elective affinity" (Howe 1978) of capitalism and the new form of penality? A new form of penality that could be taken to instantiate the "spirit of capitalism" itself, a stand-in for the "Protestant ethic" (Weber 1904–1905). Indeed, in a reversal of the usual structure/superstructure story, one could even dare to claim, with a touch of emphasis, that the very "invention" of capitalism took place in the invention of the workhouse![12] "The penal question" has in fact always been close to social innovators' hearts, and both reformers and revolutionaries alike have been taken in a love-hate relationship with the prison, in which they found, perhaps, the Utopia of society they wanted, especially the Utopia of "the new Man" they wanted to mould!

So, from the workhouse to the penitentiary. Then, about one century later, from the penitentiary to the Panopticon, later celebrated in Foucault's pages. Jeremy Bentham wrote on the frontispiece of *The Panopticon* that "The Panopticon... [is an] ...inspection-house: containing the idea of a new principle of construction applicable to any sort of establishment, in which persons of any description are to be kept under inspection" (1787: 40). He goes on to exemplify that the principle is therefore applicable to "penitentiary-houses, prisons, houses of industry, work-houses, poor-houses, manufactories, mad-houses, lazarettos, hospitals and schools" (ibidem). In *The Prison and the Factory* (Melossi 1977: 42–46), I called this panoply of institutions "ancillary" to "the factory", in the sense that they were crucial to constituting, and reproducing the social discipline demanded by a capitalist mode of production.

According to Marx's reconstruction, in fact, once the labourer has entered the not so metaphoric gates of the sphere of production, it is within those gates that, like by miracle, the sale of his or her labour power eventually gives more, to the capitalist, than what the latter has anticipated for the various costs of production. This difference, which is at the basis of the capitalist's profit, can come into being, however, only if the "freedom" of the sphere of circulation turns into the kind of (temporary) servitude of the "sphere of production". In fact, the capitalist will be a full-title capitalist only if, having bought the worker's labour power, he will be able, as every good proprietor, to use and enjoy his property as he likes, and therefore to impose that *discipline* of production that only warrants the difference which makes his profit. Because one has to note that, in a most "unfortunate" manner, the labour power, which is the merchandise the capitalist has bought, comes with a human being attached, often behaving in ways that are different from those predicted and demanded by the capitalist. This struggle between a human being, the labourer, and the labourer as mere carrier of labour power is the substance of "class struggle". This is the reason why it is silly to say, as it is often said, that Marx's theory is "based on the economy". Rather, it is, as the subtitle to *Capital* reads, a "*critique* of political economy" which locates the core of the matter in the conflict between capital and labour about exploitation. It is about a power struggle (which Marx called a "class struggle") over the management of human resources.[13] The society that is ruled by capital is therefore organized around the constitution and maintenance of "discipline", a discipline that permeates all the fundamental social institutions. It does not seem to be quite correct therefore to state that the "Marxist theses" on penality "do not depend upon specifically Marxist arguments such as the theory of surplus value" (Garland 1990: 130) because the concept of "discipline" could not be more strictly linked to the concept of surplus value, which is indeed the core of Marxian theory. It is in fact only if the discipline "in the sphere of production" warrants the extraction of surplus value, that a capitalist system can indeed even exist as such. Whether or not one agrees with the general validity of such a view—and that is an altogether different question—there is however no doubt that the connection between "ancillary" institutions, and the sphere of production, as institutions of reproduction of that *disciplined* labour power which is necessary to produce surplus value, is the very clear theoretical linkage between Marx, our work in *The Prison and the Factory*, and, I claim in the next section, Foucault's.[14]

The Destructuration of Authority: Struggles

What happened since the 1970s was the destructuration of this system of authority—it was not by chance that many among the most successful movements in the late 1960s called themselves "antiauthoritarian"—a system of authority that many misunderstood to be one and the same with "capitalism" (what one could probably call the most consequential quid pro quo of my generation). Destructuration, in other words, not only of the centrality of discipline in the organization of a "panoptic" society but also of the kind of homogeneous, mass, organized, disciplined, working class that, as Rosa Luxemburg had quite incredibly already divined in her invective against the "discipline" of the factory *and* especially of the Russian social-democratic party under Lenin's guidance (Luxemburg 1904), had been bred within the factory (and in fact what happened in the Left after the 1960s and 1970s was *also* the destructuration of all that). In the 1970s, the kind of society that had been built in the previous decades went into deep crisis, or at least appeared to go into crisis. Maybe we started "seeing" the crisis of authority in the "total institutions" exactly because the society that had fed them, and that had fed on them, entered into such a deep crisis.

The role of struggles in this work of material but also conceptual deconstruction can be hardly minimized. Struggles developed, at the same time, within factories, prisons, and in all "ancillary institutions" (mental hospitals being the most classical example (Goffman 1961; Basaglia 1968)). Suddenly we realized that these institutions were not eternal, would not last forever, that, as they were born, they could go. The "critique of institutions"—echoing perhaps what the German student leader Rudi Dutschke (Bergmann et al. 1968) had prophetically called "the long march through the institutions"—could not have existed apart from such struggles. David Garland (2014) has reminded us that this was indeed the case about Michel Foucault's concept of a "history of the present" in *Discipline and Punish*:

> That punishment in general and the prison in particular belong to a political technology of the body is a lesson that I have learnt not so much from history as from the present. In recent years, prison revolts have occurred throughout the world. There was certainly something paradoxical about their aims, their slogans and the way they took place. They were revolts against an entire state of physical misery that is over a century old: against cold, suffocation and overcrowding, against decrepit walls, hunger, physical maltreatment. But they were also revolts against model prisons, tranquillizers, isolation, the medical or educational services. Were they revolts whose aims were merely material? Or contradictory revolts: against the obsolete, but also against comfort; against the warders, but also against the psychiatrists. In fact, all these movements – and the innumerable discourses that the prison has given rise to since the early nineteenth century – have been about the body and material things. What has sustained these discourses, these memories and invectives are indeed those minute material details. One may, if one is so disposed, see them as no more than blind demands or suspect the existence behind them of alien strategies. In fact, they were revolts, at the level of the body, against the very body of the prison. What was at issue was not whether the prison environment was too harsh or too aseptic, too primitive or too efficient, but its very materiality as an instrument and vector of power; it is this whole technology of power over the body that the technology of the 'soul' – that of the educationalists, psychologists and psychiatrists – fails either to conceal or to compensate, for the simple reason that it is one of its tools. I would like to write the history of this prison, with all the political investments of the body that it gathers together in its closed architecture. Why? Simply because I am interested in the past? No, if one means by that writing a history of the past in terms of the present. Yes, if one means writing the history of the present. (Foucault 1975: 30–31)

This long fragment, and especially its close, is very significant in order to understand the endeavour that Foucault had set for himself in the work of writing a book about the birth of the prison.[15] In such connection, one contribution by Foucault that seems particularly relevant is an interview organized by John Simon, a professor of French and comparative literature at SUNY Buffalo, who had received Foucault in the USA and who helped him organize a visit to Attica a few months after the famous revolt and who then conducted an interview with Foucault in April 1972 (then originally published in *Telos* (Foucault 1974)). The revolt at the Attica penitentiary in the State of New York, probably the (politically) most important prison revolt in the history of the USA, generated great impact for its media diffusion, but also for the level of violence in its resolution.[16] That interview is very interesting because Foucault gave his impressions after visiting Attica, also about the "modern" aspects, the uses of psychiatry, the various forms of therapy, the aseptic character, etc. In fact, there where Foucault writes of a revolt that was also "against model prisons, tranquillizers, isolation, the medical or educational services" he seems to quote almost verbatim from the interview with Simon, which after all had taken place only a couple of years before.[17]

The Destructuration of Authority: Marx and Foucault

As already mentioned, Foucault's relationship with the Marxist tradition and Marx more specifically is quite problematic. Some have claimed that in the 1972–1973 Course of lectures at the *Collège de France* leading up to the writing of *Discipline and Punish*, and now collected in a volume called *The Punitive Society* (Foucault 1973), the influence of Marx over Foucault's analysis would show more clearly (Elden 2015: 161, Harcourt 2013: 283–289). However, it seems to me that, to the one open to see it, also *Discipline and Punish* would lend itself to such an interpretation. In the crucial pages on "Panopticism", closing the central section of the volume on "Discipline", Foucault claimed that "the two processes – the accumulation of men and the accumulation of capital – cannot be separated" (Foucault 1975: 221). Moreover, development of technology and development of disciplinary techniques were intimately related, according to this very passage, to the point that Foucault includes here in parentheses one of his very rare citations to a classic text, Marx's discussion, in chapter XIII of the first volume of *Capital*, on "Co-operation". In this chapter, Marx makes the point—essential to the concept of surplus value—that, at this stage of development in the history of capitalism (before the introduction of complex machinery), labour, after being purchased and assembled together by the capitalist, was forcibly organized by the capitalist's very physical authority, who co-ordinated the production process with his eye, his voice and his command (Marx 1867: 322–335, Melossi 1977: 43). In other words, at this time, discipline was constitutive of the organization of work and therefore also of the capitalist's profits.

In the next page, Foucault adds,

Historically, the process by which the bourgeoisie became in the course of the eighteenth century the politically dominant class was masked by the establishment of an explicit, coded and formally egalitarian juridical framework, made possible by the organization of a parliamentary, representative regime. But the development and generalization of disciplinary mechanisms constituted the other, dark side of these processes [...] The real, corporal disciplines constituted the foundation of the formal, juridical liberties. The contract may have been regarded as the ideal foundation of law and political power; panopticism constituted the technique, universally widespread, of coercion [...] The 'Enlightenment', which discovered the liberties, also invented the disciplines. (Foucault 1975: 222)

How not to read these lines as a gloss on Marx's quintessential opposition of a "sphere of circulation"—which is "a very Eden of the innate rights of man [where] alone rule Freedom, Equality, Property, and Bentham"[18]— and that "sphere of production" marked on the contrary by servitude? Re-reading these pages now, it appears a bit clearer to me why we seemed to think that in such kind of analyses we had found the answer to the question of ideology. However, ideology was now transformed from a matter of practical reason and morality to one of specific techniques of control over the body (Melossi 1977: 45). In this light, the secret that we were trying to unveil, indeed to unmask, the secret of capitalist hegemony, could be understood, with a little help from Weber, as the hegemony of a *mentalité*, of a mindset, of an ethos. Exactly as the good merchants of seventeenth century Amsterdam believed, profit was the "collateral advantage" of their good deeds!

It seems to me that, both in *Discipline and Punish* and—and perhaps even more so—in the pages of the lectures in *Punitive Society*, Foucault sounded a bit like a "New Left" Marxist, critical at the same time of Social Democracy and Stalinism (both somehow embodied at the time in the French milieu by the French Communist Party (the PCF)). Perhaps also for such reason, Foucault's statements resonated, to our ears educated in the tradition of the New Left, with the "Marxism" of the British historian E.P. Thompson and his collaborators[19] (Thompson 1975, Hay, Linebaugh, Rule, Thompson and Winslow 1975) but also, I would dare to add, with Harry Braverman's *Labour and Monopoly Capital* (1974) in the USA.

Each season reads the classics in a way that suits it, and Marx is certainly no exception to this. On the contrary. The Marx that was popular, also in Italy but not only in Italy, during the years that were bringing us up to 1968 was a Marx read through the eyes of the Frankfurt School, where the critique of authority was paramount. The structures of authority that had been set up by the modern State—especially, in Continental Europe, the French/German State structure—seemed to find a deep affinity with the "barrack discipline" exposed by Luxemburg, the discipline of the modern factory, which was in turn deeply affine with a whole host of disciplinary institutions. Foucault's fascination—as well as our own in *The Prison and the Factory*—with Bentham's *Panopticon* finds here its roots, the fact that Bentham had already conceived the Panopticon as the patterned model of all institutional structures of authority. In this sense Foucault was giving a sense of direction to what Rudi Dutschke had called a "a long march through the institutions" (Bergman et al. 1968) or to the unperishing words with which Mario Savio, a few years before, speaking on the steps of Sproul Hall, on December 2, 1964, had incited the Berkeley students—and, with them, our whole generation—to "stop the machine": "…you've got to put your bodies upon the gears and upon the wheels… upon the levers, upon all the apparatus, and you've got to make it stop!" (Rosenfeld 2012: 217).

Therefore, the disciplinary power mechanisms of Russian Stalinism or of Western "Communist" Social Democracies were part of the problem, not of the solution, were one and the same thing with "the enemy".

This, it seems to me, was the kind of "Marxism" that Foucault was criticizing, and the reason why Garland or Harcourt may today see these pages by Foucault as critical of Marx. This was also the origins of the affinity of Foucault—especially in *Discipline and Punish*—with the English historians such as E. P. Thompson, with Harry Braverman's reading of the relationship between the "scientific-technical revolution" and the "degradation of work", or even with aspects of Italian *operaismo*. In short, his penchant for a reading of Marx not as the author of the idea that economic structure "determines", even if "in the last instance", everything else—but the Marx who places at the centre of history and change, not the economy but class struggle. And what else if not class struggle is at the roots of Foucault's paean to "illegalism and refusal to work" in *The Punitive Society* (1973: 186–190, but see the whole Lecture of 14 March 1973) or of Foucault's description of a dialectic between "*illégalismes*" and "delinquency" which seems to border on a classic anarchist argument (1973: 139–151, and the lecture of 21 February 1973)? And what about Foucault's discussion of the relationship between wages and punishment in a way that is reminiscent of Evgeni Pashukanis' (1924) in *The General Theory of Law and Marxism* (see the Lecture of 31 January 1973; see also Elden 2015: 154)?

Visions of Social Control

So, we thought, factories are now obsolete (after all, a "bourgeois" sociologist, Daniel Bell, had already written, years before, of the advent of a "post-industrial society" (Bell 1960)), therefore, if the origins of the prison were irremediably tied to the origins of the factory, then also the prison was to be on its way out. And we could see sure evidence of that: at the time, everywhere emphasis was placed on the importance of "community", and the critique of "total institutions" (Goffman 1961; Basaglia 1968) had ushered in the rhetoric of decarceration (Scull 1977). The emergence of a "fiscal crisis of the State" (O'Connor 1973), connected to problems of legitimacy of the State (Habermas 1973), had translated in what seemed to be the inevitable reduction if not disappearance of the old-fashioned and costly prison institutions. It was indeed a bad timing for such prognosis—especially in the USA, very few years later would mark the start of the longest and most pronounced increase in the number of people committed and confined to prisons ever.[20]

In my own version, this meant that it was now the time to go "beyond the Panopticon" (Melossi 1979, 1980b) and realize that ghettoes of all sorts had taken the place of total institutions (Kraushaar 1978): the new places of confinement had no walls any longer! In Stanley Cohen's version (1985) instead it was a story of "net-widening" and "warehousing" the now clearly increasing number of "inmates". For Malcolm Feeley and Jonathan Simon (1992, 1994), it was now the time of replacing "actuarial" notions of "risk" for the passé concepts of "rehabilitation" and "discipline". Looking now back to what happened between the 1970s and 2008, in the USA, I have trouble with all these readings: the State of California for a good 30 years built a new prison every year, in the average, bringing the total number of inmates from 24,000 to 160,000, and the power elites of the state did not "believe" in prisons, and in the essentially disciplinary function of prisons? But if the goal had been to contain an "excess population" within walls in order to warehouse them and limit the risk they posed to free citizens outside, why bother about overcrowding? Why not set up enclosed "camps" where to detain men as cattle? After all, this had happened before! Instead, I believe prisons have kept performing their historical role as presiders to a kind of "internal" colonization (and "external" as well).[21]

Once again, I submit that there is a basic misunderstanding about the notion of "discipline" (and, indirectly, about the reading of *The Prison and the Factory*). The point of "discipline" is not really to teach actually useful skills to potential workers, in order to fit them in the historically given cycle of production, as a certain rhetoric of "resocialization" or "rehabilitation" would suggest.[22] The point of discipline rather is (at least programmatically) to teach the lesson of what we could call "subordinate inclusion", obedience, if you would rather like plain speaking. As we have seen, Marx never relented from noting that "subordination" is indeed the main issue because it is the necessary premise of "discipline". Where Marx describes the shift of analysis, and at the same time of the scene of action, from the "sphere of circulation" to "the sphere of production", he everlastingly describes the point I tried to make in *The Prison and the*

Factory and that I believe Foucault was making—among others—in *Discipline and Punish*:

> On leaving this sphere of simple circulation or of exchange of commodities, which furnishes the "Free-trader Vulgaris" with his views and ideas, and with the standard by which he judges a society based on capital and wages, we think we can perceive a change in the physiognomy of our *dramatis personae*. He, who before was the money-owner, now strides in front as capitalist; the possessor of labour-power follows as his labourer. The one with an air of importance, smirking, intent on business; the other, timid and holding back, like one who is bringing his own hide to market and has nothing to expect but – a hiding. (Marx 1867: 176)

The Revanche of Capital: Discipline and Subordinate Inclusion

We could think of the Prison therefore as a utopian representation of order consisting in the subordinate inclusion of its guests, who are the *outsiders* by definition, the perennial outsiders perhaps. What makes them outsiders of course may change. As Zygmunt Bauman stated, "all societies produce strangers; but each kind of society produces its own kind of strangers, and produces them in its own inimitable way" (Bauman 1995). And those strangers, those outsiders, so inimitably produced, are usually the guests of the prison, no matter when and where. Somewhere else, and trying to conjugate Marx with Rusche and Kirchheimer (1939), I offered the idea that there is indeed a connection between the cycle of class struggles and the "behaviour" of imprisonment rates (Melossi 2008: 229–252), according to which, in periods of strength of the working class, for a number of reasons imprisonment rates would be at a minimum (and "penal standards of life" at a maximum!). One of such periods was in the 1970s, when the political hegemony of work and labour was in fact accompanied by a minimum of imprisonment. In other words, the "refusal to work" among the marginal strata of society reached a peak in the generalization of anti-institutional and anti-authoritarian struggles of the 1970s due to the increasing questioning of the Fordist factory, struggles described in neo-Marxists' writings as well as, indirectly, in the emergence of Foucault's very relevant concept of *illégalismes* in *Discipline and Punish.*

The problem therefore, from the perspective of capital, was the restoration of command discipline. Nowhere this was clearer—it seems to me—than in the USA, especially in relation to the issue of "*illégalismes*" and "delinquency". As Jonathan Simon reminds us (2014), the (generally very young) leaders of the Black Panthers in the 1960s and 1970s were in a sense second generation "migrants", the children and grandchildren of the people who had moved northward and later westward from the South. So, for instance, in the Los Angeles area, a leader of his people as Bunchy Carter had contributed to the "politicization" of the Blousons gang in the 1960s and it was only after the demise of the Black Panthers and the fall of leaders such as Carter himself and John Huggins[23] that the young poor Black people from Los Angeles were brought back to the reality once again of street gangs such as the Bloods and the Crips.[24] Hadn't been after all C. Wright Mills who wrote about the necessity of turning "private troubles" into "public problems" (Mills 1959)?[25] After the fall of the various 1960s and 1970s movements, public problems—unemployment, the lack of collective rights, the repression of labour and political opposition—became again redefined as "private troubles". But, how much they were one or the other was of course a dependent variable of a power struggle defined in terms of "class" and "race". In this sense this period represented a textbook example of transformation of "*illégalismes*" into "delinquency" in the way indicated in the last section of Foucault's *Discipline and Punish* (1975: 257–292). First, the repression of the political vanguard, then the processes of criminalization in the double meaning of the term, as helping to construct a criminal underworld[26] and as the construction and diffusion of mass imprisonment (see on the connection between mass imprisonment and criminalization in the USA the work of Philippe Bourgois (1995), Victor Rios (2011) and Alice Goffman (2014)).

The nexus of discipline to the teaching of obedience to the goal of subordinate inclusion (whether there be a rhetoric of "rehabilitation" at work or not) seems therefore to be the perennial (programmatic) *raison d'être* of the prison. This nexus always concerns, mainly, outsiders, marginal strata, even if these may be "ethnic" in some places and "migrant" in others. Considering the relationships of crime, punishment and migration in Europe, and given that a new mass of immigrants went to replenish the ranks of the lowest strata of the working class, European societies recently have done nothing less but treat the immigrants as they were accustomed to treat the most disadvantaged among their own—something that had become hard to do after the workers' militancy of the 1960s and 1970s (Melossi 2015). We went therefore from the low levels of incarceration around 1970 (in spite of the cry of "repression repression!") to those much higher later on. But even in the days of the Great Recession, the prisons—the literally[27] monumental gateways conducing from the abstract sphere of equality and rights to the concrete one of discipline and subordination—seem to stand as tall as ever, presiding to the social processing of outsiders of all qualities and stripes, in a sort of "internal colonization". Whether Black and Latino people in Los Angeles and New York, or Africans and Eastern Europeans in the hundred lands of Europe, whether Arabs in Israel or Asians in the Gulf States, whether peasants *sin tierra* in Colombia or Brazil or peasants without legal residence in Shenzhen or Shanghai, they seem to huddle in slums and crowd jails in ways not too dissimilar from those described by Frederick Engels (1845) in 1844 Manchester. The process we described in *The Prison and the Factory* and that we deemed to have arrived at its final crisis when we were writing it seems to have instead developed much beyond the borders of Europe and North America, accompanying the "enlarged reproduction" of capital together with its geographic and military spread. Prisons have generally followed not far behind troops, and this also where very few factories have appeared on the scene. If capitalist society—whether characterized by private or by public capital—is essentially marked by class struggle, the idea of subordination seems to constitute its original and dominant principle, even *vis-à-vis* the very goal of production.

Notes

1. The original English version was published in 1981 by Macmillan (Melossi and Pavarini 1981).
2. At the time, a *laurea* was the only possible university degree in Italy and, according to how the "*tesi di laurea*" was developed by the candidate, its value could vary from that of a BA to that of a PhD. If I remember correctly, Massimo got his *laurea* in 1971, I in 1972.

3. Alessandro Baratta was Professor of Philosophy of Law at the University of Saarland, Saarbrücken, Germany, but in a close collaboration with Bricola in those days.

4. CNR is ConsiglioNazionaledelleRicerche, the Italian National Council of Research.

5. The NDC had been formed in July 1968 by Kit Carson, Stanley Cohen, David Downes, Mary McIntosh, Paul Rock, Ian Taylor and Jock Young. In the early 1970s the NDC—about which I recommend reading the pages written by Jock Young in the new Introduction to *The New Criminology* (2013: xxii–xxv)—somehow segued into the creation of the "European Group for the Study of Deviance and Social Control" which met the first time in September 1973 in Florence, Italy.

6. Massimo and I will then owe to our very dear and unforgettable friend Jock Young the decision to translate and publish *The Prison and the Factory* as one of the titles in the Macmillan "Critical Criminology Series".

7. The origin of the article is to be found in a paper given at the "Autorenkolloquium" organized by Alessandro Baratta and Karl Schuman in Bielefeld (FRG) on November 1–3, 1974 with Ian Taylor, Paul Walton and Jock Young, as a discussion of their *The New Criminology* (1973). See Melossi (1975b).

8. *Crime and Social Justice* was the main expression, in form of journal, of the American branch of "critical" or "radical" criminology, published by those who had given life to the brief (but long-lasting as heritage) Berkeley School of Criminology, closed by the University of California in 1974 also because of the political pressure coming from the Governor of the State, Ronald Reagan, who would then go on to becoming one of the most important political leaders in the "neo-liberal" "revolution" of the 1980s as president of the USA!

9. The authors were Gian Guido Balandi, Fabrizio Corsi, Dario Melossi, Marcello Pedrazzoli and Massimo Nobili. Marcello Pedrazzoli, who was several years our senior, was the author of great part of the document. He and Balandi went on to become Professors of Labour Law. Massimo Nobili was then Professor of Criminal Procedure. I lost track of Fabrizio Corsi. No matter our oppositional stance, we were rather pleased to be noted by some of the philosophers of law of the time such as our own Guido Fassò, in Bologna, who reviewed our document (Fassò 1969) or, even, Norberto Bobbio (1987: 308) about 20 years later (Balandi 2012).

10. Later on, in my work on Georg Rusche's biography (Melossi 1980a: 57), I discovered that Maurice Dobb had also helped Rusche to settle in London in the mid-1930s, writing letters of reference for him.

11. Also in the Lectures collected in *The Punitive Society* where, contrary to *Discipline and Punish*, Foucault (1973) sees the importance of the role of Quakers, he does not see however the importance of the workhouse and its constituting a very important link towards the penitentiary, especially by the action of William Penn and the Quakers. Penn had very probably met what was at the time the very new institution of the Workhouse—of which the Amsterdam *Rasphuis* was the most famous example—during his travels to the Netherlands and Northern Germany in 1677 (Lewis 1922: 10, Seidensticker 1878). In his penal reform a few years later (1681), part of the broader Quaker "holy experiment" of Pennsylvania, he established the clearest and most explicit link between the workhouses and the modern penitentiaries when he decreed that "all Prisons shall be workhouses for felons, Thiefs, vagrants, and Loose, abusive, and Idle persons, whereof one shall be in every county" (Dumm 1987: 79).

12. This was suggested to me, in a sense, by my mentor at UCSB, Don Cressey. I was discussing with him the relationship between economic change and imprisonment rates and, if we were quite certain about the way in which we should "measure" penality, through imprisonment rates, it was hard to identify a measure of the economy that would be able to express also the cultural changes accompanying economic change. After some running in a circle, Don looked at me and, with his rather typical manner of a good boy who knows he's doing something bad, asked, "What about the imprisonment rates?"

13. And, by the way, this is also why Socialism does not solve anything insofar as it shifts the nature of capital from "private" to "public" (which is of course sort of a joke in contemporary societies) but leaves the question of the extraction of surplus value untouched. At most, if our hypothetical Socialist society were to be organized along truly democratic principles, would make the issue of class struggle internal to the working class and to each individual member of the working class. The distinction between self-government and self-control would then be abolished (Dumm 1987) and self-control would be also, at the same time, self-government and self-exploitation. Finally there would be no distinction left between Marx's theory and Freud's and the command of the Super-Ego would be one and the same with the command of Capital!

14. In the "ancillary institutions", rules an authoritarian style that is however geared to producing self-governing, and therefore "free" Subjects. Subjects are also able to govern themselves collectively in the historical trajectory from the social contract to the Republic to democracy. These Subjects—capable of self-government because capable of self-control—would soon become those individuals endowed with "free will" by criminal and penal theorists of the Enlightenment. In the years of American independence, Benjamin Rush will call such Subjects, supposedly forged also by the newly discovered "penitentiaries", "republican machines" (Dumm 1987: 87–112).

15. See Harcourt (2013). Michael Welch (2010, 2011) has written in recent years on the relationship of Michel Foucault with the "Groupe d'information sur les prisons"—an activist group in France, in the early years of the 1970s, in which Foucault participated, trying to expose what was happening inside prisons, and connect with the prisoners' movement. In answering a letter that I had written to him on April 20, 1974, asking, among other things, whether "your group" had published on the prison, Foucault answered, on May 2, 1974, that "*we* have published a few pamphlets about the situation in French prisons" but adding right away that "*I* am going to complete a work on the history of prisons in a few months" (my transl. from French).

16. On September 9, 1971, the prisoners had managed to take the prison, and held a group of prison guards hostage. And while the Governor of the State of New York, Nelson Rockefeller, gave to understand that it was possible to generate a negotiated solution, at the same time prepared an armed intervention of the National Guard together with the prison guards who had escaped the hostage-taking situation, who eventually, on September 13, 1971, stormed the prison and produced something like 39 dead, 10 hostages and 29 prisoners. See the special issue of *Social Justice* of Fall 1991 dedicated to a commemoration of the events. See also, now, the reconstruction by historian Heather Ann Thompson (2016) according to whom both the prisoners and the hostages were killed by the indiscriminate shooting during the retake of the prison.

17. In the interview Foucault refers what he has seen in Attica and how Attica operates but nothing about the Attica rebellion. This is certainly quite bizarre, especially because in that very interview Foucault makes reference to the struggles of prisoners in France.

18. Marx (1867: 176) (quoted in Melossi 1977: 43).

19. Referenced more than once in the Lectures of *The Punitive Society* (see also Elden 2015: 160, Harcourt 2013: 277–278). Cf. Jock Young (2013) in the new Introduction to *The New Criminology* on the importance of British social historians on the emergence of the new deviancy theorists.

20. The prognosis however was not entirely wrong: there was no Franco Basaglia in the USA but drugs produced the same result as far as psychiatric institutions were concerned. Bernard Harcourt has shown that summing up psychiatric and criminal commitments there has indeed been an overall deinstitutionalization in the last half a century or so, even in the USA (Harcourt 2010).

21. As Angela Davis claims in an interview on *Social Justice* commenting on the building of new prisons in Latin America, "more prisons are being built to catch the lives disrupted by […] movement of capital. People who cannot find a place for themselves in this new society governed by capital end up going to prison" (Davis 2014: 51).

22. After all, already Bentham had to recognize that, in his Panopticon, solitary confinement had to give way to cell cohabitation if one wanted to keep up with the "modern" production of the end of the eighteenth century!

23. Who were both gunned down by members of a competing organization on the campus of UCLA on January 17, 1969.

24. See the 2006 documentary film *Bastards of the Party,* produced by Antoine Fuqua and directed by former Bloods gang member Cle Sloan. See also the interview with Ericka Huggins (2014), former BP member and widow of John.

25. I believe we should distinguish between what Taylor Walton and Young defined as "romanticisation of crime" in *Critical Criminology* (1975) and what I would call a "dialectic of crime and politics" here, that is the back and forth between a tradition of criminal behaviour of the lower classes wholly subordinated to the hegemony of power elites and the transformation instead of such behaviour into a political action able to challenge such hegemony. What looms in the background is of course the traditional debate, within the workers' movement, about the so-called *lumpenproletariat.*

26. Once again specific to the LA area, see the story about the CIA carrying drugs to the LA African American community in order to finance its own dirty wars—a story "discovered" by journalist Gary Webb with articles in the *San José Mercury Journal* in the 1990s and who was then perhaps too quickly later discredited as another "conspiracy theorist" (see www.huff-

ingtonpost.com/2014/10/10/gary-web-dark-alliance_n_5961748.html
accessed 29 October 2015). Of course the 1990s were the years of the
"crack cocaine epidemic" (and related "murder epidemic") in the USA.
27. See Foucault's description of Attica's entrance, "that kind of phony fortress *à la* Disneyland" (Foucault 1974: 26).

References

Balandi, Gianl Guido 2012 "Era una sera calda e afosa". Pp. 39–46 in Luca
Nogler and Luisa Corazza (Eds.), *Risistemare il diritto del lavoro. Liber amico-
rum Marcello Pedrazzoli*. Milano: Franco Angeli.
Basaglia, Franco (Ed) 1968 *L'istituzione negata*. Torino:Einaudi.
Bauman, Zygmunt 1995 "Making and Unmaking of Strangers." *Thesis Eleven*,
November, 43: 1–16.
Bell Daniel, 1960, *The End of Ideology: On the Exhaustion of Political Ideas in the
Fifties*, Cambridge: Havard UP, 2000.
Bentham Jeremy, 1787 "Panopticon". Pp. 37–66 in *The Works of Jeremy Bentham*.
New York: Russell & Russell, 1971.
Bergmann, Uwe, Rudi Dutschke, Wolfgang Lefèvre and Bernd Rabehl, 1968
Die Rebellion der Studenten oder Die neue Opposition Berlin: Rowohlt.
Bobbio, Norberto, 1987 "Ricordo di Giovanni Tarello", *Materiali per una Storia
della Cultura Giuridica* 17:303.
Bourgois, Philippe, 1995 *In Search of Respect: Selling Crack in El Barrio*.
Cambridge: Cambridge University Press (see also the "Preface to the 2003
Second Edition". Pp. xvii–xxiii).
Braverman, Harry 1974 *Labour and Monopoly Capital: The Degradation of Work
in the Twentieth Century*, New York: Monthly Review Press.
Cohen, Stanley 1985 *Visions of Social Control*. Cambridge: Polity Press.
Davis, Angela 2014 "Interview with Angela Davis" *Social Justice* 40 (1–2): 37–53.
Dobb, Maurice 1946 *Studies in the Development of Capitalism* London: Routledge.
Dumm, Thomas L. 1987 *Democracy and Punishment: Disciplinary Origins of the
United States*. Madison: The University of Wisconsin Press.
Elden, Stuart 2015 "A More Marxist Foucault? Reading *La société punitive*"
Historical Materialism 23:149–168.
Engels, Friederich 1845 *The Condition of the Working Class in England in 1844*.
New York: International, 1975.
Fasso', Guido 1969 "Il positivismo giuridico 'contestato'", *Rivista Trimestrale di
Diritto e Procedura Civile* 22:289.

Feeley, Malcolm M. and Jonathan Simon 1994 "Actuarial justice: the emerging new criminal law". Pp. 173–201 in D. Nelken (Ed.), *The Futures of Criminology*, London: Sage.

Feeley, Malcolm M. e Jonathan Simon 1992 "The New Penology: Notes on the Emerging Strategy of Corrections and Its Implications," *Criminology* 30:449–74.

Foucault, Michel 1973 *The Punitive Society. Lectures at the Collège de France 1972–1973*. Houndmills: Palgrave Macmillan, 2015.

Foucault, Michel 1974 "Michel Foucault on Attica: An Interview", *Telos* 19:154–161 (reprinted in *Social Justice* 1991, 18 (3), 27).

Foucault, Michel 1975, *Discipline and Punish*. New York: Pantheon, 1977.

Garland David, 2014 "What is a 'history of the present'? On Foucault's genealogies and their critical preconditions", *Punishment and Society* 16:365–384.

Garland, David, 1990, *Punishment and Modern Society: A Study in Social Theory*. Co-published by the University of Chicago Press and Oxford University Press, 312 pages.

Goffman, Alice 2014 *On the Run. Fugitive Life in an American City*. Chicago: University of Chicago Press.

Goffman, Erving 1961 *Asylums: Essays on the Social Situation of Mental Patients and Other Inmates*. Garden City (NY): Anchor Books.

Habermas, Jürgen 1973 *Legitimation Crisis*. Boston: Beacon, 1975.

Harcourt, Bernard E. 2013 "Course Context". Pp. 265–310 in Michel Foucault, *The Punitive Society. Lectures at the Collège de France 1972–1973*. Houndmills: Palgrave Macmillan, 2015.

Harcourt, Bernard E., 2010, "Neoliberal penality: A brief genealogy." *Theoretical Criminology* 14: 74–92.

Hay, Douglas, Peter Linebaugh, John G. Rule, E. P. Thompson, and Cal Winslow 1975 *Albion's Fatal Tree: Crime and Society in Eighteenth-Century England*. New York: Pantheon.

Howe, Richard H. 1978 "Max Weber's Elective Affinities: Sociology within the bounds of pure reason", *American Journal of Sociology* 84:366–85.

Huggins, Ericka 2014 "Two Interviews with Ericka Huggins" *Social Justice* 40:54–71.

Kraushaar Wolgang (Ed.), 1978, *Autonomie Oder Getto, Kontroversen über die Alternativbevegung*, Frankfurt: Verlag Neue Kritik.

Lewis, Orlando F. 1922 *The Development of American Prisons and Prisons Customs 1776 to 1845*. Whitefish: Kessinger, 2005.

Luxemburg, Rosa 1904 "Organizational Questions of the Russian Social Democracy" in Rosa Luxemburg, *The Russian Revolution and Leninism or Marxism?* Ann Arbor: University of Michigan Press, 1961.

Marx, Karl 1867 *Capital. Volume I.* New York: International Publishers.

Marx, Karl 1859 Preface to *A Contribution to the Critique of Political Economy.* Moscow: Progress Publishers, 1977.

Melossi, Dario 2015 *Crime, Punishment and Migration.* London: SAGE Publications.

Melossi Dario 2008 *Controlling Crime, Controlling Society: Thinking about Crime in Europe and America.* Cambridge: Polity Press.

Melossi, Dario 2003 "The Simple 'Heuristic Maxim' of an 'Unusual Human Being'". "Introduction" (pages 9–46) to the Transaction Edition of G.Rusche and O.Kirchheimer, *Punishment and Social Structure,* New Brunswick: Transaction Publishers.

Melossi, Dario 1980a "Georg Rusche: A Biographical Essay." *Crime and Social Justice* 14:51–63.

Melossi Dario, 1980b, "Oltre il 'Panopticon'. Per uno studio delle strategie di controllo sociale nel capitalismo del ventesimo secolo", *La questione criminale,* VI, 2–3, 277–361.

Melossi, Dario 1979 "Institutions of Social Control and Capitalist Organization of Work." Pp. 90–9 in Bob Fine et al., (eds.) *Capitalism and the Rule of Law: From Deviancy Theory to Marxism.* London: Hutchinson.

Melossi, Dario 1977 "Prison and Labour in Europe and Italy during the Formation of the Capitalist Mode of Production". Pp. 9–95 in Dario Melossi and Massimo Pavarini, *The Prison and the Factory: Origins of the Penitentiary System,* 1981.

Melossi, Dario 1976 "The Penal Question in 'Capital'." *Crime and Social Justice* 5:26–33.

Melossi, Dario 1975a "Criminologia e marxismo: alle origini della questione penale nella societa de 'Il capitale'." *La questione criminale* 1:319–38.

Melossi, Dario 1975b "Da Colchester a Bielefeld." *La questione criminale* 1:189–95.

Melossi, Dario and Massimo Pavarini 1981 *The Prison and the Factory: Origins of the Penitentiary System.* London: Macmillan and Totowa (NJ): Barnes and Noble (translation of Dario Melossi and Massimo Pavarini, *Carcere e fabbrica: alle origini del sistema penitenziario.* Bologna: Il mulino, 1977).

Melossi, Dario and Massimo Pavarini 1977 *Carcere e fabbrica: alle origini del sistema penitenziario.* Bologna: Il mulino.

Mills, C. Wright 1959 *The Sociological Imagination.* New York: Oxford University Press.

O'Connor, James 1973 *The Fiscal Crisis of the State* New York: St.Martin's Press.

Pashukanis, Evgeni 1924 *The General Theory of Law and Marxism.* Pp. 37–131 in P. Beirne and R. Sharlet (Eds.), *Pashukanis: Selected Writings on Marxism and Law.* London: Academic Press, 1980.

Rios Victor M., 2011, *Punished. Policing the Lives of Black and Latino Boys*, New York, New York University Press

Rosenfeld, Seth 2012 *Subversives: The FBI's War on Student Radicals, and Reagan's Rise to Power*. New York : Farrar, Straus and Giroux.

Rusche, Georg and Otto Kirchheimer, 1939, *Punishment and Social Structure*. New Brunswick (NJ): Transaction Publishers, 2003.

Scull, Andrew T., 1977, *Decarceration: Community Treatment and the Deviant – A Radical View*. Englewood Cliffs (NJ) : Prentice-Hall.

Seidensticker, Oswald 1878 "William Penn's Travels in Holland and Germany in 1677", *The Pennsylvania Magazine of History and Biography* 2(3):237–282.

Sellin, Thorsten 1944 *Pioneering in Penology*. Philadelphia: University of Pennsylvania Press.

Simon Jonathan, 2014, "A Radical Need for Criminology", *Social Justice*, 40, 1–2, 9–23.

Taylor, Ian, Paul Walton, and Jock Young 1973 *The New Criminology: For a Social Theory of Deviance*. London: Routledge.

Taylor, Ian, Paul Walton, and Jock Young (eds) 1975 *Critical Criminology*. London: Routledge.

Thompson, Edward P. 1975 *Whigs and Hunters: The Origin of the Black Act*. London: Penguin.

Thompson, Heather Ann 2016 *Blood in the Water: The Attica Prison Uprising of 1971 and its Legacy*. New York: Pantheon.

Weber, Max 1904–5 *The Protestant Ethic and the Spirit of Capitalism*. New York: Scribner's, 1958.

Welch Michael, 2011, "Counterveillance: How Foucault and the Groupe d'information sur les prisons reversed the optics", *Theoretical Criminology*, 15,3, 301–313.

Welch Michael, 2010, "Pastoral power as penal resistence: Foucault and the Groupe d'information sur les prisons", *Punishment & Society*, 12, 1, 47–63.

Young, Jock 2013 "Introduction to 40th anniversary edition". Pp. xi–li in Ian Taylor, Paul Walton, and Jock Young *The New Criminology: For a Social Theory of Deviance. 40th anniversary edition*. London: Routledge.

Part 1

Prison and Labour in Europe and Italy During the Formation of the Capitalist Mode of Production
Dario Melossi

Creation of the Modern Prison in England and Europe (1550–1850)

Dario Melossi

Bridewells and Workhouses in Elizabethan England

The process, therefore, that *clears the way* for the capitalist system, can be none other than *the process which takes away from the labourer the possession of his means of production*; a process that *transforms*, on the one hand, the social means of subsistence and of production *into capital*; on the other hand, the immediate producers into *wage-labourers*. The so-called '*primitive accumulation*' therefore, is nothing else than the *historical process of divorcing the producer from the means of production*. It appears as primitive because it forms the *pre-historic stage of capital* and of the mode of production corresponding with it. The economic structure of capitalistic society has grown out of the economic structure of feudal society. The dissolution of the latter set free the elements of the former.[1]

This well-known passage in which Marx outlines the essential meaning of the 'so-called primitive accumulation' is the key to a reading of those historical events which are the subject of our enquiry. The same process, *of divorcing the producer from his means of production*, is at the root of a dual phenomenon: the transformation of means of production into

© The Author(s) 2018
D. Melossi, M. Pavarini, *The Prison and the Factory (40ᵗʰ Anniversary Edition)*,
Palgrave Studies in Prisons and Penology, DOI 10.1057/978-1-137-56590-7_2

capital; and the transformation of the immediate producer tied to the soil into a *free* labourer. The process manifests itself concretely in the economic, political, social, ideological and moral dissolution of the feudal world. The first aspect of the question, the creation of capital, does not concern us here. Rather it is the second aspect, *the formation of the proletariat*,[2] that constitutes the more fruitful area of research.

The disbanding of feudal retainers, the dissolution of the monasteries, the enclosures of land for sheep-farming and changes in the methods of tillage each played their part'[3] in the great expulsion of peasants from the land in fifteenth- and sixteenth-century England. But according to Dobb's classic thesis, the feudal mode of production was being drained by its own inefficiency even before these events[4]; as the system demanded heavier workloads of the peasants, the only escape routes left open to them were vagabondage in the countryside or flight to the towns. The decline of feudalism and the corresponding brutality in social relations was marked by the intensification of the class struggle in the countryside, the prime expression of which was the desertion by the peasantry from increasingly intolerable conditions.[5]

Thousands of dispossessed workers in the countryside flocked to the towns which, with the development of economic activity, especially commerce, already represented a notable pole of attraction; the dispossessed now became the mass of the unemployed – beggars, vagrants and in some cases, bandits.

In its quest for expansion, capital displayed its most ruthless class savagery in the movement for the enclosure of common land. When referring to the relevant eighteenth-century legislation, Marx was to define the rape of the countryside which drove the first ranks of the future proletariat into the towns, as 'decrees of expropriation of the people'.[6] Thomas More gave this lucid description of the phenomenon in his *Utopia* as early as 1516:

> Your sheep that were wont to be so meek and tame, and so small eaters, now as I hear say, be become so great devourers and so wild, that they eat up, and swallow down the very men themselves ... For look in what parts of the realm doth grow the finest and therefore dearest wool, there noblemen and gentlemen ... leave no ground for tillage, they inclose all into

pastures; ... by one means therefore or by other, either by hook or crook they must needs depart away, poor, silly, wretched souls, men, women, husbands, wives, fatherless children, widows, woeful mothers, with their young babes, and their whole household small in substance and much in number, as husbandry requireth many hands ... And when they have wandered abroad till that be spent, what can they then else do but steal, and then justly pardy be hanged, or else go about begging.[7]

The state's initial response to what was at the time a social phenomenon of unprecedented proportions is quite clearly described by Marx:

The proletariat created by the breaking up of the bands of feudal retainers and by the forcible expropriation of the people from the soil, this 'free' proletariat could not possibly be absorbed by the nascent manufacturers as fast as it was thrown upon the world. On the other hand, these men, suddenly dragged from their wonted mode of life, could not as suddenly adapt themselves to the discipline of their new condition. They were turned *en masse* into beggars, robbers, vagabonds, partly from inclination, in most cases from stress of circumstances. Hence at the end of the 15th century and during the whole of the 16th century throughout Western Europe a bloody legislation against vagabondage. The fathers of the present working class were chastised for their enforced transformation into vagabonds and paupers. Legislation treated them as 'voluntary' criminals, and assumed that it depended on their own good will to go on working under the old conditions that no longer existed.[8]

Marx goes on to cite examples of the growth during the fourteenth, fifteenth and sixteenth centuries of draconian legislation against vagabondage, begging and – to a lesser extent – crime, in the face of which traditional medieval structures, based as they were on private and religious charity, proved impotent. Moreover, the secularisation of ecclesiastical wealth following the reformation in England and Europe had the twofold effect of contributing to the expulsion of peasants from church property and of leaving those hitherto dependent on the charity of the monasteries and religious orders without means of subsistence. The greater the scale of proletarianisation, therefore, the less the effectiveness of the campaign of terror,[9] while, at the same time, the development of the economy, and of manufacture in particular, demanded an ever greater quantity of labour from the countryside. More pointed out the only logical solution as early as 1516 when he strongly advocated the necessity of placing this 'idle sort'[10] in useful employment. An Act of 1530 made the registration of vagrants compulsory. For the first time a distinction was made between those unable to work ('the impotent poor'), who were authorised to beg, and the rest, who were forbidden any kind of charity on pain of being flogged until the blood ran.[11] The principal instruments of English social policy remained whipping, banishment and capital punishment until the middle of the century, by which time conditions were evidently ripe for what was to prove a model experiment. At the request of certain representative clerics alarmed at the amount of begging in London, the King consented to the use of Bridewell Palace as a place where vagrants, idlers, thieves and petty criminals would be housed.[12] The aim of the institution, which was to be run with an iron hand, was threefold: to reform the inmates by means of compulsory labour and discipline; to discourage vagrancy and idleness outside its walls; and, last but not least, to ensure its own self-sufficiency by means of labour.[13] Work mainly centred around textiles in accordance with the need of the time, and the experiment must on the whole have been crowned with success since houses of correction, indiscriminately referred to as Bridewells, soon appeared in various parts of England.

Even so a comprehensive policy was reached only under the various acts of the Elizabethan Poor Law, which were destined to remain in force without any real alteration until 1834. An act dated 1572 set up the general system of relief based on parishes. Parishioners paid a poor rate for the maintenance of their local 'impotent poor' whilst sturdy 'rogues and vagabonds' were to be furnished with work.[14] Since this last provision was to be satisfied only when the impotent poor had been catered for,[15] in fact no effective assistance was given to the unemployed, who simply continued to be the object of repression.[16]

Four years later, the entire problem was tackled by the introduction of houses of correction throughout the country so that refractory or unemployed workers could be set to work.[17] As in Bridewell, the prototype, their population was extremely mixed: paupers' children 'so that youth might be accustomed and brought up to labour', those looking for work, and all the categories noted in the first Bridewells: petty offenders, vagabonds, petty thieves, prostitutes and poor people refusing to work.[18] If the inmates received differential treatment at all, it was based on the grading of heavy jobs. The only act to which a real criminal intention seems to have been attributed was the refusal to work. As we can see, under the Act of 1601 (wrongly judged to be the principal statute of the old Poor Law whereas it merely completed preceding legislation) judges were vested with powers to despatch 'idle blockheads' to the common gaol.[19] However, it is necessary to clarify exactly what 'refusal to work' actually meant in the sixteenth century. A series of statutes promulgated between the fourteenth and sixteenth centuries fixed maximum wages. It was unlawful for anyone to exceed the stated limits. It was impossible for workers to negotiate wages or to conduct collective bargaining. Labourers were obliged to accept the first available job on whatever conditions the employers cared to establish.[20] In this way, forced labour in workhouses or houses of correction was geared towards breaking working-class resistance; it compelled labourers to accept the most exploitative conditions.

On this point, it is interesting to consider the hypothesis advanced by G. Rusche and O. Kirchheimer. Their view is that the introduction of forced labour in Europe during the late sixteenth century and in particular, as we shall see, the early seventeenth century, is related to the seventeenth-century population decline throughout Europe which must have contributed to the strength of the working class on the market.[21] They argue that the period between the fifteenth century and the early sixteenth century witnessed a bloody and ruthless repression of the mass of the unemployed at a time when there was a plentiful supply of labour. But with the approach of the seventeenth century, the labour supply dwindled and nascent capital needed state intervention to guarantee the high profits brought about by the so-called 'price revolution' of the sixteenth century.[22] Even if all this holds good it is also necessary to consider, as Marx noted[23] in the above passage, that the demand for labour by no means proceeded *pari passu* with labour supply, particularly in the 'primitive' phase of capitalism, where organising sufficient capital to make full use of the available labour is much the slower process. In fact, the growing supply of labour in the second half of the sixteenth century could not meet the demands of the prosperous and turbulent times of

Elizabethan England. Forced labour had to be resorted to if the new proletariat was to be prevented from taking advantage of this situation. It thus kept down labour costs on the free market right from the start. Nor must one forget, as Marx noted, that this newly formed proletariat was reluctant to enter the totally alien world of manufacture. As F.F. Piven and R.A. Cloward observed:

> Bred to labour under the discipline of the sun and season, however severe that discipline may be, they may resist the discipline of the factory and machine, which, though it may be no more severe, may seem so because it is alien. The process of human adjustment to these economic changes has ordinarily entailed generations of mass unemployment, distress and disorganisation.[24]

I will return to this problem later, since it is fundamental in understanding the historical role of forced labour in segregated institutions such as the Elizabethan houses of correction. Suffice it to say, for the moment, that this type of institution was the first and most important example of secular detention involving more than mere custody in the history of prison; its characteristic features, its social function and its internal organisation are, as far as the final form of the institution is concerned, already *to a large extent* those of the classic nineteenth-century model of prison.

Manufacture and the Amsterdam Rasp-Huis

It was, however, in Holland during the first half of the seventeenth century[25] that the new institution of the workhouse reached its highest form in the period of early capitalism. A juridical history (that is, the history of ideas, the history of 'the spirit') would characteristically have us believe that this new and original form of punitive segregation sprang from the individual genius of some reformer. However, given that the earlier English initiatives (Bridewells) had no *direct* influence on those of the seventeenth-century Dutch ones, it is apparent that the origins of the workhouse were rooted in the whole of capitalist development.[26] We can point to two factors around the late sixteenth and early seventeenth centuries impelling Holland to adopt a system of forced labour which was to become a model for the whole of Reformation Europe: first, as a result of the struggle for independence led by the urban mercantile class and sanctioned by the Union of Utrecht in 1579, the northern provinces of the Netherlands took over the secular state of Flanders which suffered impoverishment and strangulation at the hands of Philip II.[27] The golden age of Amsterdam followed. Secondly, the precipitant growth of trade inflated the demand for labour without a plentiful supply being available on the market (as there had been in England) at a time when Europe was undergoing a serious decline in population.[28] There was a risk that rising Dutch capital would find itself faced with a high cost of labour and a proletariat which would in some way be in a position to bargain over the sale of its labour-power despite repressive constraints. According to Rusche and Kirchheimer's interpretive hypothesis,[29] this was the economic and social situation which caused the young Dutch Republic to change its punitive methods in an effort to avoid wasting as little of the workforce as possible whilst controlling and regulating its use as capital required.

It needs to be stressed, of course, that a hypothesis restricted largely to the relationship between the labour market and forced labour (in the sense of unfree labour) cannot exhaust the entire thematic of workhouses. As we have already seen in the English case, these institutions were by no means the only instrument used in the attempt to depress wages and control the labour force. Nor, for that matter, was this the only use to which workhouses were put. As regards the first point, such instruments were accompanied, (as we have seen in England, although the point is generally valid for this period) by legally fixed maximum wages, the lengthening of the working day and the prohibiting of association and meetings, etc.[30] In reality, the fact that they were always confined to a relatively small scale means that it is better to see them as an *index* of the general level of class struggle rather than as an influencing factor. The function of workhouses was undoubtedly much more complex than that of being a simple regulator of free labour. To put it a different way, one could say that this last objective taken in its fullest sense means *control of the labour force*, its education and training. As

Marx states in a passage already cited,[31] adaptation 'to the discipline of their new condition', that is, the transformation of the ex-agricultural worker expelled from the land into wage labourer, with all that that implies, is one of the principal tasks the first capitalists had to undertake. Workhouses and many other similar organisations respond especially to this need. Evidently this question is inseparable from that of labour supply. This is not simply because the institutionalisation of (however limited) a section of the labour force in workhouses has a dual effect – first on free labour as already outlined, and secondly on forced labour, generally the most rebellious, in the sense of learning a discipline – but also because the extent to which a nascent working class displays docility or opposition depends on its relative strength in the market. Clearly, its capacity for stubbornness, opposition and resistance grows with the scarcity of labour. It may be expressed spontaneously through crime, increased aggressiveness and revolt rather than in a conscious or organised form but it still tends to endanger the social order and becomes objectively political.[32]

In the wake of studies by von Hippel and Hallema, Thorstein Sellin's book *Pioneering in Penology*[33] provides us with the richest and most meaningful reconstruction of the structure and function of a workhouse during the seventeenth century. The intimately bourgeois character of the movement which began to emerge on the penal question around the time of the Renaissance and which found its first expression in English and particularly in Dutch Humanism, appears very clearly in the principal thesis of a pamphlet on vagabondage by D. V. Coornhert. Rather like More in *Utopia*, Coornhert reasons that since slaves in Spain are worth 100–200 guilders, free Dutchmen, the majority of whom were skilled in some way, ought to be worth more alive than dead. It would be more fitting, he argues, to put anybody committing crimes to work.[34] It was not long before the work of Coornhert (and of succeeding reformers) was put into practice. In July 1589, the Amsterdam Magistrates decided to set up a house:

> where all vagabonds, evildoers, rascals and the like could be imprisoned for their punishment and could be given labour for periods of time which the magistrates found suitable considering their offences or misdeeds.[35]

After further discussion, the new establishment was inaugurated in 1596 in what had formerly been a convent. The institution was expected to support itself by means of the inmates' labour. There was no individual profit either for the governors, who received an honorarium, or for the warders, who were given a regular wage. This distinguished it from the old English custodial prisons where warders could constantly extort money from prisoners, a factor contributing in no small measure to the terrible conditions to be found, for example, in the county gaols of late medieval England. The Dutch institution's population was similar in composition to that of its English forerunners: young petty offenders,[36] beggars, vagrants and thieves. They were admitted either by administrative or by juridical order. Sentences tended to be short and for a stated period which could be altered depending on the prisoner's behaviour. Of course, the Dutch *Rasp-huis* did not provide a complete substitute for the whole range of punitive measures already in existence any more than did the English workhouses or houses of correction or others which subsequently developed in Europe. It stood somewhere between the fine, pure and simple or light corporal punishment on the one hand and deportation, exile and the death penalty on the other hand. The important point here is that those destined for the workhouse were labelled as the 'criminological types' of the time; the origins and development of these criminal categories lay in the birth and development of capitalism itself.

The institution was based on cells, each containing more than one inmate. Work was carried out in the cells or, weather permitting, in the large central courtyards. It was a question of applying the dominant productive model: *manufacture*. Dutch workhouses became widely known as *Rasp-huis* because the type of work mainly performed was the pulverisation with a multiple-blade saw of a certain wood for use in dyeing textiles. This process could be carried out in one of two ways: either with a millstone, a method commonly adopted by employers of free labour, or, as in the workhouse, by placing the hard South American wood across a bench with two inmates standing at either side and using a heavy saw to make the sawdust. This particular method was considered most suitable for the lazy and idle, who often broke their backs – quite literally – whilst doing it. Such was the justification for choosing this most fatiguing method. Incidentally, it is interesting to note that buyers of *Rasp-huis* sawdust complained of its inferior quality compared to what they obtained from the mill, but the fact is that the Amsterdam workhouse had an effective monopoly of this sort of work and indeed, the municipality became involved in legal disputes with other local authorities seeking to establish more advanced production methods. This system, based on the distribution of privilege and monopoly, is typical of the mercantilist outlook of an age in which capital was still in its infancy and required the active support of the state to make up for its weakness.[37] The initiation of a public policy, as in the management of pauperism through poor relief and workhouses, is an integral part of this particular approach to economic relationships. What is interesting here, however, is the specific relationship that came to be established between the chosen technique of production and the aim and function of houses of correction. This can be seen from the outset in terms of the problematic nature of the economic relationship between free and forced labour which looms ever larger as the development of capital accelerates the growth of its fixed component.

During what could be described as the 'preparatory studies' carried out prior to the opening of the workhouse, Dr. Egbertszoon, whose proposals were to be adopted by the Amsterdam administration, criticised a number of points advanced in the programme of the utopian Spiegel. In particular, he attacked the latter's views on prison labour. Egbertszoon held that since most prisoners were of low intelligence, they would be most efficiently employed in a single trade because teaching them a skill involved time and money. Moreover, the work ought to be based on minimum investment and maximum profit and pay should not be fixed once and for all but left to the discretion of the warders who could regulate it according to 'behaviour'.[38] It is significant that the form of manufacture involved little use of machinery, capital being mainly invested in raw materials. Forced labour was accompanied by a minimal use of capital; production was low in quality and volume, and profits were ensured by exceptionally depressed wages. It was the very *protectionist* nature of this type of industry as against the free market that permitted its survival. In this sense, there were obvious conflicts with those seeking to introduce grinding machines. They wanted to deal with a reduction in the labour force to which workhouses largely owed their existence, by introducing machines – in this instance, one of the oldest machines of all, the mill. In other words, they sought to intensify the extraction of surplus value.[39] The curbing of the class struggle by means of segregated institutions also put an immediate restraint on the development of capital itself. It was not only free workers who opposed the idea (for obvious reasons), but also capitalist interests excluded from privilege. The choice of the roughest and most tiring production methods depended on the possibility of extracting high profits without heavy capital investment, given a situation in which the classical monopoly of mercantilism enjoyed protection against external competition. But this choice had another side to it which is hidden amongst the half-truths mouthed by the ideologues of the age about the punitive character of fatiguing work or the 'low intelligence' of the labour force which filled the *Rasp-huis*. Manufacture recruited its labour essentially from two kinds of small producer ruined by the development of capitalism: the ex-artisan and the ex-peasant. Basically it was the latter who filled the houses of correction and clearly artisans were more suited to the new mode of production than the peasantry. Furthermore, manufacture had developed, as Marx stated:

> in every ... handicraft that it seizes upon, a class of so-called *unskilled labourers*, a class which handicraft industry strictly excluded. If it develops a one-sided speciality into a perfection, at the expense of the whole of a man's working capacity, it also begins to make a speciality of the absence of all development.[40]

These 'unskilled workers' are precisely those working in the kind of production examined here which generally forms part of the first operations of production. However, such workers remained a minority in manufacturing while those who retained some residual skill as artisans displayed a capacity for insubordination and resistance towards capitalist manufacture which had not yet been shattered by the arrival of machines.[41] Hence, given the problem of managing a section of workers that needed to be disciplined and coerced into its place in the world of manufacture, clearly the most suitable method of production would tend to be that which could render workers most docile and which would demand the least knowledge and skill of them lest they be furnished with the means of resistance.

In any event, no matter where the workers came from and whether they were skilled or not, at this stage the monotonous and heavy practice of *rasping* best suited what was at the time the basic function of corrective institutions: disciplinary training for capitalist production. As Sellin notes,[42] proposals elaborated by Spiegel in his primitive programme for giving vocational training to inmates were completely rejected. Instead, it was emphasised that the aim of the institution was to prepare its guests to follow a 'life of laborious honesty',[43] an objective to be fulfilled by regulating their behaviour and by obtaining their submission to authority. This attitude must have been most evident when it came to work. It is no coincidence that the most serious infraction of discipline, necessitating reappearance in court rather than internal sanction or extension of sentence, was the refusal to work for the third time. This accords with the ascetic view of life typical of Calvinism in the young Dutch republic.[44] A view of life according to which the work ethic and ideological subordination were to be reinforced in the houses of correction, as parts of the more general bourgeois-Calvinist *Weltanschauung*. Only then did it concern itself with exploitation and the extraction of surplus value. To sum up, it seems very clear to me, even from these early examples of workhouses, that the inefficient and backward form in which exploitation took place in this institution (a backwardness which could only exist in so far as state violence permitted exceptionally low wages compared to external levels) does *not* indicate a dysfunction in relation to the system as a whole. The workhouse was not a true and proper place of production, it was a place for teaching the *discipline of production*. As a matter of fact, low wages in this sense were extremely useful in that they make work methods particularly oppressive and pave the way for obedience outside. The particularly severe conditions inside houses of correction had a further effect on the outside world: jurists call it 'general prevention', that is, the intimidation of free labourers into accepting the general conditions of life and work imposed on them as being at least preferable to those inside prisons or workhouses. Hence, quite apart from the absolute pre-eminence assigned to work, the internal regime in workhouses tended to accentuate the role of that total bourgeois *Weltanschauung* to which the free proletarian never entirely commits himself. The prominence given to order, cleanliness, uniforms, hygiene (except of course when it came to working conditions), the rules against swearing, using slang or obscene language, reading, writing or singing ballads unless allowed by the governors (in a place and time characterised by the struggle for freedom of thought!), the prohibitions on gambling and the use of nicknames, etc. – all of this constituted an attempt both to impose the newly discovered way of life and to smash a radically counterposed underground popular culture which combined forms of the old peasant way of life with new methods of resistance called forth by capitalism's incessant attacks on the proletariat. If one cannot understand the close connection between the worker in manufacture and later in the factory with social relations as a whole; if one cannot understand the thoroughness with which, even in the early stages of its development, capital tried in every possible way to pull together a proletariat for itself and to secure the most favourable conditions for the exploitation of labour, one will not succeed in seeing how a series of factors and social events, far from being insignificant, reveal meaning and direction which link them up with manufacture during this period. The general significance of this relationship is well described by Marx in his depiction of the worker in manufacture:

> … manufacture thoroughly revolutionises it, and seizes labour-power by its very roots. It converts the labourer into a crippled monstrosity, by forcing his detailed dexterity at the expense of a world of productive capabilities and instincts; just as in the States of La Plata they butcher a whole beast for the sake of his hide or his tallow.[45]

The role assigned by the worthy Calvinists to the seventeenth-century workhouse will later be assumed by the modern prison: to ensure the suppression of a *world of productive capabilities and instincts* in order to concentrate upon that minute part of the individual useful to the capitalist work process. The total impoverishment of the individual takes place in manufacture and in the factory; but preparation and training is ensured by a string of ancillary institutions from which basic features of modern life have already begun to develop by this time: the nuclear family, school, prison, the hospital and later the barracks and the mental asylum ensure the production, education and reproduction of the workforce for capital.[46] Resistance is the only alternative. At first, spontaneous, unconscious, *criminal*, later organised, conscious and *political* as the pro-letariat begins to learn opposition both in the factories and in the various institutions mentioned above. The relationship between capital and labour determines the general course of development once the new society is born and the new terms of struggle are posed. A number of observations made by Sellin in his discussion of the *Rasp-huis* may provide us with evidence on this. He reports on collective punishments meted out for refusing to work.[47] It is interesting to note that by the first half of the eighteenth century the number of blades used on saws had been reduced from twelve to eight, then to six and finally to five. At the same time, the amount of sawdust produced per week by each inmate fell from 300 to 200 lbs. Naturally this must have been due to the use of an obsolete method of production, out of date since its inception, as well as to the more general evolution of workhouses over the centuries. However, the opposition in this institution to which Sellin refers (despite his lack of interest in reconstructing this aspect of the workhouse) must have been a contributory factor of no little significance.

Genesis and Development of Prisons in Other European Countries

We will now consider the situation more generally. Before the development of capitalism in England, forms of capitalist production arose in certain areas of Italy, Germany, Holland and, somewhat later, in France.[48] It is not relevant here to examine how and through what complex of historic events the precocious development of capitalism in these areas later became much inferior to the development of capitalism in England (or indeed, how Italian capitalism actually regressed). The important thing is that capitalist development in these areas coincided with the creation of a 'roaming, landless, depressed class, competing for employment'[49] and of a vast stratum of workers excluded from corporations, for example the Florentine Ciompi (wage-earners in the wool industry).[50] The so-called 'price revolution' caused real wages to fall in sixteenth-century France, Flanders and Germany at a time when there was a plentiful supply of labour.[51] In this situation, the 'bloody repression of vegabondage' was complemented by the equally ruthless repression of the unemployed masses: free association, strike action and abandonment of work were severely dealt with, wide use being made of the *galley*. Houses of *correction* multiplied. In Paris, where the *Royaume des Truands* was built, the number of vagabonds amounted to one third of the total population.

One of the first reactions to this situation was to replace the old system of private and religious charity with public assistance coordinated by the state. This was in social terms one of the most significant consequences of the confiscation of ecclesiastical property during the Reformation.

Luther himself undertook the interpretation and diffusion of new ideas about charity in his *Letter to the Christian Nobility* which clearly stated that begging ought to be abolished, each parish providing for its own poor.[52] He later elaborated a detailed scheme of assistance which Charles V was to apply throughout the empire.[53] However, measures to remove assistance to the poor from purely private initiative were not simply confined to Protestant countries. The development of a commercial bourgeoisie and a national state in Catholic France, for example, gave rise to a similar problem and a similar solution. Take the case of Lyons, a trading and commercial centre where the population doubled during the first half of the sixteenth century.[54] After the continual agitation among artisans, day-labourers and the poor in 1529, 1530, and 1531, a decision was made to set up a centralised, comprehensive scheme of welfare. Two years later the system was extended to every parish in France by decree of Francis I. At the same time, the French created their version of the workhouse: *l'Hôpital,* which was based much more on confinement as such rather than on work as was typical of institutions in the countries of the Reformation. On the other hand, confinement only became general in France (within limits, as we shall see) during the second half of the next century – a notable delay in comparison with England and the Protestant states. Undoubtedly, however, this was not simply due to religious influences; the fact that workhouses and houses of correction flourished in Flanders, the Netherlands and Northern Germany considerably earlier had much to do with the more advanced stage of capitalism reached in these parts. Nevertheless these dynamic societies undergoing a process of total transformation did, it is true, provide the most favourable conditions for the existence and growth of both the Reformation and the new attitude to poverty alike. There is no denying that Catholicism could not compare with the various strands of Protestantism, especially Calvinism, in furnishing a complete vision of the world and of life based on the *work ethic*, that *religion of capital* which gave life to the first segregated institutions.[55]

In the transition from medieval peasant society to bourgeois-industrial society, the worker is no longer subject to the direct, immediate ties of the Seigneur – ties which were juridically and militarily guaranteed, and justified on an ideological level by a completely theocratic vision of life. Now he is governed by a much more indirect force, that of economic coercion. Moreover, it is only in its fully developed form that capitalism comes to exercise so complete a material and ideological hegemony over society that it can use need on its own as a means of compulsion in the running of society. In the long period of transition we are now considering, during which an interpenetration of peasant and urban economies persisted, the 'outlawed' worker went through the novel experience of being, as Marx observed, 'free' and 'dissolved of ties'. It was only an illusory freedom, of course – the freedom to die of hunger, a freedom to which authority frequently responded with drastic terroristic measures. None the less, the social relations which emerged in this period did present the worker with a series of alternatives which, though often quite dramatic and desperate, had not existed in previous social structures.

It is no coincidence that this was the day of the vagabond, the brigand, the rural thief, peasant revolt and the beginnings of class struggle in the towns. The bourgeois monarchies still depended on the use of violence for the control of the lower classes, although it was necessary to build a world where violence as a generally valid instrument of control could be largely avoided. The workers' 'liberty' will be expressed in the Enlightenment law through the concept of the *contract*. This marks a great change even if, as the Marxist critique was to show, this apparent liberty is nothing but the sanctioning of a different kind of force no longer juridical-military or political, but economic. Clearly, social organisation is considerably different where labour is allocated through the impersonal workings of the market (however terribly concrete), as against that in which it is exploited under the personal and perpetual supervision and control of the exploiter. This is the structure upon which the whole dialectic between the principle of liberty and the principle of authority is based. It began with bourgeois society and the Reformation was its first basic expression. Authority in the medieval system weaves together the social relations of an undifferentiated peasant community which derives internal cohesion and all-embracing structure from its very penetration by the religious, political and economic hierarchy. In the *dialectic* of the peasant *liberation* and the transformation of the peasantry into proletarians, this hierarchical order ends in destruction: while the principle of authority becomes the very basis of capitalist production *inside the factory*, it contracts and withdraws from *certain areas of external social life*. The more the principle of authority progresses inside the factory, the more it controls the organisation of exploitation, the more the struggle for liberalism and democracy advances outside (that is, at least for as long as the canons of 'classic' eighteenth-century capitalism remained valid). In any event this opened up a profound contradiction between the world of the factory and the external world. It is no coincidence that this contradiction was to become one of the major areas of struggle for the organised proletariat. Moreover, authority in the factory is an impersonal, *mute* authority; it has lost the rich ideological character of religious medieval society. Thus, authority in the factory must always be accompanied by external control over the labour force – indeed such control began to unfold on more than one level during this period. It was a question of inducing in the worker a natural and spontaneous tendency to submit to factory discipline, whilst reserving the use of open force merely for a minority of rebels. Such control – and here the importance of religious reform and its connection with the early forms of confinement is evident – developed in two ways: within the individual (and within the family) and within the *segregated institutions*.[56] In his early works, Marx very succinctly expresses all this in a few lines:

> Luther, to be sure, overcame servitude based on devotion, but by replacing it with servitude based on conviction. He shattered faith in authority by restoring the authority of faith. He transferred the priests into laymen by changing the laymen into priests. He liberated man from external religiosity by making religiosity that which is innermost to man. He freed the body of chains by putting the heart in chains … it was no longer a question of the layman's struggle with the priest outside of him, but of his struggle with his own inner priest, his priestly nature.[57]

The disintegration of the peasant community, the isolation of the worker as an individual in the face of the individual capitalist, the struggle against the Catholic church and its 'external' forms of communion devoid of inner faith, their replacement by the isolation of man from man and man before God – all these went hand in hand. When Luther spoke of divine activity, he was really talking about capital: 'For God has fully ordained that the under-person shall be alone into himself and has taken the sword from him *and put him in prison*'.[58] The struggle for freedom of conscience and of religion, the 'private' reading of the holy scripts, the direct rapport between man and God, the devaluation of good works and of the world in the face of faith are profound transformations in the religious, social and above all in the psychological *habitus* of the individual which tended to internalise authority and violence. The psychological chains of the pious man largely replaced the visible chains between serf and glebe. At the same time, extraordinary prominence is given to 'educative' instruments, *imprimis* to the family. It has been noted that it was precisely in this period and under the impact of Protestant doctrine that the classical form of the patriarchal bourgeois family assumed a new and particular vigour; it was at this point that the father became a social figure endowed with great power to whom public authorities could delegate control over his children's education and over his wife.[59] It is no accident that in this period one of the primary aims of workhouses and other institutions examined here was the socialisation of the young. It was to a case concerning a youth and to a general preoccupation with juvenile delinquency that the famous *Rasp-huis* in Amsterdam owed its existence. Houses of correction for the young appeared at the same time as those for the poor. Parts of the workhouses were often set aside for the young – some, from good families, having been sent by their fathers.[60] Clearly, it was fully recognised that the new order of ideas, without precedent from previous centuries (at least not on any large scale), the new 'spirituality' of order and repression, had to be taught and inculcated from infancy – indeed particularly in infancy. For Luther and Calvin, 'God, the Father and the Master' was the perfect trinity.[61] Other institutions gradually emerged outside the family, particularly work-houses and houses of correction. The function of these institutions was marked by a certain ambivalence: were they genuine places of production or were they educative instruments of the 'paternalistic' type? Though this ambivalence persisted, we will see that the latter gradually triumphed.

With the Reformation, poverty was seen in a different light. It no longer possessed the 'positive mystique' it had had for medieval Christianity. Now poverty was a sign of divine malediction. In the Reformation 'poverty means punishment' observed Foucault,[62] and it is easy to see how he who is cast out and punished by the wrath of God is also cast out and punished by men. All the more so if the poor cannot or will not participate in that great glorification of God which is the end of earthly works.[63] Works have no value per se. The total devaluation of the practical world denotes a society in which production is now geared towards accumulation, not towards the use and consumption of goods produced.[64] But it was precisely the absolute worthlessness of worldly activity in comparison with the only aim which had real value – achievement of the state of grace, communion with God – that made man free to increase the glory of God through his earthly life and works which he took as a *sign* of his own eternal well-being. Protestant ideology encapsulates the pessimistic vision of a world engulfed in sin, a divine epiphany in which men sing the praises of the Lord by working, and (some of them) by accumulating and by saving. Luther sees the human situation as a prison, probably a canonical prison given that he is a monk and talks about isolation. On the one hand, has not the state of the priest become the 'priestly nature' of anyone? *Ethics* have taken over religion and in the new religion priesthood is accessible to all. The experience of the ecclesiastical organisation is generalised. Already in Luther we see one of the most important values of the new society – isolation, particularly isolation from the old peasant community and from the ownership of one's own means of production.

If prison is a model of society – and here one is still concerned with metaphor – it will not take many years for the Protestant and above all the Calvinist view of society to create a model of the prison of the future in the shape of the workhouse. A couple of centuries later, in an age and region full of promise for the development of capitalism and its spirit – the English ex-colonies of North America at the beginning of the nineteenth century – the Quaker colonists of Pennsylvania rigorously interpreted Luther's words in their *cellular prisons*, the form finally discovered of bourgeois punishment. The whole secret of the workhouse and the *Rasp-huis* lay, right from the very start, in the way they applied bourgeois *ideals*[65] of life and society to the preparation of people, particularly poor people, proletarians, so that they would accept an order and discipline which would render them docile instruments of exploitation. The eighteenth-century houses of correction were filled with poor people, young people and prostitutes; it was a question of those social categories which had to be educated or re-educated for a well-mannered and laborious life in bourgeois society. They were not simply there to learn, they were there to be convinced; from its inception, it was imperative for capitalism to substitute for the old religious ideology new values and new means of gaining submission. The sword could not be wielded against the multitude indefinitely and there was always the very real fear that the lower classes would find a new solidarity, a new identity, which would enable them to break out of their isolation. Having proclaimed that the isolation of man was the will of God, Luther adds: 'If he rebels against this *and combines with others* and breaks out and takes the sword, then before God he deserves condemnation and death'.[66] Not only did Luther define the actual penal practices of his day (if 'prison' is for everyone, it is just that the poor, guilty only of so being, should end up in prison whilst the rebellious should hang – effectively this is what happened), but he opposed the movement his own words had helped to inspire – the peasant revolt. As the peasant leader correctly put it, this was revolt of the dispossessed against the many-sided process described above, which Marx refers to as 'primitive accumulation'. Such collective rebellion assumed a *political* significance going far beyond the dangers of the immediate responses of theft or banditry. Müntzer was fully aware of this. Referring to Luther, he stated:

> ... he says in his book on trading that one can with certainty count the princes among the thieves and robbers. But at the same time he conceals the real origin of all robbery ... For see, our lords and princes are the basis of all profiteering, theft and robbery; they make all creatures their property. The fish in the water, the birds of the air, the plants on the earth must all be theirs (Isaiah 5). Concerning this they spread God's commandment among the poor and say that God has commanded that you shall not steal, but it does them no good. So they turn the poor peasant, the artisan and all living things into exploiters and evil-doers.[67]

But for Luther such rebellion is the worst thing of all. Marcuse remarks, citing Luther:

> The robber and murderer leave the head that can punish them intact and thus give punishment its chance; *but rebellion 'attacks punishment itself'* and thereby not just disparate portions of the existing order, but this order itself.[68]

Throughout the period of absolute monarchy the crime of *lèse-majesté*, which regularly carried the death penalty, constantly increased; for these offenders there was no real possibility of 'correction'. Teaching by dint of flogging and work could only be fruitful as long as rebellion against the dominant social relations was expressed in terms of simply not conforming, however serious this might be in itself (though this depended, on the other hand, on the current need for labour). But if rebellion is directed – even in mystified, unclear forms – against the social relations themselves, against *authority*, clearly nothing can be done. He who rebels against discipline as such rather than against some particular application thereof is not open to *correction*: he deserves death.

The type of workhouse built in Amsterdam was copied in many European towns, particularly throughout the German-speaking regions.[69] The generalisation of the Dutch initiative was no chance happening. Workhouses appeared wherever there was a notable development of mercantile capitalism: in the Hanseatic League houses of correction (or *Zuchthause*) were established at Lubeck and Bremen (1613), at Hamburg (1622), Danzig (1630) Switzerland was another area in which they developed a few years after the Dutch initiative: at Bern (1614), at Basle (1616), and at Fribourg (1617).

The *Rasp-huis* was visited a number of times by people sent by the various cities that were later to set up similar institutions.[70] Again, the fact that these different regions were linked together by the same connective tissue of economy and religion, especially Calvinism, was undoubtedly a factor of some weight favouring the spread of the workhouse. The various institutions had similar features. Generally they housed beggars, the idle, vagabonds, prostitutes, thieves, petty offenders, young criminals, or juvenile offenders and the insane. Here as well, work for the men mainly consisted of making sawdust for dyeing while the women, who were usually prostitutes or vagabonds, had to spin. The immediate success of these institutions was due above all to their profitability. In the case of Amsterdam, for example, where the institution was protected by monopoly, profits were described as exceptional. These institutions generally had two purposes: on the one hand, they were purely disciplinary, which, as we have already underlined, is what gives them the element of continuity; on the other hand, a scarcity of labour in the first half of the seventeenth century emphasised the need to give some vocational training to the inmates (a fact which frequently led the municipalities responsible for these houses into conflict with local guilds).[71]

As the institutions developed over time, those convicted of more serious crimes and sentenced to longer terms were admitted in increasing numbers. Thus, in the long run, imprisonment came to replace other forms of punishment. For some time, there was no rigid classification or separation of the various human and juridical categories. As Rusche and Kirchheimer note, it is possible to formulate a distinction between the *Zuchthaus*, which was meant to be a true and proper prison, and the *Arbeitshaus*, which was meant for the poor, the vagabonds and those imprisoned by police measures, but it was a formal difference of no effective consequence.[72] On the whole, however, it was during the seventeenth and eighteenth centuries that, little by little, there came into existence an institution of a kind which the Enlightenment, and subsequent nineteenth-century reform were to bring to fruition in the form of the modern-day prison. Thus, write Rusche and Kirchheimer, 'The early form of the modern prison was bound up with the manufacturing houses of correction'.[73] The workhouse was, at its inception, undeniably a part of the Protestant, and above all Calvinist, heritage and it is significant that a Dutch pamphlet dated 1612, polemicising against Catholicism, holds the miracles of the church saints up to ridicule by contrasting them with the miracles actually performed in the workhouse by St Raspinus, St Ponus and St Labour in reforming vagabonds and criminals.[74]

But confinement soon became general in Catholic countries as well, particularly in France. We have already seen how, in the middle of the sixteenth century, an *Hôpital* came to be set up in Lyons; however this remained a rather isolated case. It was only in 1656 that the *Hôpital*

Général was set up in Paris and then spread throughout the French kingdom by the edict of 1676.[75] But the time-lag between the French- and German-speaking regions was not the only factor which distinguished them. Poverty in Paris had reached a remarkably high level and the *hôpital* – which was a regrouping of existing institutions – was oriented more towards the provision of social welfare. In this way, it differed from the corrective and productive bias of workhouses and the *Zuchthaus*. The French admitted large numbers of widows and orphans to their institutions. Their population was vast and heterogenous.[76] Although the importance of work was also strongly emphasised, the Paris *hôpital* seems to have made a heavy financial loss within ten years of its birth.[77] Rusche and Kirchheimer insist that religious differences were of no real relevance to the spread of these institutions. In fact their own evidence shows that the economic situation of France was somewhat different to that of Holland or the Hanseatic League; and because of this it was difficult for both the workhouse and, above all, the new vision of life appropriate to capitalism, to take full root. This was even more obvious when it came to the other Catholic countries.[78]

Despite the fact that *hôpitaux* were the result of a royal initiative, they owed their extension throughout France to the energetic activity of the Jesuit priests, Chauraud, Dunod and Guevarre.[79] In a booklet dated 1639, Guevarre clearly and simply justified confining both the 'good' and 'evil' poor on grounds familiar in Protestant and Catholic workhouses alike: the *good* deserved confinement, which would assist them and make work opportunities available to them; the *evil* would be justly deprived of liberty and punished by having to work. In this way, Guevarre, like Solomon, resolved the contradiction – though it was not recognised as such at the time – between workhouses for the poor and houses of correction for vagabonds and criminals. Both institutions served the same purpose because the real crime was poverty and both had the aim of inculcating a discipline which was perceived as punishment. As Foucault observed:

> Confinement thus came to be doubly justified, in an un-dissociable equivocation, in the name of good and in the name of punishment. It simultaneously recompensed and punished according to the moral value of those the

confinement was imposed upon. Until the end of the classical age, the use of confinement was to be a prisoner of this equivocation; the peculiar reversibility of confinement enabled it to change meaning according to the merit it was accorded to those it was applied to.[80]

In the course of the seventeenth and eighteenth centuries, a marked sensitivity to the concrete aims of punishment pervaded the Catholic world. Reviewing the use of prison punishments made by canonical courts in a work written at the end of the seventeenth century and published posthumously in 1724, the French Benedictine Father Mabillon formulated a series of considerations which anticipated by some decades a number of typical Enlightenment assertions on the penal question. Mabillon was one of the first to put forward the new idea that punishment should be proportionate to the gravity of the offence and to the bodily and spiritual strength of the offender, and to raise the problem of reintegration into the community.[81]

Later Developments with Regard to English Institutions

In the age of mercantile capitalism, young national monarchies sought to prop up the development of capital, which still lacked confidence and security and needed protection and privilege. Workhouses were a typical result. The rising capitalist mode of production needed 'the power of the state, the concentrated and organised force of society'[82] not only 'to "regulate" wages ... to lengthen the working-day and to keep the labourer himself in the normal degree of dependence',[83] but also in the relations between states and – in a more and more obvious way – when it came to the colonies.[84] However:

> The advance of capitalist production develops a working class which by education, tradition, habit, looks upon the conditions of that mode of production as self-evident laws of Nature. The organisation of the capitalist process of production, once fully developed, breaks down all resistance. The constant generation of a relative surplus-population keeps the law of

supply and demand of labour, and therefore keeps wages, in a rut that corresponds with the wants of capital. The dull compulsion of economic relations completes the subjection of the labourer to the capitalist. Direct force, outside economic conditions, is of course still used, but only exceptionally. In the ordinary run of things, the labourer can be left to the 'natural laws of production' i.e. to his dependence on capital, a dependence springing from, and guaranteed in perpetuity by, the conditions of production themselves.[85]

Marx's analytical model of the origins of capital provides us with a synthesis of the essential development of class relations between the seventeenth century and the first half of the nineteenth century.

The next phase in the history of English houses of correction fits into this background. The scarcity of labour throughout the seventeenth and a good part of the eighteenth centuries posed a serious problem for capital which feared a rise in the level of wages above all else.[86] However, the problem was not nearly as serious as it had been in the first years of the seventeenth century. This was due both to renewed population growth and to the continuing rise in the expulsion of the English peasantry from the land and in the expropriation of their property. None the less, it is significant that continued demands were made for the use of forced labour,[87] since it took the capitalist mode of production quite some time to smash residual resistance on the part of a proletariat which retained traces of the old mode of production.

The more the expropriation of the peasantry advances, the less possibility it has of defending itself. It is only the growth of the market that gradually destroys the peasant subsistence economy.[88] In this context, it is hardly surprising that the Elizabethan Poor Laws suffered a major onslaught which continued until 1834 when, shortly after the formal assumption of power by the bourgeoisie, the demands made time and time again were incorporated into the New Poor Law. As is commonly agreed, the various provisions of the Old Poor Law, dating from 1572 to 1601, effectively transformed a system of private charity into a system of public charity; they imposed an obligation on the local community to furnish work for the able-bodied poor. However, the sections of this legislation seeking to provide relief outweighed those which dealt with the provision of work. Critics voiced the unanimous opinion that the provision of a system of relief tended to reduce the availability of labour and thus kept wages at an unnecessarily high level.

> This mischief of high wages to handicraftsmen is occasioned by reason of the idleness of so vast a number of people in England as these are: so that those that are industrious and will work make men pay what they please for their wages: but set the poor at work and then these men will be forced to lower their rates.[89]

A chorus of voices was therefore raised in unanimous praise of the benefits to be had from the wide and fairly exclusive use of workhouses.[90] The first result of this was the introduction of the Workhouse or General Act of 1722–3 which permitted groups of parishioners to build workhouses designed to receive anyone requesting some form of assistance.[91] But, as Marshall observes, the provisions of the Old Poor Laws were powerless in the face of structural unemployment.[92] Sufficient capital could not be raised to find work for all the poor and fewer houses of correction were actually built than originally envisaged by the Old Poor Laws.[93] As a contemporary text reports, those still condemned as idlers and vagabonds to flogging or banishment openly cursed the magistrates for their inability to provide them with jobs.[94] All this occurred, as we have already mentioned, during a period marked by the relative scarcity of labour. It is only with great difficulty that one can distinguish the development of true and proper houses of correction from the workhouse or poorhouse. As we have already made clear, no such distinction was made under the Old Poor Law which assigned the ordinary unemployed worker, the vagabond, the thief, etc. to the houses of correction to be built in every parish. This system worked for a time but gradually it broke down. Work in the houses of correction became scarce. Once again vagabonds were whipped or branded rather than being placed in confinement. None the less, the existence of houses of correction did increase the predisposition towards punishment by detention which gradually embraced the old custodial gaol. Although it was only in 1865 that the Prison Act formally eliminated the difference between gaol and Bridewell, it was already possible in 1720 to condemn petty criminals to either institution on purely discretionary grounds. The line formally dividing the workhouse (meant solely for the poor) from the *penal* institution, the Bridewell, as a section thereof (or vice versa) in the same building, was frequently blurred.[95]

Despite continual pressure and repeated efforts to 'set the poor to work' during this period, the overwhelming affinity between houses of correction and the old custodial gaols resulted in a reversion to late medieval methods at least as far as the internal regime of custodial gaols was concerned.[96] Work disappeared completely. There was a return to the dreaded practice of private gain for the warder; all former classifications or ways of differentiating between inmates, however crude they may have been, now disappeared. The female sections of prisons became brothels directed by the gaolers; thus the situation arose which was later to prompt the work and writings of so many reformers in the second half of the eighteenth century. Its most sinister aspect was the scourge of gaol fever which carried off about one fifth of the inmates every year. It spared neither judges, gaolers, witnesses nor the whole apparatus connected in some way or other with prisons. In this period, then even if there was a consolidation of, rather than any change in, the historic trend towards replacing the old forms of corporal and capital punishment with forms of detention, the latter was becoming increasingly pointless and painful for the inmates.

We can trace the roots of this progressive degeneration to the great transformations of the second half of the eighteenth century. The exceptional acceleration in the tempo of economic development – the industrial revolution[97] – shook traditional social equilibrium in England. A revival in population growth coupled with the introduction of machinery and the passage from manufacture to a true and proper *factory system* simultaneously produced a golden age for young capitalism and the darkest age in the history of the proletariat. The remarkably accelerated rate at which capital penetrated into the countryside and the consequent expulsion from it of the peasantry, particularly as a result of the bills for enclosures of commons,[98] helped to throw an unprecedented supply of labour on the market. From about 1760 to 1815 workers had to endure yet another round of wage cuts. The phenomena of urbanism, pauperism and 'criminality' grew to proportions hitherto unknown. The 'dull compulsion of economic relations' replaced statutory violence. It was the age of liberalism: capital could now stand on its own two feet and proudly proclaim itself confident, self-sufficient and scornful of the system of privilege, inequality and authority to which it owed its development in centuries gone by. However this phase did not last very long. Soon, 'direct force outside economic conditions' had to be invoked against the workers' first attempts to organise themselves. The implications of the French Revolution were already clear. The new Napoleonic state was very much stronger, very much more centralised and efficient than that of the *ancien régime*. From the outset, liberalism meant that capital was *free from the state*, that the state was a thing on its own – as the young Marx was to write some decades later[99] – and that the state must render its services to *Monsieur le Capital* – a fact that was made very clear in relation to welfare and prison matters. 'Crime, revolt and incendiarism' are necessitated and spontaneous responses of the poorest section of the proletariat.[100]

The first response to the great rise in pauperism, which was due, among other things, to a rise in the price of corn, was made with the revised provisions of the Old Poor Law. Between 1760 and 1818, the poor-rate tax increased six times to keep up with the growth of pauperism. A series of instruments used earlier now became more widespread: the deterrent workhouse, the roundsman system, the allowance in aid of wages.[101] Under these new circumstances and in the light of an increasingly costly relief system, the criticisms regularly raised in previous centuries grew to a climax. After 1815, it was particularly the allowance in aid of wages or Speenhamland system – that is, a payment given to the poor according to the current price of bread (in fact, a way of avoiding having to pay a minimum wage) – which aroused the fiercest criticism. The traditional and recurrent criticisms that such assistance would encourage indolence and refusal to work and would thereby maintain high wage levels was reinforced by the Malthusian vision of population growth – the extreme form of economic *liberalism*. Relief permitted the survival and reproduction of a surplus population which was both useless in itself and actively harmful to economic development. This was the basic view of the Commission of Inquiry of 1832–4, the product of whose labours was the New Poor Law.[102]

Convinced with Malthus and the rest of the adherents of free competition that it is best to let each take care of himself they would have preferred to abolish the Poor Law altogether. Since, however, they had neither the courage nor the authority to do this, they proposed a Poor Law constructed in harmony with the doctrine of Malthus, which is yet more barbarous than that of *laissez-faire* because it interferes actively in cases where the latter is passive.[103]

What then was the solution adopted and championed by Nicholls and other reformers? The ideal workhouse had been defined as a house of terror[104] as early as 1770 – though this way of looking at the workhouse had existed earlier. The solution that the English bourgeoisie hit upon shortly after its definitive accession to power was that of the deterrent workhouse, that is, the substitution of all forms of outdoor relief by confinement and forced labour. But what was the aim of this measure and in what sense did the reformers see the workhouse as a deterrent? Living and working conditions in workhouses were to be such as to discourage all but the most desperate from entering them. In this respect the words of the commissioners are very revealing:

Into such a house none will enter voluntarily; work, confinement, and discipline, will deter the indolent and vicious; and nothing but extreme necessity will induce any to accept the comfort which must be obtained by the surrender of their free agency and the sacrifice of their accustomed habits and gratifications.[105]

Once more, then, the aim of the workhouses was to make the poor accept any conditions imposed by an employer.[106] Life in the workhouse had to be less bearable in every way (particularly, of course, when it came to living standards) than the life of the lowest stratum of free workers.[107] Thus workhouse detention was to have an effect on the market – not so much because one sector of production enjoyed forcibly reduced labour costs (which had happened before) but rather, because the institution openly terrorised the worker into keeping away from its doors at all costs. The law sought to give a directly political content to formal control over the wage-earning proletariat, coming as it did after the French Revolution and the first struggles of the English workers. Sir George Nicholls, the principal architect of the New Poor Law, regarded the poor as 'potential Jacobins', 'ready to prey on the property of their richer neighbours'.[108] Engels very clearly described life in the workhouse which was so similar to prison in every detail that the poor renamed them 'poor-law bastilles'.[109] Not only did the workhouse ensure a standard of living frequently lower than that of prison, it also imposed a similar series of limitations on individual liberty. Among other things – and this is particularly significant – the work was usually pointless, having no real importance, being designed more for the needs of discipline and training than for profitability.[110] In brief, as Disraeli was to declare, the reform of 1834 'announced to the whole world that in England poverty is a crime'.[111]

I have dwelt at length on the question of relief not only because it can be seen to be directly linked with the rise of the modern prison – indeed the two are confused with each other – but above all because throughout the industrial revolution, this link clearly persisted over and above the variety and scope of the institutions. Throughout the preceding period, an apparent contradiction had been observed in the development of a policy of assistance. This was being challenged more and more by the demand for workhouses, together with the withdrawal of work from prisons, which were very much in decline – at least in the case of houses of correction – not so much in terms of their numbers, which continued to rise, as in the significant worsening of their internal conditions. However, as we have said, this contradiction is only apparent. Not only did the workhouse and the prison share a common destiny but both were also involved in a significant change of direction during the industrial revolution.

The same outlook which stimulated appeals for workhouses and which played a prominent part in the new Poor Law of 1834 can be encountered in the evolution of prisons during this period. The growth of pauperism during the age of industrial revolution was coupled with a growth in crime and rebellion.[112] The cry 'bread or blood' spread through the English industrial districts. It was not only the continental aristocracy but also the English bourgeoisie whose slumbers were disturbed by the spectre of Jacobinism. However, the only way in which the impoverished masses managed to express their opposition at this stage was through individual crime and violence.[113] In the general climate of post-Napoleonic restoration, it was hardly surprising, therefore, to hear voices raised in favour of a return to the gallows and so on. The attack on the Enlightenment's so-called philanthropic attitude towards criminality and prison – for example, as it was represented in England through Howard[114] – became a leitmotiv of the reaction against the French Revolution. However, this reaction did not bring about a return to pre-prison punitive forms. Instead it made prison itself more rigid and punitive. On the other hand, in by-passing Enlightenment notions of prison reform based on rationalisation and the introduction of greater decency and dignity, it established some continuity with the events of the preceding century. The root cause here, as has already been seen, lies in an extraordinary increase in the supply of labour which made the old formula for convict labour totally obsolete. It was superseded by an age in which the workhouse and to an even greater extent the prison were distinguished by intimidation and terror. Prison labour was not rejected a priori, nor did it cease; it was simply that its punitive and disciplinary aspect became more important than its economic role. This was also because (as a report pointed out at the time) with the introduction of machines, the level of capital investment in all forms of production had risen so much that prison labour could not be carried on without serious risk of loss.[115] On the other hand, the plentiful supply of free labour meant that forced labour no longer functioned as any kind of regulator on external wages as it had done in the age of mercantilism. This made it acceptable to express sympathy with the free workers' protests that convict labour was unfair competition.[116] In any event, even where the provision of work for the poor was supposed to be the sole aim of workhouses, labour was typically intimidatory and useless. In addition, it is useful to take account of the dimensions of the phenomena of pauperism and poorhouses as against those of prison. According to the Webbs' estimate, around 12–13 per cent of the English population was being assisted by parishes in 1820 (that is, under the old Poor Law system).[117] In 1845, out of a total of 1,470,970 being assisted, it was estimated that some 215,325 English citizens were being confined as a result of the new Poor Law.[118] In 1782, Howard's findings had shown that a total of 4439 people were being detained in English prisons (of whom about half were debtors).[119] By 1869, the number of registered inmates was 8899.[120] Considering that the real figure may have been appreciably higher in view of what was happening between 1820 and 1840, then, taking the figures as a guide, the imbalance between the size of the problem of poverty and what we can call its criminal emergence is immediately apparent.[121] One can easily understand, therefore, how hardly any attention came to be paid to prisons, in socio-economic terms, compared with the energy expended on the whole problem of pauperism. On the other hand, however, prisons now acquired a *symbolic, ideological* connotation.

In the proposals advanced by Jeremy Bentham, a major representative of the ascendant English bourgeoisie, prison has reached its intermediate stage: the productivist and rehabilitative aims of its earlier days – aims which were revived during the Enlightenment – began to be overtaken by pure control and deterrence. As in any transitional period, the whole question of prisons became a political football. As theorists adjusted their ideas and proposals, intellectual camps were formed now on one position, now on another. Bentham's *Panopticon*[122] was a naive attempt to combine a system of intensified punishment and control with productive efficiency which was never put into practice but which already showed signs of the tendency to favour the first aspect in the years to come. The *Panopticon* is at one and the same time an architechtonic concept and the embodiment of its own ideology:

> The formal principle upon which the Panopticon is based consisted of two multi-floored coaxial cylindrical containers, each having opposing and complementary functions: the circular crowns in correspondence to the floors of the outer cylinder, were placed between six radials in cellular units completely opened out towards the central space and lit by the outer perimeter; this section was allotted to those to be controlled. The inner coaxial cylinder, concealed by thin, opaque partitions placed along the length of the perimeter was for the warders – very few, it was specified – who, without any chance of being seen, could have exercised tight and constant control at every point of the outer cylinder by means of well placed peep-holes; nothing could have escaped their scrutiny.[123]

Life in the 'rudimentary cell' was connected with the introduction in Bentham's first project (1787) of the idea of permanent solitary confinement but in his *Postscript* four years later, the cells were enlarged so that the number of inmates could be increased to four.[124] Without any doubt, however, the 'inspection principle', that is, the possibility of keeping every inmate under constant surveillance (or of making the inmates believe that this was so) with the use of few men, was the essential element in the project. If solitary confinement (which later disappeared) and inspection were the two features the *Panopticon* had in common with modern penitentiaries based on cells, contemporaneously emerging in the United States,[125] then what remains uniquely Benthamite is the prominence given to productivity.[126] Bentham is staunchly utilitarian on this point: 'I would do the whole by *contract*,'[127] Work should not have any punitive dimension but should be administered on purely capitalist criteria: 'I must confess I know of no test of reformation so plain or so sure as the improved quantity and value of their work.'[128] Even with regard to work, the essence of the penalty resides in the privation of liberty, conceived above all, in the form of the privation of the freedom of contract: there is a monopoly of employment to which the inmate is subject, a very convenient situation for the contractor: 'confinement, which is his punishment, preventing his carrying the work to another market subjects him to a monopoly; which the contractor, his master, like any other monopolist, makes, of course, as much of as he can.'[129] But punishment by isolation on the one hand and by simple privation of liberty on the other, which still coexist here, are to become increasingly incompatible. Bentham's architectonic project suits his foremost concerns – control, custody and intimidation – but certainly not the introduction of productive work in prison. Not at a time when the use of a vastly increasingly number of machines was based more and more on co-operation between workers. Perhaps Bentham's later plan to house four inmates in each cell is related to this. It certainly suggests why Bentham's project was not applied in practice despite the fact that in the first years of the nineteenth century the prevailing pressure for reform centred around his appeal for the productive use of prisons.

But there is another element that needs highlighting in Bentham's project – and it is perhaps the most significant one for the epoch and its ideology. The following appears on the frontispiece of the volume in which the *Panopticon* was outlined:

> 'PANOPTICON' or, the inspection-house: containing the idea of a new principle of construction applicable to any sort of establishment, in which persons of any description are to be kept under inspection; and in particular to penitentiary-houses, prisons, houses of industry, work-houses, poor-houses, manufactories, mad-houses, lazarettos, hospitals and schools.

In the opening passages of this work, Bentham repeats that this idea is applicable:

> Without exception, to all establishments whatsoever, in which, within a space not too large to be covered or commanded by buildings, a number of persons are meant to be kept under inspection. No matter how different, or even opposite the purpose: whether it be that of *punishing the incorrigible, guarding the insane, reforming the vicious, confirming the suspected, employing the idle, maintaining the helpless, caring the sick, instructing the willing* in any branch of industry, or *training the rising race* in the path of *education*: in a word, whether it be applied to the purposes of *perpetual prisoners* in the room of death, or *prisoners for confinement* before trial, or penitentiary-houses, or *houses of correction*, or *work-houses*, or *manufactories*, or *mad-houses*, or *hospitals*, *or schools*.[130]

With particular diligence Bentham now sets about dealing with the application of his project to the model prison in which 'the objects of safe custody, confinement, solitude, forced labour, and instruction were all of them to be kept in view.'[131] One cannot sufficiently emphasise the interchangeable character of the various segregated institutions recently created by bourgeois society when Bentham wrote these pages. Over and above their specific functions, one overall aim united them: control over a rising proletariat. The bourgeois state assigns to all of them a directing role in the various moments of the formation, production and reproduction of the factory proletariat: for society they are essential instruments of social control, the aim of which is to secure for capital a workforce which by virtue of its moral attitude, physical health, intellectual capacity, orderliness, discipline, obedience, etc., will readily adapt to the whole regime of factory life and produce the maximum possible amount of surplus labour. But it is the *inspection principle*, more than any other feature of these institutions, that guarantees the observance of discipline. The *panopticon's* ability to control its subjects at any time and in any place within its walls, is, to put it crudely – and bourgeois theories in this period *were* crude, that is, they were simple, clear and (almost) uncontested – an extension of the *master's eye*. We can see this quite literally in the contemporary organisation of factory work from which Bentham patently drew a utopia of control for the various segregated institutions.

At this stage, co-operation could not be secured by the automatic workings of the productive process[132]; given machinery from the prehistory of modern technology, labour had to be forcibly organised by the physical authority of the capitalist (or that of his overseer) who co-ordinated the smooth running of the production process with his eye, his voice and his command.

In this respect, it is useful to trace the history of capitalism from its origins in the process of primitive accumulation to the analysis of the essence of capital in its classic eighteenth-century form in the first volume of *Capital* (Part VIII back to III). At this point Marx arrives at an explanation of what lies at the very heart of his theory, the production of surplus value, or rather, the *process of capital valorisation*.[133] At the end of Part II, Marx invites us to follow his analysis of the problem he has posed of that extraordinary exchange of equivalents between capital and labour which has the property of *creating value*, beyond the *sphere of circulation* in the 'secret laboratory of production'.[134] Here the 'secret of the production of surplus-value' is unveiled.[135] As we desert this 'sphere', Marx describes it as follows:

> The sphere of circulation or rather the exchange of commodities within the limits of which moves the purchase and sale of labour power, is in reality a veritable Eden of the natural rights of man. There reigns only Liberty, Equality, Property, and Bentham.[136]

This is not by any means just an exercise in irony. Before this remark, Marx explains how the sale of labour-power respects the general principle of the exchange of equivalents: labour-power is effectively 'paid for at its price'.[137] At this stage there is no question of exploitation. Up to this point, the juridical deception of the contract and the illusion that people freely dispose of their commodities exchanging them at equal values has yet to be revealed. However, the enigma arises from the fact that even by paying for what he buys at its price, the capitalist ends up with a greater value than he had at the beginning: he possesses what he has paid for plus a *surplus value*. Thus, the enigma must reside in the peculiar nature of the commodity he buys, in labour-power.[138] The *use-value* of this commodity clearly no longer belongs to the seller, the worker, but to the capitalist who has bought it. And it is the peculiar nature of this commodity that the consumption of its use-value *produces value.*[139] But this is only true if the use of labour is such as to produce in the working day a greater value than the capitalist originally advanced. If this is to occur, it depends not only on the amount of time during which the labour power is employed but also on the capitalist's capacity to obtain from the workforce an *average* hourly yield that does not fall short of his expectations, that is, it depends on his ability to bend his labour force to his will and his intelligence (as is in any case his contractual right; but labour-power, just as it possesses the peculiar characteristic of producing value, is also marked by another opposing and complementary peculiarity: its tendency not to let itself be consumed). If this is true, therefore, and if it is true that the extraction of surplus value is a question of life and death which decides the very existence of capital as such; then, de facto, *authority in the process of production, authority in the factory*, which is the power of the capitalist to do as he likes with the commodity he has bought in exactly the same way as any other buyer, is a question of life and death.[140] The history of the relationship between capital and labour, history *tout court*, which is the history of class struggle,[141] becomes then the history of capitalistic relations inside the factory, the history of the authority of capital in the factory and correspondingly the history of the *discipline* of the worker and of everything which serves to create, maintain or subvert such authority. It is precisely the irreducible class character of this particular commodity which means it cannot be handed to capital on a plate without a series of complementary treatments which precede, accompany and follow its induction into the productive process. This is the specific task, invented by the bourgeois capitalist class and cited by Bentham, of the segregated institutions, institutions which can be defined as ancillary to the factory in the proper sense. They have the same relationship with the world of production as civil and political equality has with the sphere of circulation, as Marx observes above. The sphere of circulation, of the exchange of equivalents, is the realm of liberty and equality, the realm of the *declaration of rights*; the sphere of production is the realm of exploitation, of accumulation and therefore of authority, of the factory and of other segregated institutions.

Departing from this point, one can comprehend the content of that *religion of capital*[142] which is the dominant ideology in these years, particularly inside the segregated institutions. The great merit of Michel Foucault's recent book[143] is that it places the relationship between *technique* and the *ideology* of control back on its feet, demonstrating how ideology (obedience and discipline) does not come to determine the *practical* reason, the morality, but how on the contrary this is produced by specific techniques of control over the body (in military art, school, ateliers, etc.).[144] However, what is presented to us as the 'political economy of the body' is 'political economy' *tout court*; it is already locked in the concept of labour-power. It should be sufficient to recall the writings of Marx on manufacture already cited or perhaps we should even return to his early work in the *Manuscripts of 1844*.[145] This bourgeois *construction* of the body in the school, the barracks, the prison and the family remains completely incomprehensible (except in terms of an ineffable moment of the history of the spirit) unless we start from the capitalistic management of the labour process (and *at this moment* in the history of capitalism). This had to set itself the task of structuring the body as a machine inside the productive machine as a whole, that is, we must understand that the organisation of work does not treat the body as something extraneous, it *steps through* the body into the muscles and into the head, reorganising simultaneously with the productive process that fundamental part of itself constituted by the labour-power of the body.

In sum, in this age the *machine* constitutes a compound invention in which there resides a dead, inorganic, fixed element and a live, organic variable one. On the whole, therefore, the physical sciences and moral (later social) sciences, sciences of nature and human sciences are placed in an integrated relationship with the technique of formation, of exploitation and of 're-education' of fixed capital ('machinery' in fact) and labour-power (the body, man, the spirit, etc.). The history of segregated institutions and of their prevailing ideology can be reconstructed from capital's fundamental need to extend its command: The history of their ancillary nature can be traced to the factory, which is no more than the extension of the capitalistic organisation of labour above and beyond the factory, the *hegemony* which capital exercises on the whole of social relations. This hegemony should not in any way be understood in terms of an analogy between the factory and the outside world even if it appears as such at first sight; rather, it forms a continuum which pervades every aspect of personal life, commanding remodelling (or creating) social institutions in which the process of formation occurs. As Foucault observes with reference to Bentham,[146] prison is the experimental laboratory of the whole design; the 'Panoptic machine' has the task of producing a type of human being which will constitute the fundamental articulation of the productive mechanism.

Once again, it is not a question of institutions which serve the capitalist organisation of labour but a question of this very organisation as such which, from the family to the school, from the hospital to the prison and so on, organises an essential component of itself, that part of capital from which it is possible to extract surplus value. These institutions, their formative practices, the ideologies and theories prevailing within them, can only be understood in the light of capital's essential need to reproduce itself as it passes through various social moments, thereby producing a new society.

The contradictions at the root of Bentham's hypothesis became more and more obvious in the first decade of the nineteenth century and later on after the 1815 Restoration. In the first years of the nineteenth century, the refusal of reformers to embrace the idea of solitary confinement clearly revealed the impossibility of coupling moral reform and intimidation with productive efficiency and reform by means of labour.

Howard's basic orientation on reform prevailed in the laws of 1810 and later on in Peel's Gaol Act of 1823.[147] The idea of group classification, segregation of the sexes, nightly cell isolation and daily communal work, the abolition of private profit for warders, of corporal punishment and the ending of some of the worst abuses of the preceding period were all realisations of the contributions which had been made to the struggle for prison reform by Enlightenment figures from Howard and Bentham to Sir Samuel Romilly and Elizabeth Fry. But the movement in favour of reform was bound to clash increasingly with a reaction in favour of repression which arose out of the socio-economic situation created by the industrial revolution. The fear of Jacobinism, the extreme growth of pauperism and criminality accompanying an immense industrial reserve army and an extremely low standard of living for the proletariat, the appearance of forms of crime which had an unmistakeable *class* content even if they were not yet *political*, made the demands for a return to the good old days of terror and harsh methods grow ever more numerous.[148] The full force of the contradiction between the bourgeoisie and the proletariat, which for some centuries had been apparent on a secondary level (compared with the contradiction that existed between the aristocracy and bourgeoisie), now moved into the centre of the stage. This growth of reaction over the question of crime coincided with a Europe-wide dispute on the Philadelphian *separate* system and the Auburn *silent* system.[149] The first system which, given the different set of social circumstances,[150] had had little success in the United States, was regarded increasingly favourably in Europe as it exactly suited the need for a punitive and deterrent prison without 'useful' labour which was already taking shape in Europe and especially in England. Work in the system of isolation in cells retains only the repetitive, fatiguing, monotonous aspects of work outside. In brief it is still punitive but completely useless. The tread-wheel or crank were simple structures which could be installed in a cell and whose real purpose, despite the appearance of being instruments of labour, was torment and torture. In the period 1840–65 the principle of terror and with it those of cellular isolation and useless work triumphed in England.[151]

Establishment of Modern Prison Practice in Continental Europe Between the Enlightenment and the First Half of the Nineteenth Century

John Howard, appointed sheriff of Bedford in 1773, took an active interest in prison conditions throughout his county. Indeed he was to dedicate the remainder of his life to the question of prison reform, for which purpose between 1770 and 1780 he travelled extensively throughout Britain and Europe. His account provides us with the fullest survey we have of the way prisons were developing in the latter part of the eighteenth century.[152]

If as we have seen, the English prisons were in serious decay, things were different in the German-speaking areas of Europe which had become the natural breeding-ground of houses of correction. Throughout the seventeenth and eighteenth centuries, houses of correction and workhouses had also flourished in countries not mentioned here but above all, in Germany. In particular this widespread growth took place at the same time as a decline in the usage of old punitive forms consistent with capital or corporal punishment and frequently coincided with the general economic, political and cultural awakening of the Enlightenment (some of the institutions Howard visited were in fact of recent construction). Thus Rusche and Kirchheimer's thesis, according to which there was an overall decay in prisons during this period, should be treated with a certain amount of caution.[153] To be precise, by decay these authors do not mean that there was a reduction in the use of *detentive* punishment or, therefore, in the growth of institutions designed for this purpose, that is, houses of correction (as opposed to the old custodial gaols which Howard frequently found to be semi-deserted). What they are referring to is the deterioration in their internal regimes in which economic functions – and indirectly rehabilitation – were increasingly abandoned in favour of punitive and repressive aims. They attribute this new course to the social consequences of the industrial revolution which through the creation of an enormous reserve army of unemployed throughout Europe, made prison labour (underpaid labour) redundant and the need for open intimidation and socio-political control, if anything, more urgent than ever. If, as Rusche and Kirchheimer contend, the process of decline is linked with the industrial revolution, then we should hardly be surprised to find that most of the evidence supporting their view comes from England. In the same way, it is no surprise that Howard could only discover sporadic signs of deterioration in a more backward country such as Germany, or that the process did not become really general until the influence of the French Revolution and of the English industrial progress was felt in the first years of the nineteenth century and, above all, after the 1815 Restoration.

Howard reserved his highest praise for the Dutch prisons,[154] most of which were still *Rasp-* or *Spin-huis* with a distinctly higher criminal population than had been the case in the seventeenth century. The internal organisation of these institutions was still quite similar to their earlier form. Most of the practical work consisted of rasping wood for dyes; however, as Sellin points out,[155] the daily workload had been reduced by a third and the prisoners fashioned small objects in their spare time to sell to visitors.

About sixty workhouses existed throughout Germany[156] at the end of the eighteenth century. Howard visited many of them[157]: Osnabrück, Bremen, Hanover, Brunswick and Hamburg. The actual gaols housing debtors and those awaiting trial or execution were usually in a horrendous condition: old, unhygienic, often with secret underground floors packed with instruments of torture. However, their population was sparse and many were actually empty. On the other hand, the houses of correction and workhouses were more highly populated; here the men worked on wood (following the Dutch model) whilst the old, the young and women did spinning. There was a great confusion of petty criminals locked up with beggars, vagabonds and those merely suffering from poverty. Often, the only distinction between them was the fact that they were prohibited from mixing or trading with each other. Workhouses thrived in Hamburg in particular, which was a highly developed city rich in trade: when Howard made his later visits, the Hamburg authorities were preparing a scheme based on workhouses to employ the city's numerous poor.[158] The introduction of the scheme had remarkable effect and Hamburg proudly proclaimed that begging had disappeared from its streets. But then ten years later, in 1801, the administration fell into heavy debt. The appearance of spinning machines had reduced the competitiveness of the old methods of production. In these circumstances the rapid propagation, primarily of the technological results of the English industrial revolution, effectively made itself felt even when it came to forced labour in Germany. The importation of English machinery and French revolutionary ideas prompted a return to methods of prison control based on terror, which was to characterise the major part of the nineteenth century, long before it produced any great changes in the labour market (though the introduction of machines, among other things, did swell the ranks of the unemployed).

Howard visited other workhouses: in Copenhagen, Stockholm (founded in 1750), Petrograd (still under construction at the time of his visit), in Poland (where, however, there was no work), Berlin (founded in 1758), Spandau, Vienna, in Switzerland, Monaco and Nuremberg (the German and Swiss ones were generally much older). There were numerous houses of correction in Austrian Flanders (Belgium), the most famous of which was the *Maison de Force* at Ghent. This was completely rebuilt in 1775, under Maria Theresa, on the foundations of an old house of 1627.[159]

The *Maison de Force* in particular must have had a great impact. It was one of the first great prison establishments built in the form of an eight-pointed star. The building was divided into sections, each corresponding to a different classification. Whilst criminals had separate cells and were subject to nightly separation, the women and vagabonds slept in dormitories. Textile manufacturing was carried out in large communal areas. However, Howard's enthusiasm for its order, moderation and hygiene waned during his last visit in 1783:

> I found here a great alteration for the worse; the flourishing and useful manufactory destroyed; and the looms and utensils all sold, in consequence of the Emperor's too hasty attention to a petition from a few interested persons – that which ought to be the leading view in all such houses is now lost in this house.[160]

Even the food had deteriorated and the small wage earned by each inmate had been reduced to little or nothing. The 'few interested persons' were probably producers competing with the institution; they were in fact the source of most attacks on prison labour. For as long as the development of industry depended on the mercantilist system of privilege and monopoly, the authorities could easily get the better of opposition from competing producers, as we have seen in seventeenth-century Holland. But as capitalism grew and imposed the new doctrine of laissez-faire, forms of enterprise outside the laws of the free market, such as those making use of forced labour, began to meet with successful opposition. As a result, prison work either tended to disappear or to become totally unproductive with purely disciplinary and deterrent aims. Opponents could now embroider their attack on convict labour with the very convenient excuse that in a situation of extensive unemployment from which *they* prospered, this kind of work endangered the livelihood of the free unemployed labourer. As a matter of fact, the first working-class organisations increasingly adopted a similarly hostile stance towards convict labour.

There were hardly any examples of this sort of institution in Portugal[161] or Spain.[162] In France, the system was seen right from the start much more as a means of suppressing mendicity rather than as a way of providing work.[163] The late economic development of the *ancien régime* weighed heavily upon France. But the abysmal functioning of the *hôpitaux* was primarily attributed to the idleness of the residents, despite all the efforts of the Constituent Assembly's Committee on Mendicity.[164] Howard found thousands of inmates of every kind in the various *hôpitaux généraux*: debtors, criminals (awaiting sentence), the poor, prostitutes, the insane and those suffering from venereal diseases. Continual revolts broke out and torture was widely used. Many died of frostbite during the bitter winters. There was hardly any work.[165] Howard concluded his analysis of Parisian prisons with a description of the Bastille. He was obliged to rely on second-hand information here since he was rudely refused permission to make a personal inspection of the building.[166]

Looking at Howard's account, it is important to realise that the relationship between prison labour and the standard of living of inmates is more than casual. It would be wrong to establish a strict correlation between work and a rehabilitation attitude on the one hand, or between the non-existence of work and a deterrent attitude on the other. These attitudes have been in constant interaction since the institution's earliest days, a fact that is readily apparent from the conception of the *punitive* character of prison labour (though it should be remembered that capitalist ethics also apply this conception to 'free' labour). Nevertheless, it is true that the very conditions of prison life (the level of hygiene, the possibilities of communication and solidarity between inmates, the standard of food, the possibility of earning small personal allowances, etc.) vary according to how far the internal organisation is part of a framework based on productive or unproductive work. Obviously, in the former case, whoever is in charge is presented with the twofold task of exploiting the labour force as rationally as possible while ensuring their daily reproduction (which is more than simply a question of physical subsistence). This produces a situation in which the standard of living of inmates must be inferior to that of employed workers in the outside world (in accordance with the *less eligibility* principle), although it may well be superior to that of someone who is unemployed outside and may, paradoxically, imply a 'material improvement' for the *lumpenproletariat*. This explains why tough methods are revived and the internal conditions of institutions become most harsh when unemployment rises – as tended to happen in the whole of Europe during the first half of the nineteenth century. In general, at least in the period examined up to this point, one can see that the inmates' strength and their living and working conditions tended to keep one step behind that of the proletariat as a whole. As a matter of fact, if this did not happen, prisons would lose all their deterrent power as far as the ruling classes are concerned. At times of great poverty and social change, it is not unusual for the most dispossessed sections of society to rise up in protest in a context in which even prison living standards are superior to those they must endure outside. In his description of conditions in poorhouses resulting from new legislation, Marx observes that prison rations were better than those received by the poor.[167] This is because prisons (which had less social impact in any case on account of their sparse population) were part of the reform movement of the previous century – which from the Restoration onwards was to be derisively termed as Enlightenment philanthropy – while the new English workhouse of 1834 conformed to the objectives laid down by the bourgeoisie. A few years later, the English institution, like those in Europe, took a sharp turn away from the principle of productive work towards a drastic tightening up of its deterrent role.

In the climate of heated ideological debate during the second half of the eighteenth century, a discussion on pauperism, crime and its remedies developed in France. In 1777 the *Gazette de Berne* held a competition to find 'a complete and detailed plan for criminal legislation'. The future revolutionary leader, Dr. Jean-Paul Marat, took part with his *Plan de législation criminelle*, published at Neuchatel in 1780.[168] Having dealt with social order and laws in the first part, entitled *fundamental principles for good legislation*, Marat dealt with *the obligation to submit to the law*.[169] Let us take a close look at Marat's argument in order to appreciate fully the consciousness and sensitivity shown by this epoch towards the whole problem.

Marat based his whole argument on an analysis of the concrete situation to which law related. Having noted how 'wealth quickly accumulates in the bosoms of a restricted number of families', producing as a result, 'a multitude of needy persons who will leave their offspring in poverty',[170] he continues:

Here is why they must die of hunger: the earth has become other people's property and they have no chance of getting anything for themselves. Now, since this disadvantage excludes them from society, are they obliged to respect its laws? Definitely not. If society abandons them they returns to a state of nature. So when they forcefully vindicate the rights they have lost with the sole aim of improving their lot, any authority which stands in their way is tyrannical and the judge who condemns them to death is nothing but a vile murderer. If it is true that society must oblige them to respect the established order for the sake of its own self-preservation, it is also true that society must before all else, shelter them from temptation born of need. Society must therefore assure them of adequate means of subsistence and of the chance of suitable clothing, guaranteeing moreover to give them the best possible protection, to look after them in time of illness and old-age: they cannot renounce their natural rights until society has made available to them a way of life that is preferable to the state of nature. Society has no right therefore to punish those who violate its laws without having made shift in this way to fulfil its obligations towards all its members.[171]

Marat then goes on to examine these principles in relation to a particular crime: theft. But 'any theft presupposes property rights'[172] and, having challenged the various contemporary theories on the origins of such rights, Marat hands over to 'someone unfortunate enough to find himself before the judges':

> Am I guilty? That's not the point. The real point is that I've done nothing I shouldn't have done. The first right of man is to keep body and soul together and you know yourselves that there's no more important right than that; he who has no way of keeping himself alive other than by stealing is only exercising his rights. You accuse me of disturbing law and order. But how do you expect me to care about your precious law and order when it only reduces me to such misery? It doesn't surprise me at all that you go around preaching that everyone should obey the law – it's the law that allows you to rule over so many unfortunate people. You tell us we've got to work. Easier said than done. What sort of chance did I have? Reduced to poverty through the injustice of a powerful neighbour, in vain I sought the refuge of a peasant's cottage: I was torn away from the plough by a cruel illness which consumes me and made me a burden to my master. There was nothing left for me to do but beg for my bread: but even this pathetic expedient failed me ... your turning me away made me desperate, having nothing and driven by hunger I took advantage of the darkness of the night to snatch the alms your hard hearts had denied me from a passerby. It's because I've used my natural rights that you've condemned me.[173]

So what is the answer? The authorisation of theft and anarchy? Certainly not!

> Evil doing is warned against; but what is done to remedy it? Beggars are classed as vagabonds and put in prison. This is not good politics: I will not discuss whether the government has the right to deprive them of their liberty in this way but I will merely observe that the houses of detention in which they are locked up can only be maintained at public expense, and that the spirit of idleness which they nourish rather than remedying the poverty of the individual, can only raise the general level of poverty. Very well then, what is the remedy? Here it is. Don't keep the poor in idleness, give them work, make it possible for them to satisfy their wants through labour. They

must be given a trade, they must be treated as free men. This means that numerous public workshops must be opened for the use of the poor.[174]

During the deep-seated economic crisis which preceded the great revolution, this problematic imposed itself on everyone who lived in France. In town and country alike, the endless 'reserve army' of unemployed were forced to beg, thieve and turn to vagrancy or in the last resort to banditry, if they were to avoid starvation.[175] The revolt of the poor against the process Marx describes as 'primitive accumulation' worked its way through the countryside without pause. By the second half of the eighteenth century, the collective rights, which had always greatly assisted the poor peasants, had been severely eroded by the great property owners and government supported tenants.[176]

At the end of the *ancien regime*, people everywhere were searching for land; the poor took over the common land, overran forest, open country and the borders of marshland; they complained about the privileged classes who used bailiffs and foremen to farm their land; they demanded the sale or even the free distribution of the King's estates and sometimes of the clergy's property too; there was a very strong movement against the existence of the great estates, for their division into small lots would have provided work for many families.[177]

As a result, 'at least one tenth of the rural population did nothing but beg from one year to another'.[178] The local communities were not always hostile to vagabonds; in certain 'pamphlets of complaint', protests were made against the confinement of vagabonds in houses of detention. The arguments were probably similar to those of Marat. Bands of unemployed beggars and vagabonds roamed town and country; the greater their numbers, the greater the poverty and as their numbers grew so did their sense of desperation: beggars gravitated towards brigandage. Even if those not paying the requested alms did not take the lead from an Arquebus, they still ran the risk of finding their crops dug over, their cattle mutilated or their houses burned down.[179] It was quite clear from the fact that 'when the almshouses were full, the doors were opened'[180] that they were quite inadequate. In fact, objections were raised because of the contamination that resulted from allowing the poor to mix with real criminals. Lefebvre states that this was not the least cause of the 'great fear' pervading France when revolution was imminent in 1789.

The revolutionary penal code of 25 September 1791 crowned the intense agitation for reform of the preceding half-century with the introduction of the principle of legality both in relation to crime and punishment and with the declaration that detention should reign supreme over any other punitive form. At the same time it was emphasised that *hôpitaux* and prisons must be made into places where society would be truly defended on the basis of labour.[181] The idea that punishment should no longer be arbitrary but should be proportional to the gravity of the crime, as laid down in an explicit legal code, played an important role in the struggle of a now confident and developed bourgeoisie against the old state forms (though this approach to penal practice had been formulated as much as two centuries earlier). As the Russian, E. B. Pashukanis, very acutely observed in 1924:

> Deprivation of freedom, for a period stipulated in the court sentence, is the specific form in which modern, that is to say bourgeois-capitalist, criminal law embodies the principle of recompense. This form is unconsciously yet deeply linked with the conception of man in the abstract, and abstract human labour measurable in time … For it to be possible for the idea to emerge that one could make recompense for an offence with a piece of abstract freedom determined in advance, it was necessary for all concrete forms of social wealth to be reduced to the most abstract and simple form, to human labour measured in time … Industrial capitalism, the declaration of human rights, the political economy of Ricardo, the system of imprisonment for a stipulated term are phenomena peculiar to one and the same historical epoch.[182]

The notion of proportionality in relation to punishment had already assumed this significance for a writer representing the summit of bourgeois consciousness in its 'classic' period-Hegel.[183] The refusal to use corporal and capital punishment, the notion that a specific crime must correspond to a *quantum* of punishment and that internal prison conditions must be 'humane' therefore began with the practice established in workhouses under the direction of public authorities and merchants. To this the revolutionary impulse of the eighteenth-century bourgeoisie added its struggle for the establishment of a legal code. The origin of this struggle lay not in the confrontation between the bourgeoisie and the proletariat but in the confrontation between the bourgeoisie and the absolute state. Nevertheless, it is important to understand that it was no accident that such principles were to become an increasingly strong weapon in the hands of the proletariat. Enlightenment thought of the second half of the eighteenth century explains and summarises this development. The spread of houses of correction throughout Europe was by no means the only reason why such thought was not simply confined to a declaration of principles. Nor is it at all the case that reformers and politicians were the only ones who saw the connection between penal reform and workhouses; in those works dedicated to law, discussion was not limited merely to principles of natural law but for example it was made very clear that there were connections between poverty, unemployment and the widely varying forms of delinquency.

On the other hand, Hegel and Pashukanis were to express in the most theoretically rigorous terms the formalisation of criminal law according to revolutionary principles: the concept of *labour* represents the necessary welding of the institution's content to its legal form. To calculate, to *measure* a punishment in terms of labour-value by units of time is possible only when the punishment is filled with this significance, when one labours or one is trained to labour (to wage labour, capitalistic labour). This is also true if one does not work in prison: time (measured, broken up and regulated time) is one of the great discoveries of this period in relation to other ancillary institutions such as the school.[184] Even if the time spent in prison does not reproduce the value of the injury (the basis of retaliatory punishment as Hegel observes), the propaedeutic, ancillary nature of the institution is precisely such as to exact retribution through the very fact of having to serve time, calculable time, measured time, that 'empty form' which is never a mere ideology but which gnaws away at the body and mind of the individual to be reformed, and which shapes him according to *utilisable* parameters for the process of exploitation.

The content of the punishment (the 'execution') is thus linked to its juridical form in the same way as authority in the factory ensures that exploitation can assume the character of a contract. After all, is it not *value* which determines, in Hegel's view, as much the equality between the two sides of the bargain in contractual exchange as that between the two sides of retribution, crime and punishment?[185] Again, it is not a question of analogy, but an expression of the two mutually essential moments in the capitalist structure: circulation and production. Once more, the realm of law (the circulation of goods), the great pride of the revolutionary bourgeoisie in the sphere of law, is intrinsically linked to the relationship of exploitation, that is, the authority and violence which reigns in production (in the factory, in the prison). Such bourgeois conquests, therefore, have much more to do with the consolidation of class hegemony over the social structure as a whole and therefore objectively against the proletariat *as such*, than with bourgeois defence against the absolute state. In any case, in so far as the latter adopts such principles itself, it is increasingly in bourgeois hands.

These are therefore genuine bourgeois-revolutionary conquests in the sense that they revolutionise old methods of handling punitive problems by the application of the new criteria of capitalist relations of production (as workers destined to find themselves behind bars – 'dangerous classes' – will very quickly come to appreciate). And, in fact, whilst the revolutionary bourgeoisie found that a sentence served by working was a concretisation of its conception of life based on labour-value measured in terms of time, the lower classes, in their turn protagonists of the Great Revolution that shook Europe, viewed prisons in a totally different light. The destruction of the Bastille was no isolated fact; although it is true that it was a specific type of prison, that is a fortress for political prisoners, it is not without some irony that the English workhouses of 1834 were, as we have seen, immediately renamed 'poor-law bastilles'. From then on, attacks on prisons and the liberation of prisoners were a constant feature of every uprising and popular insurrection. Although assaults on prisons usually had the aim of releasing 'political' prisoners or at least popular leaders and brigands, etc., to whom the masses felt some kind of affinity, things did not stop there; guided by an acute class instinct, they also unlocked the cells of ordinary thieves, vagabonds and so on without any moralism.

After some delay, the more backward regions of Europe were also affected by the growth of an immeasurably large industrial reserve army, with a concomitant growth in pauperism and criminality. Indeed after the revolution and Jacobinism, whilst working-class organisation was still in its infancy, class war was largely fought out on the terrain of criminality, the violent individual solution. This period was fraught with massive unemployment, extreme poverty and disorganisation of the masses; real wages plummeted to what was possibly an all-time low in the history of capitalism; the masses were driven into begging, stealing and, in some circumstances, violence, banditry and primitive forms of class struggle, for example, incendiarism and machine-breaking. In the face of this phenomenon, the creation of capital itself, its bourgeois political agents no longer had to rely on forced labour in order to drive down free labourers' wages, nor did they have to worry about training and returning the forced labourers to factory work. Prison remained the definitive and increasingly dominant acquisition of bourgeois punitive practice, but its function throughout Europe – at least while the circumstances described above prevailed (until just after the middle of the century) – increasingly acquired a bias towards terror and direct social control; the principle of discipline *tout court* prevailed over that of *productive* factory discipline.

In the more advanced countries the reactionary turn of the 1815 Restoration brought about an alliance between the victorious bourgeoisie and what remained of the old absolutist order together with its theoretical and practical remnants. This turn was an expression of anti-liberal resistance on the one hand, and a growing anti-working-class stance on the other. From the Restoration onwards, the emergence of an incipient political potential among the lower classes made it impossible to divorce the question of crime and prison in particular from the more general class struggle. What had been an unconscious relationship between the new classes of capitalism during its formative period now emerged as a conscious relationship of *political* hostility. During the first decades of the last century, various European governments demonstrated a mounting concern over the question of prison reform as a result of the 'terrible rise in recidivity'.[186] Foreign observers were sent out to other countries, particularly the United States.[187]

It is no accident that statistical research into criminality began in this period and revealed a particularly rapid rise in crimes against property in England and France.[188] A slow but continuous movement in favour of greater severity in penal doctrines and practices began with the Napoleonic Code of 1810 and joined in the attack on revolutionary *philanthropy*.[189] The French code essentially envisaged three types of sanction: capital punishment; forced labour; and the house of correction. The death penalty, however, was not the exceptional measure it had tended to be in earlier revolutionary legislation but was applied to practically all crimes threatening state security, counterfeiting, larceny and arson; in this way, it struck at every kind of subversion which had immediate political–military repercussions and at the two crimes common to the urban and country masses. For the less serious crimes of these classes – vagrancy, mendicancy, rebellion not constituting a serious threat to state security, the offences of striking and of association, etc. – the use of the house of correction·was envisaged, of a short, sharp punishment, and above all, one that centred on compulsory labour; in this way, the practice we have seen being used from the foundation of the very first workhouses or houses of correction was formalised. The refinement of legal technique; the ever more complete incorporation in penal law of fundamental civil rights; both went hand in hand with the strengthening and stiffening of repression in other codes as well, such as the Bavarian Code of 1813, which was the work of Anselm Feuerbach.[190]

As we have already seen, one of the main aims to be achieved by coerced labour since prisons first began was the levelling down of wages outside. This could only partially be achieved, however, by means of an economic mechanism pure and simple, that is, by placing unfree labour at the disposal of certain branches of production (if for no other reason than the scarcity of those kinds of labour). It was due, more than anything, to the terror struck in those refusing to work, either at all or in particularly bad conditions, by the idea of prison as their unavoidable fate. Then according to the less eligibility principle, freedom and outside work must always be preferable to confinement. In the period of mounting unemployment and pauperism now being examined, the only possible way of intimidating people who had no chance of finding work anyway was politically, in the sense of deterring the unemployed, the vagabond, etc. from turning to crime, begging and so on, in the attempt to keep alive. But the risks at stake for the poor and the unemployed in these first decades of the nineteenth century were precisely those of survival or of starving to death with their families, and not just of haggling over the *conditions* of exploitation. It was extremely difficult for prison to intimidate them in the light of this, as it only had to provide the bare minimum necessary for subsistence to be preferable to freedom.

Thus, in this period, protests against the work of reform carried out in the late eighteenth century multiplied. Whilst it was conceded that reforms contained some merit, objections were raised as to the excessive improvement of prison conditions. It was said that too much attention had been paid to the *material* aspect and too little to the *spiritual* aspect of detention.[191] That prisoners should enjoy a standard of living similar to that of any free 'artisan', whose own standard was in any case frequently below the minimum level of subsistence, was held to be an impossible state of affairs.[192] As a result, prisoners became ill and died of starvation; Malthusianism was being taken towards its logical conclusion – genocide of the proletariat.[193]

It was in this climate that the reformers now turned their attention towards the American scene. By the end of its first century, the Quaker state of Pennsylvania had already established a prison regime based on solitary confinement: this typically Calvinist system was entirely founded upon the *spiritual* work ethic (just what they were looking for in Europe!) and had no place for productive work. Production, by contrast, was at the basis of the Auburn *silent* system which envisaged solitary confinement at night and silent collective labour during the day.[194] In the new and rapidly growing states of North America, this system soon gained ground as a result of the great shortage of labour that had arisen, in contrast to Europe.[195]

At this point in the history of the Old World, the debate on prison reform fused with a discussion on the merits of these two systems, cross-fertilising each system into a number of possibilities which generated new solutions.

Though some taking part in the debate propounded what was by now a different ideology, they carried on in their activity the tradition of Enlightenment *philosophes*: as scholars representing the widest range of human sciences, they frequently wrote essays, articles and travelogues. Though these projects for reform dealt with different matters, they all had in common the overall organisation, in its multifaceted complexity, of nascent bourgeois civilisation and especially of its state. They were often personally involved in legislative or administrative activity and their interest in the prison question, as it came to be known, was never casual but was always with an eye to the possibilities of practical application. Carlo Ilarione Petitti di Roreto from Piedmont was typical of this breed. In his work of 1840, *Della condizione attuale delle carceri e dei mezzi di migliorarla* (The present condition of prison and ways of improving it),[196] he provides an extensive survey on the state of reform in the nations of Europe at the time and the accompanying theoretical discussion.[197]

Both positions presupposed that it was necessary to avoid the corruption of contact between the various categories of prisoners. Such corruption was said to form the basis of what was considered to be the most worrying phenomenon in the prison question, the rise in recidivism. The supporters of the Auburn system, who were however, in the minority,[198] denounced the remarkable rise in cases of insanity and suicide found in prisons conducted on the Philadelphian model of solitary confinement. At the same time, the supporters of the Philadelphian system made use of the Quaker theory of the great moral effectiveness of meditation and of the comfort offered by sound and reliable visitors, who were allowed for despite the system's rigidity.[199] They further accused the silent system of being very difficult to put into practice and of giving the warders too much scope for the excessive use of violence in the attempt to ensure adherence to the rules. The marked lack of interest shown by European culture on the question of convict labour showed itself in the fact that the fundamental difference between the two systems – the one facilitating the installation of real productive work, the other not – was usually missed or at least was not seen for what it was. For the treasuries of various states, however, the consideration that the Philadelphian system with its costly requirement of cellular buildings would involve great expenditure was much more important. This was later the reason why a number of states which had declared themselves in favour of this solution in principle did not put it in practice.

The system of solitary confinement was the final outcome of a series of international prison conferences, the first one of which took place in Frankfurt. The reasons for this were precisely those stated at the start: the lack of interest in forced labour (provided for under the Auburn-system) when labour was abundant; a preference for the use of terror, never openly admitted but embodied in the choice of the 'Philadelphian System': an awareness of the horror inspired in the potential offender by the prospect of spending a five, ten or twenty-year sentence in solitary confinement – often relieved only by some form of 'work' so pointless and repetitive that it would really amount to physical torture. Again, for the complex reasons we have tried to explain, the serious decline in prison conditions was thus accompanied by an ever more limited use of work. Moreover, the use of work was also impeded by technical considerations: in an age which gave birth to the real modern factory, with its expensive and cumbersome machinery, with the first development of a more structured organisation of labour, only a very single-minded policy bent on transforming prison into factory through capital investment, etc., could have sustained efficient use of convict labour.

On the other hand, it was not only the reservations of reactionaries that discouraged this kind of prison regime. The popular masses themselves were very conscious of the menace convict labour represented in competition with free labour, especially in a situation of widespread unemployment. For many years, the working-class movement thus became one of the principle obstacles to prison labour. In the United States, for example, perhaps the only country which had had significant experience of convict labour, its continual decline from the end of the last century up to 1940 was above all due to the hostility of a strong and organised workers' movement. Even in a situation closer to that under examination – the 1848 Revolution in Paris – one of the first victories of the popular masses was the abolition of work in prisons, promptly restored after their defeat.[200] However, it is interesting that the fundamental social struggle of the 1848 Revolution was around the demand for 'the right to work'. This led to the opening of the *Ateliers Nationales* along the lines proposed by Considérant and Fourier. Even if the consciousness of the time probably did not make a link between the two problems, it seems to me that there is a direct connection from the workers' point of view between the fight for the right of everyone to work and the fight against convict labour. Free labour must be available to all without the economic and political blackmail of the house of correction! The views of the Parisian Proletariat were to be echoed by Marx many years later in his comments on a demand relating to convict labour in the German Social Democratic Party's Gotha Programme.[201] Marx wrote that prisoners should neither be deprived of 'productive labour' nor be treated 'like animals' from fear of their competition. However, the organised working class's attitude *vis-à-vis* prison work belongs to a history which begins where we finish. Towards the middle of the last century, prison came of age and was able to take its place in line with the other bourgeois social institutions of capitalism. Its further history is above all the history of a *crisis* which, like the history of the organised working class, already belongs to a different sort of capitalist society.

Notes

1. K. Marx, *Capital*, vol. I (London: Lawrence and Wishart, 1977) p. 668; see the whole of Part VIII.
2. M. Dobb, *Studies in the Development of Capitalism* (London, 1963). Cf. particularly chs 4, 5 and 6: 'The Rise of Industrial Capital', 'Capital Accumulation and Mercantilism' and above all, 'Growth of the Proletariat'.
3. Dobb, ibid., p. 224 Cf. Marx, *Capital*, vol. I, ch. XXVII, pp. 671 ff.
4. For a discussion on this thesis see R. Hilton (ed.), *The Transition from Feudalism to Capitalism. A Symposium* (New York 1954).
5. Dobb, *Studies in the Development of Capitalism*, p. 42.
6. Marx, *Capital*, vol. I, ch. XVIII, p. 678.
7. Sir Thomas More, *The 'Utopia' and The History of Edward V, with Roper's Life*. Edited, with Intro, by M. Adams, London, n.d., pp. 89–90.
8. Marx, *Capital*, vol. I, ch. XVIII, p. 686.
9. More, '*Utopia*', p. 98: W. J. Chambliss, 'A Sociological Analysis of the Law of Vagrancy', *Social Problems*, vol. 12, no. 1 (Summer 1964) p. 67.
10. More, '*Utopia*', pp. 92 ff.
11. F. Piven and R. A. Cloward, *Regulating the Poor* (London, 1972) p. 15.
12. A. van der Slice, 'Elizabethan Houses of Correction', *Journal of the American Institute of Criminal Law and Criminology*, vol. XXVII (1936–7) p. 44; A. J. Copeland, 'Bridewell Royal Hospital', *Past and Present* (1888); Max Grünhut, *Penal Reform* (Oxford, 1948) p. 15; S. and B. Webb, *English Prisons Under Local Government* (London, 1963) p. 12.

13. Grünhut, *Penal Reform*, pp. 15, 16 and van der Slice, *Elizabethan Houses of Correction*, p. 51.

14. F. M. Eden, *The State of the Poor* (London, 1928) p. 16; G. Rusche and O. Kirchheimer, *Punishment and Social Structure* (New York, 1968) p. 41; Piven and Cloward, *Regulating the Poor*, pp. 15, 16; Grünhut, *Penal Reform*, p. 16; van der Slice, *Elizabethan Houses of Correction*, p. 55.

15. Eden, *The State of the Poor*, p. 16.

16. Van der Slice, *Elizabethan Houses of Correction*, p. 54.

17. See Eden, *The State of the Poor*, p. 17; S. and B. Webb, *English Prisons Under Local Government*, p. 13; Rusche and Kirchheimer, *Punishment and Social Structure*, p. 51; van der Slice, *Elizabethan Houses of Correction*, p. 55; Grünhut, *Penal Reform*, p. 16.

18. Eden, *The State of the Poor*, p. 17.

19. Ibid., p. 19.

20. See Piven and Cloward, *Regulating the Poor*, p. 37; also Marx, *Capital*, vol. i, chs. xxviii-xxix, pp. 686–96; and Dobb, *Studies in the Development of Capitalism*, pp. 231 ff.

21. Details here and in subsequent passages on the demographic situation are drawn from A. Bellettini, 'La popolazione italiana dall'inizio della era volgare ai giorni nostri. Valutazioni e tenderize', in *Storia d'Italia*, vol. v, 1 (Torino, 1973) p. 489. This essay relates the Italian demographic situation to that of Europe in general.

22. Dobb, *Studies in the Development of Capitalism*, pp. 237 ff.

23. See above, p. 13.

24. Piven and Cloward, *Regulating the Poor*, p. 6.

25. Marx defines Holland as 'the head capitalistic nation of the seventeenth century', *Capital*, vol. i, ch. xxxi, p. 704.

26. T. Sellin, *Pioneering in Penology* (Philadelphia, 1944) p. 20; Grünhut, *Penal Reform*, p. 17; R. von Hippel, 'Beiträge zur Geschichte der Freiheitsstrafe', *Zeitschrift für die gesamte Strafrechtswissenschaft*, vol. xviii (1898) p. 648.

27. See Sellin, *Pioneering in Penology*, pp. 1, 2.

28. Cf. Rusche and Kirchheimer, *Punishment and Social Structure*, p. 42 and Bellettini, *La popolazione*.

29. See Rusche and Kirchheimer, *Punishment and Social Structure*, p. 42.

30. Marx, *Capital*, vol. i, Part viii, p. 686 ff. and Part iii, ch. x: *The Working Day*, pp. 222 ff.

31. See above, p. 13.

32. Piven and Cloward have especially emphasised this, for example in the first chapter of *Regulating the Poor*.

33. I have already cited Sellin; cf. von Hippel, 'Beiträge zur Geschichte', pp. 437 ff. A. Hallema has contributed widely to this theme: A. Hallema, *In em om de Gevangenis, Van vroeger Dagen in Nederland en Nederlandsch-Indie* ('s Gravenhage, 1936) pp. 174–6. Most historical research on penology refers to Dutch workhouses. In Italian see: C. I. Petitti di Roreto, 'Della condizione attuale delle carceri e dei mezzi di migliorarla (1840)' in *Opere scelte* (Torino, 1969) p. 369. M. Beltrani– Scalia, *Sul governo e sulla riforma delle carceri in Italia* (Torino, 1867) p. 393.

34. See Sellin, *Pioneering in Penology*, pp. 23, 24. All the following information on the Rasp-huis is drawn from Sellin.

35. Ibid., p. 26.

36. It was calculated that in the city of Amsterdam, with a population of 100,000, at the time of the opening of the institution there were about 3500 'juvenile delinquents' (ibid., p. 41).

37. Dobb, *Studies in the Development of Capitalism*, pp. 193 ff.

38. See Sellin, *Pioneering in Penology*, pp. 29, 30.

39. For a theoretical discussion on this theme see Dobb, *Studies in the Development of Capitalism*, pp. 281 ff.

40. Marx, *Capital*, vol. I, p. 331.

41. Ibid., pp. 346, 347.

42. Sellin, *Pioneering in Penology*, p. 59.

43. Ibid., p. 63.

44. Cf. pp. 23 ff.

45. Marx, *Capital*, vol. I, p. 340.

46. See pp. 33 ff.

47. See Sellin, *Pioneering in Penology*, p. 68.

48. See Dobb, *Studies in the Development of Capitalism*, pp. 151 ff.

49. Ibid.

50. Ibid., p. 158. On the 'Ciompi' see V. Rutenberg, *Popolo e movimenti popolari nell' Italia del '300 e '400* (Bologna, 1971) pp. 157–329.

51. See Dobb, *Studies in the Development of Capitalism*, pp. 235 ff. and bibl.

52. Referred to in Rusche and Kirchheimer, *Punishment and Social Structure*, p. 36; Piven and Cloward, *Regulating the Poor*, p. 9; Grünhut, *Penal Reform*, p. 14.

53. In Piven and Cloward, *Regulating the Poor*, p. 9.

54. Ibid., p. 11. Specifically on Lyon, also see: J. P. Gutton, *La Société et les pauvres. L'exemple de la généralité de Lyon, 1534–1789* (Paris, 1971); N. Z. Davis, 'Poor Relief, Humanism and Heresy: The Case of Lyon', in *Studies in Medieval and Renaissance History* (1968) p. 217; R. Gascon, 'Immigration et croissance au XVIe siècle: l'exemple de Lyon (1529–1563)', *Annales* (1970) p. 988.

55. On this specific theme cf. Rusche and Kirchheimer, *Punishment and Social Structure*, pp. 33–52; more generally, see: J. B. Kraus, *Scholastik, Puritanismus und Kapitalismus* (München, 1930); P. C. Gordon Walker, 'Capitalism and the Reformation', *Economic History Review*, vol. VIII (1937) p. 18 and, of course, M. Weber, *Protestant Ethic and the Spirit of Capitalism* (London, 1976), int. A. Giddens.

56. See pp. 33 ff. In the same way, the influence of methodism grew in Great Britain during the industrial revolution: see E. P. Thompson, *The Making of the English Working Class* (Harmondsworth: Penguin Books, 1968) pp. 385 ff. It is no accident that Marx refers to 'the methodist cell system' in *The Holy Family* (Moscow, 1956), though, as we will see, this system was originally more Quaker than Methodist. On this theme, cf. D. Melossi, *The Penal Question* in *'Capital'*, *Crime and Social Justice*, no. 5 (1976) pp. 26–33.

57. K. Marx, *A Contribution to the Critique of Hegel's 'Philosophy of Right'*, ed. O'Malley (Cambridge U.P., 1977) p. 138.

58. Cited by H. Marcuse in his 'Study on Authority', *Studies in Critical Philosophy* (London, 1972) p. 65.

59. Marcuse puts this forward in the above study (p. 49 ff.) It is enough simply to mention the fact that it is this family structure which lay at the basis of Freudian theory. A theory, that is to say, which rose to prominence in this century as the bourgeois consciousness of the crisis in this particular *form* of the family. But see below, note 133.

60. See below, pp. 67 ff.

61. Marcuse, *Study on Authority*, pp. 56 ff.

62. M. Foucault, *Storia della follia* (Milan, 1963) pp. 91, 92. Eng. Trans: *Madness and Civilisation. A History of Insanity in the Age of Reason* (London, 1965).

63. M. Weber, *The Protestant Ethic and the Spirit of Capitalism*, pp. 159 ff.

64. That is to say, as Marx explains with magnificent clarity, this devaluation of the *significance* of works as such as against their value in the eyes of the deity, as a *sign*, exactly corresponds to a society in which works

do not imply production for immediate consumption (as in peasant society) but for the market, for exchange (i.e. the difference between *use-value* and *exchange-value*): *work* has value not for what it is but for what it can obtain (*accumulation* or *grace* – it makes no great difference to the *religion of capital*).

65. 'An ideal house of terror', see below, n. 104.
66. *Selected Writings*, vol. III, p. 466, quoted in Marcuse *Study on Authority*, p. 65. My emphasis.
67. Quoted in Marcuse, *Study on Authority*, p. 64n. It is symptomatic that the social strata to which Müntzer refers as the victims of the predatory princes are 'the poor peasant, the artisan', i.e. precisely those who bore the main brunt first of expropriation, then of proletarianisation. On the peasant revolts in Germany, see Engels's classic, *The Peasant War in Germany* (London: Lawrence & Wishart, 1969).
68. Marcuse, *Study on Authority*, p. 65. This conception is essentially at the basis of Hegelian penal theory.
69. Cf. Rusche and Kirchheimer, *Punishment and Social Structure*, p. 44, von Hippel, *Beitrage zur Geschichte der Freiheitsstrafe*, pp. 429 ff.
70. As in von Hippel, 'Beiträge zur Geschichte', p. 648.
71. See Rusche and Kirchheimer, *Punishment and Social Structure*, p. 44.
72. Ibid., pp. 63 ff.
73. Ibid., pp. 65.
74. Ibid., p. 51, n. 139. Von Hippel's 'Beiträge zur Geschichte' contains a full summary of this booklet in German.
75. See Foucault, *Storia della follia* (Madness and Civilisation) p. 82.
76. See Rusche and Kirchheimer, *Punishment and Social Structure*, p. 43; Foucault, *Storia della follia*, pp. 126 ff.
77. See Rusche and Kirchheimer, *Punishment and Social Structure*, pp. 45, 48.
78. See the section in this chapter on the establishment of modern prison practice in continental Europe, and Chap. 3, which deals with Italy. Rusche and Kirchheimer conclude: 'the fact that both the old and new religious doctrines collaborated in the mutual development of the new institution goes to prove that purely ideological viewpoints took second place to economic motives as driving forces in the whole movement.' p. 52(*Punishment and Social Structure*).
79. Ibid., p. 43; Foucault, *Storia della follia*, p. 85 and pp. 95 ff.
80. Foucault, *Storia della follia*, pp. 98–9.

81. See Rusche and Kirchheimer, *Punishment and Social Structure*, p. 69 ff; Jean Mabillon, 'Reflexion sur les prisons des ordres religioux' in *Ouvrages Posthumes de D. Jean Mabillon et de D. Thierri Ruinart…* (Paris, 1724) pp. 321–35, edited in English in T. Sellin, 'Dom Jean Mabillon – A Prison Reformer of the Seventeenth Century', *Journal of American Institute of Criminal Law and Criminology*, vol. xvii (1926–7) pp. 581–602.

82. Marx, *Capital*, vol. i, p. 694.

83. Ibid., p. 702 and pp. 716 ff.

84. Ibid., p. 702.

85. Ibid., p. 694.

86. See Dobb, *Studies in the Development of Capitalism*, pp. 226 ff.

87. Ibid.

88. Ibid., p. 225.

89. Cited in T. E. Gregory, 'The Economics of Employment in England, 1660–1713', *Economica*, vol. i (1921) p. 44. For a survey of various views on this see R. Bendix, *Work and Authority in Industry* (New York – London, 1956) pp. 60 ff; also interesting is D. Defoe's 'Giving Alms No Charity', in *A Select Collection of Scarce and Valuable Economic Tracts* (London, 1859) p. 40; Bendix is very important in relation to the whole of English social policy from the sixteenth century to the nineteenth century (Bendix, first part, Ch. II).

90. See Eden, *The State of the Poor*, pp. 25, 34, 35.

91. See J. D. Marshall, *The Old Poor Law 1799–1834* (London, 1968) p. 14.

92. Ibid., p. 15.

93. See Eden, *The State of the Poor*, pp. 25 ff.

94. Ibid., p. 27.

95. See S. and B. Webb, *English Prisons Under Local Government*, pp. 15–17; L. W. Fox, *The Modern English Prison* (1934) p. 3; Grünhut, *Penal Reform*, p. 17.

96. On the following see S. and -B. Webb, *English Prisons Under Local Government*, pp. 18 ff.

97. See Dobb, *Studies in the Development of Capitalism*, pp. 256 ff.

98. See above, n. 6.

99. See 'Debates on the Law on Thefts of Wood' in K. Marx and F. Engels *Collected Works* (London: Lawrence & Wishart, 1975) vol. i, pp. 224–63. See also P. Linebaugh, 'Karl Marx. The Theft of Wood and

Working Class Composition: A Contribution to the Current Debate',
Crime and Social Justice, vol. 6 (Fall–Winter 1976) p. 5.

100. See Piven and Cloward, *Regulating the Poor*, p. 29, cf. Thompson, *The Making of the English Working Class*, pp. 59 ff.

101. In relation to these, see Marshall, *The Old Poor Law*. On the Poor Laws in a broader economic and ideological context, see K. Polanyi's *The Great Transformation* (Boston, 1957).

102. For an elaboration on the new poor laws, see Marshall, *The Old Poor Law*, p. 17; Piven and Cloward, *Regulating the Poor*, pp. 33, 34; Rusche and Kirchheimer, *Punishment and Social Structure*, p. 94; F. Engels, *Conditions of the English Working Class in 1844*.

103. Engels, ibid., p. 312.

104. See Marx, *Capital*, vol. I, p. 263.

105. Piven and Cloward, *Regulating the Poor*, pp. 33, 34.

106. Ibid.

107. Ibid., p. 35. This came out of the so-called 'less eligibility' principle.

108. In Marshall, *The Old Poor Law*, p. 30. For the relationship between what nowadays we would define as 'political criminality' and 'common criminality' and which then took on various forms, primitive and barely different form of class struggle in Britain of the industrial revolution, see Thompson. *The Making of the English Working Class*, pp. 61 ff.

109. See Engels, *Conditions of the English Working Class in 1844*, p. 287.

110. Ibid., p. 288.

111. Piven and Cloward, *Regulating the Poor*, p. 35.

112. See Rusche and Kirchheimer, *Punishment and Social Structure*, pp. 95 ff.

113. See ibid., pp. 96, 97 for an account of the rapid rise in the crime rate in England especially from 1810 onwards. It is no accident that the themes of pauperism, alcoholism, prostitution and crime continually crop up in the young Engels's work cited above. The actual situation before Engels, was one in which *mass criminal activity* had barely been superseded by class struggle. This is summed up in Engels' exclamation: 'And he among the "surplus" who has courage and passion enough openly to resist society, to reply with declared war upon the bourgeoisie to the disguised war which the bourgeoisie wages upon him, goes forth to rob, plunder, murder, and burn!' (p. 87) He then describes how the British working class passed through crime, revolt and Luddism to political struggle as a result of winning the right to organise (pp. 214, 215). It is not inappropriate to note, *en passant*, that Marx's

well-known judgements of the *lumpenproletariat*, which sparked off a famous politico- philological *querelle* (see *Il Manifesto*, 16 and 23 Jan and 6 Feb 1972) were all delivered, like those presented by Engels, within a particular socio-political context from which they derive their own special validity. It was the particular task of the socialist movement in the last century to transform, willy-nilly, criminal behaviour into mass *political* activity while such behaviour remained characteristic of a section of the working class: the lumpenproletariat, to be precise, which was often used in an anti-working-class way. It was quite obvious that with such a *political* perspective Marx and Engels would denounce the *lumpen* elements. It should also be stressed that the question of the lumpenproletariat as a question of class analysis has not the slightest connection with those of violence and illegality as forms of political struggle. On this point see M. Foucault, *Surveiller et Punir* (Paris, 1975) pp. 261 ff.

114. See J. Howard, *Prisons and Lazarettos, I: The State of The Prisons in England and Wales* (Montclair, New Jersey, 1973) particularly: 'Proposed Improvements in the Structure and Management of Prisons', p. 19.

115. See Rusche and Kirchheimer, *Punishment and Social Structure*, p. 110.

116. Ibid., p. 111.

117. In Marshall, *The Old Poor Law, 1795–1834*, p. 33. The basic text on this problematic in the industrial revolution period is (regarding English history) the work of S. and B. Webb, *English Poor Law History*, vols VII, VIII and IX of their *English Local Government* (London, 1929).

118. See Piven and Cloward, *Regulating the Poor*, p. 35.

119. See Howard, *Prisons and Lazarettos*, p. 492.

120. From the official *Prison Report* by the Home Office for that year.

121. We should also remember that in the transition from one social situation to another, the same results can be achieved with other means, for example other segregated institutions, transportations, etc.

122. See J. Bentham, *Panopticon*, in *The Works of Jeremy Bentham*, vol. IV (New York, 1962) p. 37.

123. See V. Comoli Mandracci, *Il carcere per la società del Sette-Ottocento* (Turin, 1974) pp. 36, 37. Also R. Evans, 'Bentham's Panopticon. An Incident in the Social History of Architecture', *Architectural Association Quarterly*, vol. 3, no. 2 (April/July 1971).

124. See *Postscript* in Bentham, *Panopticon,* pp. 71 ff.

125. Cf. M. Pavarini's essay in the second part of this book.

126. See Bentham, *Panopticon*, p. 47 ff.

127. Ibid., p. 47.

128. Ibid., p. 50.

129. Ibid., p. 54.

130. Ibid., p. 40.

131. Ibid.

132. On the concept of co-operation see Marx, *Capital*, vol. i, pp. 305 ff.

133. See ibid., pp. 181 ff. The thesis set out below is more widely developed in D. Melossi, *The Penal Question* in *'Capital'*; D. Melossi, 'Institutions of Social Control and the Capitalist Organization of Work', in NDC/CSE (eds) *Capitalism and the Rule of Law* (London: Hutchinson, 1979) pp. 90–9; D. Melossi, 'Strategies of Social Control in Capitalism: a Comment on Recent Work', *Contemporary Crises*, 4 (1980), pp. 381–402. Particularly the last two essays seek to understand this process from the standpoint of changes in social control as capitalism has developed. It should be stressed that here, on the contrary, the discussion specifically centres on the period of the prison system's maturity, i.e. 'classical' capitalism of the nineteenth century. It is from this starting point (and that of the first volume of *Capital*) that I write here.

134. Marx, *Capital*, vol. i, p. 172.

135. Ibid.

136. Ibid.

137. Ibid.

138. Ibid.

139. Ibid.

140. Marx clearly demonstrates how the principle of authority is incorporated into the capitalist process of production itself in the chapter on co-operation: 'By the co-operation of numerous wage-labourers, the sway of capital develops into a requisite for carrying on the labour- process itself, into a real requisite of production. That a capitalist should command on the field of production, is now as indispensible as that a general should command on the field of battle': in *Capital*, vol. i, p. 313. Also pp. 305 ff.

141. See K. Marx and F. Engels, *The Manifesto of the Communist Party*.

142. See the section above on the genesis and development of prisons in other European countries.

143. *Surveiller et punir*, already cited. We were able to see Foucault's book only after our own work here had been completed. M. Foucault's book is a brilliant discourse on prison rather than a history of the same. It is

thus of little use here if only for its extreme Franco-centrism (every twist and turn is modulated on French history – if this leaves the philosophical discussion relatively unharmed, it is, as I think I have shown, quite misleading from a historical perspective). But I repeat, it seems to me that Foucault's aims (and that which is of most interest in his work) are other than 'historical'. For a debate on this, cf. *La Questione Criminale*, vol. 11, no. 2/3 (1976).

144. See V. Cotesta, 'Michel Foucault: dall 'archeologia del sapere alia genealogia del potere', *La Questione Criminale*, vol. 2, no. 2/3 (1976).

145. On man's estrangement from his body, on the reduction of man to worker, on the whole thematic of the senses and *needs* (pp. 322 ff.) in K. Marx, 'Economic and Philosophic Manuscripts 1844', in *Early Writings*, Intro. L. Colletti (Harmondsworth: Penguin, 1977).

146. See Foucault, *Surveiller et punir*, pp. 197 ff. And as we have seen in Bentham, *Panopticon*.

147. Fox, *The Modern English Prison*, pp. 6, 7; G. C. Marino, *La formazione dello spirito borghese in Italia* (Firenze, 1974) pp. 353–5.

148. See Rusche and Kirchheimer, *Punishment and Social Structure*, pp. 95 ff.

149. See pp. 47 ff.

150. Cf. Pavarini's essay, below.

151. Cf. Fox, *The Modern English Prison*, pp. 14 ff; Rusche and Kirchheimer, *Punishment and Social Structure*, pp. 132 ff.

152. The complete title of Howard's first volume cited here is: *The State of the Prisons in England and Wales, with Preliminary Observations, and an Account of some Foreign Prisons and Hospitals*.

153. Cf. Rusche and Kirchheimer, *Punishment and Social Structure*, ch. vi, pp. 84 ff.

154. See Howard, *The State of the Prisons*, pp. 44 ff.

155. See Sellin, *Pioneering in Penology*, p. 59.

156. See Grünhut, *Penal Reform*, pp. 19 ff.

157. See Howard, *The State of the Prisons*, pp. 66 ff.

158. See Rusche and Kirchheimer, *Punishment and Social Structure*, p. 91.

159. See Howard, *The State of the Prisons*, pp. 145 ff. which includes a reproduction of the plan of the *Maison de Force*; Grünhut, *Penal Reform*, p. 22; L. Stroobant, 'Le Rasphuis de Gand, Recherches sur la repression du vagabondage et sur le système pénitentiaire établi en Flandre au xviie et au xviiie siècle', *Annales de la Soc. d'Histoire et d'Archéologie de Gand*, vol. iii (1900) pp. 191–307. It was due to the work of the Count Hippolyte Vilain that the new building was made possible. He espoused

his programme in an essay which Howard also cites: *Mémoire sur les moyens de corriger les malfaiteurs et les fainéants a leur propre avantage et de les rendre utiles à l' Etat* (Ghent, 1775). The prison at Ghent was generally considered to be the fundamental starting point for the development of the modern prison; it is cited in practically all historic studies on this subject.

160. Howard, *The State of the Prisons*, p. 148.
161. Ibid., p. 150.
162. Ibid., p. 153. For Italy cf. pp. 63 ff.
163. See Foucault, *Storia della follia*, pp. 109 ff.
164. Ibid., p. 110; Rusche and Kirchheimer, *Punishment and Social Structure*, p. 91.
165. See Howard, *The State of the Prisons*, pp. 165 ff. For an analysis of the various human types locked up in the Parisian hospitals, see Foucault, *Storia della follia*, pp. 126, 127.
166. See Howard, *The State of the Prisons*, p. 174.
167. See Marx, Capital, vol. i.
168. See J. P. Marat, *Disegno di legislazione criminale* (Milano, 1971). Refer to the preface by M. A. Cattaneo and the scholarly introduction by M. A. Aimo for further material on this work.
169. Ibid., pp. 71 ff.
170. Ibid., p. 72.
171. Ibid., pp. 72–3.
172. Ibid., p. 73.
173. Ibid., pp. 74–5.
174. Ibid., p. 78.
175. Cf. G. Lefebvre, *The Great Fear of 1789, Rural Panic in Revolutionary France* (London, 1973). There is extensive material in French on this subject. I will limit myself to citing the following: C. Paultre, *De La répression de la mendicité et du vagabondage en France sous l'Ancien Régime* (Paris: 1906); L. Lallemand, *Histoire de la Charité, t. IV, Les temps modernes*, (Paris: 1910 and 1912); 'Crimes et criminalité en France sous l'Ancien Régime, XVIIe–XVIIIe siècles', *Cahier des Annales*, vol. 33 (Paris, 1971); A. Vexliard, *Introduction à la sociologie du vagabondage* (Paris, 1956).
176. See Lefebvre, *The Great Fear*, pp. 10, 11.
177. Ibid., p. 14.
178. Ibid., p. 14.
179. Ibid., p. 17. Brigandage in Italy is more specifically dealt with later in Chap. 3.

180. G. Lefebvre, *The Great Fear, p.* 21.
181. Cf. Rusche and Kirchheimer, *Punishment and Social Structure,* pp. 81–2, 91–2; Foucault, *Storia della follia,* p. 110.
182. E. B. Pashukanis, *Law and Marxism: A General Theory,* ed. C. Arthur (London, 1978).
183. In para. 101 of his *Philosophy of Right,* trans. S.W. Dyde (London 1896), Hegel states in relation to the *lex taliones*: 'This identity, involved in the very nature of the case, is not literal equality, but equality in the inherent nature of the injury, namely, its value.' And: 'Value as the inner identity of things specifically different, has already been made use of in connection with contract, and occurs again in the civil prosecution of crime. By it the imagination is transferred from the direct attributes of the object to its universal nature' (pp. 98, 99, 100).

    The young Marx was to develop this concept in an article on the law against thefts of wood. 'Proceedings of the Sixth Rhine Province Assembly. Third Article. Debates on the Law on Thefts of Wood,' in K. Marx and F. Engels, *Collected Works* (London, 1975) vol. I, pp. 224–63. The scope of our research does not permit any discussion of penal theory. It is, however, necessary to mention the profound contradiction which permeates the Hegelian doctrine of retribution. This doctrine is, on the one hand, a philosophical expression of the bourgeoisie's increasing harshness on the question of crime once in power: the rejection of Enlightenment utilitarianism derives, above all, from the need to assert the general and universal validity of order and respect for law. Equally, it is, in Hegel's own words, an identification of the criminal as a "rational being" (see para. 100 of the *Philosophy of Right*) and it is no coincidence that Marx shapes his particular view of the penal question through a discussion of the Hegelian Theory: see Bottomore and Rebel (eds.), *Karl Marx. Selected Writings in Sociology and Social Philosophy* (London, 1956) pp. 228–70 ('Capital Punishment,' from an article in the *New York Daily Tribune*). On the function of the Hegelian theory in this respect see Rusche and Kirchheimer, *Punishment and Social Structure,* p. 101.
184. Cf. Foucault's brilliant discussion in *Surveiller et punir,* pp. 158 ff. on the new mode of controlling time 'par découpe segmentaire, par sériation, par synthése et totalisation.' On a more general discussion than is dealt with here in this relation, see pp. 222 ff.
185. See above, note 183.
186. These words are from Petitti di Roreto, *Della condizione attuale delle carceri,* p. 372.

187. Probably the best-known reports came from G. de Beaumont and A. de Tocqueville, *On the Penitentiary System in the United States and its Application in France* (Southern Illinois University Press, 1964). In Petitti's book cited above, these reports are fully documented (pp. 372–3). Also see M. Pavarini's essay below.

188. See Rusche and Kirchheimer, *Punishment and Social Structure*, pp. 96–7.

189. Ibid., pp. 98, 99. In the nineteenth century this came to be a common point from which eighteenth-century social policy was attacked.

190. Ibid., pp. 99–100.

191. See Petitti, *Della condizione attuale delle carceri*, pp. 374–5 and 469.

192. See Rusche and Kirchheimer, *Punishment and Social Structure*, pp. 106–7.

193. See information recorded in Rusche and Kirchheimer, p. 109.

194. See ibid., ch.VIII, p. 127; ch. III of Petitti's study is entirely dedicated to the various systems and contains a full bibliography.

195. See Rusche and Kirchheimer, p. 130.

196. See note 33 above.

197. See Petitti, *Della condizione*, p. 374 ff.

198. Petitti lists the following as being amongst the supporters of this system: 'Messrs Lucas, Mittermaier, Béranger, Madam Fry, Aubanel, Leone Faucher and Grellet Wammy and himself', p. 450.

199. The following supported solitary confinement: 'Moreau-Cristophe, Aylies, Demetz, Blouet, Julius, Crawford, Russel and Ducpetiaux' (p. 452). The people cited here and in note 198 above are amongst the main artificers, both in practical and theoretical terms, of European social policy during the first half of the nineteenth century.

The connection between isolation, the penal or *spiritual* conception of punishment, as it was called, and madness, is thus synthesised by Marx in *The Holy Family*: '... correctly describes the conditions to which isolation from the outer world reduces a man. For him who sees a *mere idea* in the *perceptible world, mere idea*, on the other hand, becomes a *perceptible being*. The figments of his brain assume corporeal form. A world of perceptible, sensible ghosts is begotten within his mind. That is the mystery of all pious visions and at the same time it is the general form of insanity' (Marx and Engels, *The Holy Family*, pp. 244–5).

200. See Rusche and Kirchheimer, pp. 94–5.
201. Marx comments: 'Kleinliche Forderung in einem allgemeinen Arbeiterprogramm. Jedenfalls musste man klar aussprechen, dass man aus Konkurrenzneid die gemeinen Verbrecher nicht wie Vieh behandelt wissen und ihnen namentlich ihr einziges Besserungsmittel, produktive Arbeit, nicht abschneiden will. Das war doch das Geringste, was man von Sozialisten erwarten durfte' (K. Marx, *Kritik des Gothaer Programms*, in MEW, Band 19 (Berlin, 1962) p. 32). Translations are often a little ambiguous. The sense, however, is:

'A petty demand in a general workers' programme. Anyway, it should have been made quite clear that there is no desire to treat run-of-the-mill criminals like animals through fear of competition and especially not to cut them off from their only means of improvement, productive labour. This was surely the least one might have expected from socialists.'

On the positions of the French workers' movement on this subject at the beginning of the last century, see also Foucault, *Surveiller et punir*, pp. 291 ff.

Genesis of the Prison in Italy

Dario Melossi

The Sixteenth and Seventeenth Centuries

Compared with England and the other great national monarchies, we face considerable difficulties in the reconstruction of the historical development of the Italian prison even with regard to its essential features. General material on Italy's socio-economic development and studies on our specific theme are thin on the ground. The lack of a unified central power – both a cause and an effect of Italy's historic backwardness – and the lack of a national monarchy which proved elsewhere to be of fundamental importance especially during the formative period of capitalism (the age of mercantilism) certainly present us with major problems. It is perhaps superfluous to add that this lack of unity failed to boost economic development in Italy thus preventing the generalisation of a whole series of experiences, ideas and measures such as prison. In Italy these experiences can only be seen as the heritage of individual states or regions. Thus it is arbitrary to consider Italy as a single entity, especially in relation to our subject, whereas in other countries, economic homogeneity and state intervention were the basis on which it was possible to develop initiatives in the sphere of prison.

© The Author(s) 2018
D. Melossi, M. Pavarini, *The Prison and the Factory (40ᵗʰ Anniversary Edition)*,
Palgrave Studies in Prisons and Penology, DOI 10.1057/978-1-137-56590-7_3

'In the Netherlands and in certain Italian cities these developments of capitalist production that we meet in Elizabethan and in Stuart England are to be found already matured at a much earlier date.'[1] In Florence, for example, as early as the end of the thirteenth century and particularly in the fourteenth century, there was considerable growth of a proletariat consisting of labourers excluded from the guilds following the expulsion of the peasantry from the countryside,[2] which in turn resulted in class conflict inside the town.[3] It is no accident that in this political context, a series of repressive penal measures were enacted against labourers: 'controlling his wages, enjoining the strictest obedience on him to his master, and ruthlessly proscribing any form of organisation or even meetings of journeymen (which were invariably denounced as "covins" and "cabals")'.[4] It was not uncommon for the more powerful authorities of the *Comuni*, characteristic of this period in which state power was still in the course of construction, to hold debtors and to carry out corporal punishment in their own custodial gaols. As Dobb notes, in Italy, Flanders, Germany and Holland, commercial capital and usury could not be transformed into industrial capital, as was to be the case in England later on, except in very partial terms.[5] In Italy in particular, the power of the Church and the feudal princes, closely allied in every *Comune* and republic with the commercial aristocracy, was strong enough to prevent further industrial and political development which could otherwise have been mutually supportive.[6]

Even if, then, seventeenth-century Italy received its *coup de grâce*[7] from shifts in trade patterns and the rise of other manufacturing powers, it was the internal structural causes to which we have referred which lay at the basis of its weakness and slow pace of development. During the whole of the sixteenth century, the economic ideal was based on the ennoblement of money and contempt for trade. Capital was immobilised in grandiose public works or returned to the countryside – though not in any productive sense or as a stimulus for change as had happened in the fourteenth century.[8] Even so, the sixteenth century was a period of transition whose effects were still to be felt: the profound stagnation, the political and cultural backwardness and the isolation which were to characterise the seventeenth century of the Counter-Reformation are here still in their initial phase.

As we shall see, in relation to social and criminal policy in the various Italian states, the differences between the sixteenth and seventeenth centuries are crucial. There was still some expansion in textile manufacture in the sixteenth century whilst in the seventeenth century wool manufacture slumped and the new silk industry fared differently in each area, at times expanding, at times contracting.[9] Although, as in Europe as a whole, widespread vagrancy and brigandage arose from the process of primitive accumulation, it was also the result of mass unemployment in the true meaning of the term – the consequences of redundancies in manufacture. There are numerous cases of repression against vagrancy and mendicancy. Fanfani records attempts similar to those in France and England to throw the unemployed masses out of towns in Southern Italy, the Papal States, Tuscany, Lombardy, Piedmont and Venice. In particular, thousands of textile workers, metal workers and workers from the arsenals found themselves out of work in the central and northern regions.[10] Whilst social control in the south relied on the gallows for centuries,[11] in the remaining states attempts were made during the sixteenth and seventeenth centuries to introduce measures similar to those contemporaneously adopted in England, Germany, etc.: prohibitions on begging, internment in hospices, assistance for the impotent, efforts to procure work for the able-bodied.[12] Naturally, this last aim was the *punctum dolens*. Faced with unemployed workers, the efforts of the various Italian statelets to conduct mercantilist investment policies in terms of public manufacture were very rare indeed.

Again, it was in Florence that the initial stages of capitalist development saw a certain revision in the totally religious medieval conception of charity in relation to attitudes on poverty and almsgiving. As early as the beginning of the fifteenth century, the practical and theoretical work of Antonino of Florence anticipated the more bourgeois approach embodied both in Lutheran reform more than a century later and in the writings of Muratori in the eighteenth century.[13] Though there was no provision for the organic reform of assistance in his work, Antonino had already replaced medieval values on poverty with the bourgeois and lay conception of *labour* seen as the principal obligation of the ordinary people.

On the other hand, his preaching was against a background in which hospices for the poor and the infirm, etc., had already been set up in the

Italian *Comuni*.[14] However, in the face of a serious economic crisis in Europe and growing deterioration in Italy in the first half of the sixteenth century, measures of a wider and more radical nature were necessary. Around 1530 in Venice, attempts were made to set paupers and vagabonds to work in the arsenals at a payment of half the average wage.[15] It was feared that assistance without work would ease the pressure of need on the lower classes – at least in the still flourishing towns like Venice. The question of law and order came to the fore in the Papal States as beggars converged on the capital of the Catholic world. Repeated attempts were made to confine paupers in recently created *Ospedali* under threat of harsher alternative penalties. But a century was to pass before these institutions formulated the obligation to work.[16] *Ospedali* were established at Parma, Turin, Modena, Genoa and Pisa.[17] In 1560 the *Ospizio di San Gregorio* was founded at Bologna where three years after its construction, beggars were led in procession through the town as was the custom:

> And as it pleased God, on a holy day which fell on the 18th April in the said year 1563 all the poor beggars to be found in the city at that time were indiscriminately gathered together in the courtyard of the Bishops Palace and taken in solemn procession with much almsgiving from the populace as they were led in order by the divine Maiestade: and they then began to be furnished not only with food and clothing but also with godly instruction and teachings as much in religious matters as in good behaviour and various skills for those who were willing and able, women as much as men, being provided with masters schooled and expert in these skills.[18]

The teaching of skills was also one of the functions of other *ospedali* or institutions often designed for the young. However, the extreme rarity of cases in which even this limited vocational preparation was mentioned leads one to suspect that it was not put into practice and that the Italian *ospedali* limited their aims to a rationalisation and centralisation of the old private form of charity. The great lack of industrial capital and hence the possibility of work discouraged any activity similar to contemporary English or Dutch initiatives.[19] It is superfluous to note that no initial distinction was made in Italy between the poor and the petty criminal: repressive legislation *created* the crimes of vagabondage and begging and, to put it in modern terms, the poor were already stigmatised as tending towards immorality, petty theft, etc. If anything, the distinction lay along the lines set down in the famous pamphlet by Andrea Guevarre which we have already discussed[20]: the *good* poor graciously received confinement as a gift; the confinement of the *wicked* poor was justified simply on the grounds that their resistance to confinement made such a measure necessary and fair.[21] If anything, the fact that there was no true and proper *punitive* internment for certain crimes, as was the case in Dutch and German workhouses, bears witness to the limited development of Italian initiatives; so much so that bad behaviour inside the *ospedali* or persistent begging were not punished by confinement as such but by being 'imprisoned either in the prisons of the institution [of the *ospedali*] or in those of the city, the *director* punishing *"according to demerit"*,[22] that is to say, it was traditional punishment.

One of the first modern Italian prisons was established in Florence by Filippo Franci in the middle of the seventeenth century – not much later than the period we have just considered.[23] The basic structure of this institution designed for the young was similar to other contemporary *ospedali*. Abandoned children were gathered together in Florence, assisted, housed and sent to work in local workshops. But its unusual feature was the special section (named San Filippo Neri) built in 1677 (or shortly after), which was referred to as 'corrective'. On the whole, this was intended for youth from respectable families who were entrusted to Franci because they showed some signs of maladjustment to normal bourgeois values.[24] This section was made up of eight small single cells. The offending youths from good families were committed to solitary confinement day and night: in exceptional cases, other assisted youths were committed to this institution for punishment. According to Sellin, this is the first recorded case of solitary confinement with the aim of reformation and correction. Certainly two things contributed to its creation – though like all Italian initiatives we shall examine, this example was very restricted in numerical terms. The combination of the religious revival of the Counter-Reformation and the sluggish state of Italian manufacture prevented the development of labour as a basis for a more 'material' reform as had been the case in other countries for some decades.

The Eighteenth Century

The work of Luigi Dal Pane, *Storia del lavoro in Italia* (A History of Work in Italy) provides both documentation and an invaluable analysis of the development of social and criminal policy in Italy from the beginning of the eighteenth century to the Napoleonic age.[25] By the eighteenth century the nadir of Italian economic, political and cultural collapse had passed. Even if the process was somewhat slow, the following century was marked by fresh advances – above all in agriculture.[26] The rise in population, which shot up from between 13 and 14 million to 18 million in the first years of the nineteenth century was symptomatic of this.[27] Primitive accumulation in Italy, which had begun earlier than anywhere else in Europe – only to be abruptly interrupted by the Renaissance[28] – was revived, albeit with great effort.

A sure sign of this was the continual worsening of the lower classes' living standards, especially in terms of real wages (in many cases, workers were still paid in kind).[29] This deterioration in living conditions was accompanied by the growing *proletarianisation* of the peasant strata and artisans. Even if this did not occur on the same scale as elsewhere in Europe, it does point to development along capitalist lines. 'A fact associated with the fall in real wages of agricultural labourers and industrial workers from 1700 to 1815 is that in that period their numbers grew to the detriment of other occupations.'[30] This process was greatly accelerated in the second half of the eighteenth century and received a decisive push forward in the north during the French occupation. The dynamic of feudal decay had the same effect in Italy as they had already had in other countries: on the one hand redistributed parts of the *latifundia* to the advantage of the new bourgeois strata, favouring the concentration of capital and more intensive agricultural production; on the other hand, the precarious subsistence economy of the old feudal world was wiped out, creating an army of vagabonds. Moreover, the crisis of the *Mezzadria* system also arose at this time (*Meteyer* share system), a crisis which has persisted to the present day. This system had a crucial effect on the development of social relations in the Po Valley and was a barrier to agricultural change from this time on. Various sections of the peasantry fell deeper and deeper into debt as a result of continual price rises, while the terms of contracts worsened.[31] Many were forced to become day-labourers, common rural workers. Obviously this situation generated increasingly wide strata of poor people and beggars who failed to find work in manufacture.

Furthermore, the eighteenth century saw the rapid growth of an approach to social policy based on exactly the same idea of *restricted charity*[32] to be found in mercantilist ideas in other countries. An increasingly rigorous distinction was made between the able-bodied poor and those deemed impotent. Only the latter were afforded any assistance and in the fierce struggle against private charity and begging, attempts were made to force the former into work. Once again, the specific aim was to make labour available cheaply, to force workers to accept work no matter what the conditions. In this respect, I feel that Dal Pane brings out the similarity between measures in the Italian states and those in other European countries, while at the same time pinpointing the specificity of the Italian situation:

> they wished to drive down wages, to obtain a workforce which would accept work no matter how low the pay. In the documents … one comes across the complaint that workers do not want or know how to live within their means – thus the blame is put on the workers. They wished to put them at the mercy of the employers … The laws of the Italian principalities against begging are thus on a parallel with those of the thriving European countries such as England and France. Seen in relation to the proletarianisation of the peasants described earlier, they indicate a tendency to bend a displaced rural population, reduced to vagabondage, to the discipline of the wages system. But in a country like Italy, where industrial development met with very serious hindrances and obstacles, such policies were bound to produce much more pernicious consequences than elsewhere unless they were carried out with great restraint. However, the observable fact of proletarianisation in the countryside together with the difficulty of absorbing the workforce explains the growth of a great number of robbers who overran the streets, stole from the fields and lined the way of the traveller with the dismal sight of their hanging bodies.[33]

The continuing surplus of labour over and above the demands of industry was to give rise – with specific exceptions in certain states and in certain periods – to a protracted policy of Malthusianism on the part of Italian capital, particularly in relation to the southern masses: Italian capital sought to obviate the problem posed by insufficient industrial development first by hunger and the gallows and then, after unification, through emigration. And this also explains why the Italian prison never (or almost never) saw the extensive use of industrial labour, that is, productive labour: on the one hand, it would have taken work away from free workers; on the other hand, there was no need to put pressure on the labour market in this way.

However, particularly in the eighteenth century, and especially in the more developed states such as Piedmont and Lombardy, where the imbalance between labour supply and demand was less marked, industrial development was accompanied by the attempt to utilise productively and economically a workforce locked in *ospedali* and charitable institutions.[34] There was intensive activity in the field of assistance and *correction* (before the proper prison) in the Savoy states (Piedmont).[35] Vittorio Amedeo II promulgated the *Istruzioni e regole degli Ospizi generali per i Poveri* (Instructions and Rules for General Hospices for the Poor) in 1717, which clarified the discussion outlined earlier on the century-old concept of *restrictive charity*: the only form of relief offered to the able-bodied was help in finding work even if they were unemployed through no fault of their own. Their only alternative was emigration, since mendicancy was outlawed.[36] This derived in part from the same principles as did the reforms of legislative and penal practices a few years later (1723–9), introducing as they did the principles of legality and proportionality between crime and punishment (to a very limited extent).[37]

Later, in the middle of the century, an establishment for dissolute youth was set up by the Marquis of Giallone.[38] This *Casa del Buon Consiglio* (House of Good Advice) had an interesting regime. It was one of the first in Italy to be run on corrective and educational lines of purely bourgeois inspiration. The institution was based on 'frugality and labour'. A maximum level of isolation was sought and attained through the 'maxims of the workhouse' – a rule of absolute silence (which, inter alia, demonstrates how the famous American systems which were to develop a few decades later were in reality, the fruit of ideas and practices common to the most economically and socially developed areas). The idea of work as a corrective is essentially Calvinist in origin and already shows distinct signs of what were to be the pedagogic attitudes of the Enlightenment. The individual is seen as a wild beast whose instincts must be tamed by labour and obedience:

> It is quite clear how necessary this labour is for them, entirely removing them from idleness, the cause of all the sins of the degenerates brought to this place: and it is consequently the remedy adopted above all others to reform them, as being the most opposed to their acquired habits, for which reason it is fitting to occasion that this exercise tames the ferocity and indolence of these souls, before promising to demand a true conversion of them ...[39]

As in the case of the Amsterdam workhouse, it was corrective policy *vis-à-vis* the young which enlarged the scope of penal reform; all of these Italian initiatives, from Franci's to the *Ospedale di S. Michele* in Rome,[40] started as houses of correction for the young. The belief that youth was susceptible to pedagogy obviously enhanced the hopes of reforming and re-educating the lower age-groups. At the same time, adolescents and even children were constantly in demand as workers in industry for similar reasons. They were the most amenable to correction, they were more malleable and less resistant to integration into the world of exploitation. In this way, houses of correction were accompanied by the foundation of training schools, orphanages and a whole range of institutions which sought from the outset to mould the kind of human being who could adapt to wage labour. The conditions of the Turin prisons described by Howard at the end of the century were abysmal.[41] The inmates did not generally work but were sent to the galleys. Their sad and battered faces demonstrated the little attention which was devoted to them.'[42]

However, it was above all in Lombardy under Austrian domination that the concrete measures of a new social and criminal policy were closely welded to renewed economic initiative. At the beginning of the eighteenth century, the embryonic industrial capitalism of Milan sought to assert itself 'outside the closed shop of the guilds'.[43] This public initiative tended to assume the same importance that it had once had in other European states. The employment of the mass of idle and vagabond proletarians excluded from the guilds became the natural point of reference for this policy. 'In 1720 the government had solicited, discussed and approved the *Ronzio* project which was designed to stimulate commercial activity by establishing a workhouse that would put vagabonds to work by force.'[44] In the course of the struggle against the guilds and against a nascent working class, numerous regulations governing the discipline of workers were planned and put into practice: under the edict of 30 May 1764 (inspired by earlier Piedmont regulations), 'those who offered high wages, thereby bribing workers to violate the agreement signed with their contractor, did so under pain of tough penalties and those workers who deserted their employer leaving work unfinished ran the risk of imprisonment'.[45]

Other projects of this kind (which were also connected with clashes in Como between the civil guard and workers in 1790) were prepared by Bellerio and Beccaria.[46] Milan's induction into the Austrian commercial, cultural and normative system created opportunities previously impossible in the absence of a great national Italian monarchy. Milanese Enlightenment culture became closely linked to the reformist policies of both Maria Theresa and then of Joseph II and to the great French Enlightenment. The 1760s and 1770s were years of intensive production of new institutions and ideas. The group around Pietro Verri provided the reforming practice of enlightened absolutism with a kind of Italian bourgeois *Encyclopedie*, ranging from economics to law, from literature to philosophy, from social policy to natural science. Lombardy's much-needed revival depended on the bourgeoisie's ability and will to win hegemony. But before it can exercise hegemony, the bourgeoisie must be capable of sweeping away old conceptions and of presenting an organic, detailed and concrete world view which would include new ways of running society. Penal policy is by no means the last consideration in this respect. In fact Cesare Beccaria's *Dei delitti e delle pene* (On Crimes and Punishment) was to be the most internationally famous product of Pietro Verri's group.[47] It would not be appropriate to dwell at length on this well-known work here; it is enough to recall that the fundamental principles of criminal law, the pride of the Enlightenment and of traditional liberalism, which were to be embodied in the famous Declaration of Rights of 1791 and which Beccaria was the first to draw together lucidly and advocate, were, as I have tried to show more than once, closely linked to prison initiatives – as they had been in the more advanced European countries in preceding centuries. Above all, there was a predisposition towards a normative apparatus for codifying crimes, sanctions, penalties and their mutual relations which corresponded to a world view wherein both crime and punishment were susceptible to a rigid economic evaluation (in the widest sense of the term economic) by *calculating the labour time used up in prison*. Time is money and since any injury can be economically evaluated in a society based on exchange, a determinate time to be discounted (working) in prison, can make good the crime committed.[48]

It is interesting to consider further Beccaria's attachment to the more general movement of his time in relation to criminal social policy; with regard to the crime typical of the poor – theft – he pronounced a judgement very similar to the one Marat was to make a few years later (as we have seen).

> Thefts without violence should be punished by fine. He who enriches himself at another's expense ought to suffer at his own. But, as theft is generally a crime of wretchedness and despair, a crime of that unhappy portion of mankind to whom the right of property (a terrible and perhaps not a necessary right) has left but a bare subsistence; and as pecuniary penalties increase the number of criminals above the number of crimes, depriving the innocent of their bread in order to give it to the wicked, *the fittest punishment will be that kind of servitude* which alone can be called just, namely the temporary *servitude* of society, the personal and absolute dependence due from a man who has essayed to exercise an unjust superiority over the social compact.[49]

As Beccaria was writing this, two prisons were built along the most modern lines, a truly rare event in Italian history. The construction of the *ergastolo* and the *casa di correzione* in Milan was obviously centrally influenced, since it is accompanied by the creation of the institution at Ghent in Austrian Flanders[50] so much praised by Howard, and by the issuing in 1769 of the Austrian penal code. The conception and planning of the house of correction demonstrates the gradual slide of the workhouse for the poor towards the corrective prison for criminals.

In about 1670, while the initiatives of Franci at Florence and of the earlier Roman *Ospedale di S. Michele* were being developed, it was proposed that a hostel for the poor or a workhouse[51] with a house of correction as an annexe should be erected in Milan. However, it was only a century later that this enlightened project was taken up under the Empress Maria Theresa, the house of correction being begun in 1759 and completed seven years later.[52] This development was clearly connected with the passing of Lombardy from the backward Spanish system to the more advanced and innovative rule of Austria. The establishment had 140 cells, '25 for women and 20 for youths; but recognising what torment solitude would be it was reserved for those who had first been sent to the Venetian galleys, each day spent in confinement counting as two of the original sentence'.[53] The cells were single just as in the corrective section of the *Maison de Force* at Ghent, but isolation was not continuous because in this period, as we have seen – and all the more so in Lombardy, where the army of unemployed characteristic of the industrial revolution was yet to appear – work for the convicts was a priority and in fact they were put to work in great communal halls.[54] However, the fact that one day's isolation was counted as equal to two days of the sentence shows how distressing and intolerable solitary confinement – which was to become so familiar in nineteenth-century bourgeois society – seemed to the proletariat of Lombardy. Whether in fact isolation was rigorously maintained is hard to say; Howard maintained that about 300 inmates were under lock and key when he visited the place.[55]

This Milanese establishment marks a crucial transition in the history of the Italian prison and it is no accident that it was a product of the economically and culturally more progressive region of the time. In Howard's descriptions of various Italian prisons, this is the only one which resembles the foreign institutions examined earlier; it is already an institution for criminals, not for the poor or for the young.[56] Work is not geared towards vocational training, it is productive, consisting of operations in textile manufacture – the most important industrial sector of the time.[57] Finally, it does not seem to me irrelevant to observe that the house was built at the same time as the introduction of criminal provisions governing work relations (mentioned above) which laid down fines for employers but imprisonment for workers.

Howard's description seems to imply that while less serious offenders (for whom work was, as we have said, related to manufacture) were confined in the houses of correction, the inmates of the *ergastolo* were generally serving long or even (though not necessarily) life sentences; these people were employed in public road works. In the *ergastolo*, (presumably) built as part of the house of correction, there was no division into cells; it had 359 inmates.[58] The principles of isolation and labour were later sanctioned by the Joseph II code of 1785 for the whole of Lombardy: 'the prisoner will be locked up alone, in a well-lit place, without bars or fetters: he may not communicate with other prisoners or outsiders whilst serving his sentence. He will be given nothing but bread and water at the expense of the house, anything else coming from what he earns by his labour.'

The Venetian galleys and the *Piombi* (prisons with lead roofs which intensified the heat in summer and the cold in winter) perhaps horrified Howard most of all.[59] In the backward, decadent Venetian Republic there was no trace of any kind of penal reform.[60] It was only towards the end of the century that commissioners were appointed and studies carried out as to the general possibility of utilising the labour of inmates in public works.[61]

Tuscany, which was linked to Austria by the House of Lorena, also saw the benefits to be had from Hapsburg rule even though it was not so closely tied to it as Lombardy was and retained a greater amount of freedom in internal policy.[62] Especially under the guidance of the Grand Duke Pietro Leopoldo, from 1765 to 1790, the Tuscan region went through a period of intensive reform stimulated by local and European Enlightenment culture. This also applied to the sphere of criminal law and the *Legislazione criminale toscana* of 1786 was seen by many as embodying the theories of Beccaria and Howard.[63] The death penalty and torture were abolished (instruments of torture were publicly burnt), the crime of *lèse-majesté* ceased to have special status and the aim of punishment was clearly defined as being that of reforming the offender.

Leopoldian humanitarianism existed in a very static social context seemingly conducive to enlightened experimentation. However, this static order in which, for example, social relations in the Tuscan countryside had remained unchanged since the introduction of the *mezzadria*, aggravated the crisis of the silk industry and the poverty and unemployment affecting many craftsmen. Thus it was no accident that in 1790, at the same time as the explosion of the French Revolution, a number of different events took place: the departure of Pietro Leopoldo; popular uprisings, especially of craftsmen and workers; and the reintroduction of special measures dealing with crimes against state security. By the end of the century the brief dream of the Enlightenment monarchies and philosophers had already foundered in the class conflict which was increasingly to dominate the society in the following century.[64] Following legislative reform, efforts were made to reform the punitive system. Howard described two prisons at Florence: the *Palazzo degli Otto* and the *Stinche*,[65] both of which were run on traditional lines without any sign of innovation. The fortress at Livorno with 132 prisoners was more significant.[66] Serious offenders were sent to the galleys while the rest were employed in public works (in 1786 the death penalty was replaced by forced labour). Prison life was strictly regulated and showed signs of Leopoldian reform on the administrative side. Nearly all the classic rules of the modern prison were introduced: set hours, cleanliness, searches, uniforms, short hair, etc. The convicts, chained in twos, were paid to clean up ports and work on public buildings such as the *lazarettos*. Howard's statistics on the Grand Duchy may be of interest:

> During the 10 years preceding 1765, there were 3,076 in prison for debt, 704 for petty offences, 210 condemned to the galleys, 17 executed, 5 branded. This punishment of branding was abolished by the grand-duke, Leopold. In the 4 years preceding 1769, there was no capital punishment. In the 10 years from 1769 to 1779, the numbers imprisoned were 3,036 debtors, 1,126 petty offenders, 142 sent to the galleys, 2 executed.[67]

In the Kingdom of Naples, prison conditions largely reflected the persistence of feudalism in the region.[68] A feature characteristic of the whole peninsula appeared here in its most extreme form: impoverishment forcing great masses of peasants into vagabondage, banditry and pre-political revolt combined with an extremely sparse accumulation of capital in both agriculture and industry. Thus, there was not the slightest chance of resolving the social problems mentioned above. In these circumstances, the gallows decimated the surplus population in the South for centuries, while the intensive intellectual activity of the Neapolitan Enlightenment[69] was reduced to the mere denunciation of the gravity of the prison problem.[70] The man who fought most against pauperism in the South was Giuseppe Maria Galanti. He advocated hospices for the poor and showed how most of the crime in the Kingdom of Naples consisted of rural theft, the crime typical of poor peasants:

> ... the origins of most political disorders must be attributed to that immense fortune which society has placed in few hands. The excesses of wealth have produced the excesses of misery; the government has had to build as many vast prisons as there are magnificent palaces. Nonetheless, it is extremely difficult to contain so many discontented people, exhausted by hunger, who see so many satisfied people swamped with riches. Everything has to be guarded and kept under lock and key. Not one door can be left open with impunity. Many laws are made to protect the haves from the have-nots: moral principles – always stronger than the law – add disgrace to the legal sanctions against theft: but the poor, who see so much gold and so much wealth in the houses of the rich, are strongly tempted to steal in order to keep themselves alive. Dissipation, luxury, the extravagant profusion of opulence must lessen the injustice, if not the disgrace, of theft in their eyes.[71]

In considering the great number of inmates in Neapolitan prisons, one must bear in mind that in 1791, this city with its population of nearly half a million, was by far the biggest in Italy and amongst the largest in Europe. The main prison, *la Vicaria*, contained 980 prisoners in 1781.[72] According to Howard's description some of the inmates worked, but the majority were left idle. It was rife with dirt and infection and the intense heat forced the inmates to go about nude. About 150 prisoners were housed in three other prisons. Then there were four galleys which confined 1130 men. Finally in the *Serraglio* or Almshouse, there were 360 inmates; the able-bodied were employed as labourers. Here the old, the infirm, beggars and the idle were detained.

Howard adds some observations on *ospedali* and violent crimes in Italy. As to the *ospedali*, which he found to be numerous and well kept, he observes that 'In visiting the prisons of Italy, I observed, that in general great attention was paid to the sick; but I could not avoid remarking, that too little care was taken to prevent sickness.'[73] He then notes that crimes of violence were very much more common in Italy than elsewhere. The number of murders in one year were much higher in Rome or Naples than in Britain and Ireland put together. It was a source of pride for the inmates to state that they had used a knife but never committed theft (which amongst other things, demonstrates that there was already a clear distinction between the underworld and the mass of vagabonds, unemployed, etc. who lived by petty crime).

The Duchy of Modena was an interesting case. The extensive studies carried out by C. Poni enable us to link socio-economic changes in this area with the thematic with which we are dealing.[74] Moreover, although this small Duchy was hardly in the forefront of agitation for reform – due to considerable limitations imposed by structural backwardness and territorial fragmentation – the Modenese Lodovico Antonio Muratori carried out some of the most informed and effective work on pauperism and crime.[75] As in the case of the Lombardian and Neapolitan Enlightenment attitudes, charity and poverty were treated not in isolation but as part of the greater struggle against feudalism.[76] Muratori criticised the progressive impoverishment of the countryside but did not connect it with urban pauperism which, in his view, thrived on excessive almsgiving.[77] In fact, a modest process of primitive accumulation began in the countryside of this area in the sixteenth century. The *mezzadria* peasantry and smallholders became proletarians (*braccianti* – rural day labourers) or vagabonds, small-holdings being merged into larger estates.[78] The process was on a modest scale, first because the centuries-old *mezzadria* system involved the maintenance of numerous landless peasants and secondly, because primitive accumulation in the eighteenth century did not succeed in totally destroying it. In fact, the landowners increasingly defended the system since they feared the formation of a threatening mass of rural labourers.[79] Even so, heavy debts to landowners and usurers and exhorbitant taxes did provoke a flight from the countryside.[80] Muratori's proposals on the problem of pauperism were on the same level as contemporary deterrent measures in England.

Muratori's point of departure was that 'everyone must live by their own efforts and must earn their keep by the sweat of their brow as long as their strength permits'.[81] Since almsgiving seduces the poor and spoils their children 'who sadly lacking religious instruction and full of the vices of idleness are incited to steal by want and, having harmed many others, they finish by harming themselves, ending their lives in the galleys or on the scaffold',[82] it could even 'incite workers to resort to similar means'.[83] Although Muratori does not say so, this would obviously happen if the workers' standard of living dropped towards that of the beggars.

Starting from this assumption then, it is necessary in order to resolve the problem, to avoid the 'growth of a population made up of the lazy, the idle and who knows what other kinds of people under the cloak of poverty ... we must make wise use of the economics of almsgiving. The poor must be made to love wearing themselves out in labour and to change and improve their behaviour.'[84] This can be achieved by:

The establishment of *public hospices for the poor.* That is to say, the gathering together in one or more buildings, with a necessary division of the sexes, of all the poor who are already begging for their bread or who are on the verge of doing so; the provision of food and of the bare minimum of clothing to all and the forcing of the able-bodied to use their strength in regular work, exempting the old and the infirm; it is not fitting to live except by one's own labours ... A general hospice for all beggars: this would truly seem to be a universal remedy capable of perfectly balancing and reconciling the laws of good neighbourliness with those of wise political government. Nor is it necessary to gather all the poor together under this system which could and should easily permit those reluctant to leave their families to stay at home. If one rightly knows their needs, some discreet and regulated relief can be provided on condition that they do not beg. Besides, it is well known that many abhor the idea of being locked up in a hospice and would elect either to go with God or to earn their food through labour, that is to say, in a state of liberty rather than in that *honourable prison*, thus freeing the directors of charitable work from concern with their maintenance.[85]

In a situation such as that of Modena, in which there was an abundance of labour but a lack of capital, confinement was much more of a deterrent to those outside than a way of exploiting labour inside. It was not long before an ideal house of terror of the English type confirmed the 'abhorrence of being locked up in a hospice'.[86] As a result, 'going with God' meant choosing between emigrating, dying of hunger and, for the fortunate, taking the worst type of work. It was not until a terrible famine several years later, in 1764, that Muratori's ideas were taken up in the construction of a large *Albergo dei Poveri*[87] (home for the poor). The Modena penal code was also largely inspired by Muratori's work.[88]

Similar ideas were to be taken up later by Lodovico Ricci in his *Riforma degli istituti pii della città di Modena* (1787), a work which 'had been the delight of liberal writers for a long time'.[89] Here immoderate subsidies were criticised even more sharply as 'the main cause of persistent poverty. Where such subsidies are lacking, the poor must *shake themselves from indolence, emigrate or perish.*'[90]

In the Papal States nearly all the prisons were grouped together in Rome, with the obvious exception of the galleys at Civitavecchia.[91] Rome, the second most populous city in Italy, was characterised by the contradiction between the cosmopolitanism of being the Catholic capital and the serious economic situation of the city itself and its surrounds which, though a great centre of consumption, was also an area of minimal production. Beggars and paupers were numerous. The situation in other parts of the state was similar, if less serious. The proletarianisation of the peasants and sharecroppers and the decline of the silk industry in Bologna, once the most famous in Europe, contributed to the growing number of beggars in that city, whilst the Papal authorities were plagued with an ever greater number of brigands.[92] Brigandage was more or less widespread in all the states under Papal rule, although it was more prevalent in the South. This explains why as we have seen, the Papal authorities began sporadically to confront the problem of mendicancy and the confinement of the poor in the sixteenth century.[93] The founding in Rome at the end of the seventeenth century of an *Ospedale Generale*, which was to merge all existing institutions for the poor, the young, women, etc., marked the beginning of a new endeavour, though it was not to be completely finished for a century.[94]

The most famous – and for us, the most interesting – section of the *Ospedale di S. Michele* was the house of correction for the young built inside this vast undertaking on the basis of Pope Clement XI's *motu proprio* of 1703.[95] This decreed that all prisoners under the age of 20 must serve their sentence in the new institution until free of the corrupting influence of that environment. The same was to apply to young people committed by their parents for corrective treatment. The building, designed by the architect Carlo Fontana, was later to be described as a cell block. It was rectangular and had 60 cells on three floors overlooking a large open space.[96] Work took place in the common area and consisted of spinning cotton and knitting. The young inmates were chained to benches where they remained seated from morning to night with very little break. Prayers, hymns and severe punishment (usually flogging) filled the day. A large sign with the word *Silentium* was affixed to a wall in the work room. Juvenile delinquents committed for reform had to pay their way. According to visitors at the end of the eighteenth century, those delinquents who did not work were kept in permanent solitary confinement.[97] This situation, a resumption of Franci's initiative, is doubly interesting in that it featured a more ideological and internal compulsion on the will of these *corrigendi*, who were generally young aristocrats or members of the bourgeoisie, while the rule of labour was applied to those sentenced in court, that is, workers. Later, in 1735, a similar house of correction was set up for young women criminals and prostitutes. When Howard visited the house of correction in 1778 his impression was quite favourable. He records the two Latin inscriptions on the walls of the building: 'Pope Clement XI. For the correction and instruction of the strayed young, until they who were a burden to society become useful' and 'it is insufficient to restrain the wicked by punishment unless you render them virtuous by corrective discipline'.[98] Sellin observes, reporting Morichini's view as well, that the *S. Michele* house of correction was part of the transition from the model of the *cella* and canonical punishment to lay punishment.[99]

Various authors have suggested that the Roman prison influenced later models. This could have been the case but, in any event, the appearance of similar phenomena in widely varying circumstances bears witness to the similarity of responses in the face of comparable problems.[100] However, the severe discipline at *S. Michele* in Ripa is noteworthy in this connection. These early eighteenth-century experiences, usually designed for the young or for delinquents, mark a decisive shift from the mercantilist workhouse for the poor, with its emphasis on production, towards the prison proper of the late eighteenth and nineteenth centuries where the primary aim of punishment, the preoccupation of planners and administrators, became the deterrent and increasingly 'ideological' concern with branding the hearts and minds of the lower classes with the mark of discipline and obedience.

From the Napoleonic Period to Pre-unification

The final part of this study – from the French Revolution to the end of the Restoration period – is particularly important. There is a twofold reason for this: in many parts of Italy the bourgeoisie was by now openly trying to take advantage of social changes already underway in order to establish its own rule. Although it is not relevant here to dwell at length on the various details of this situation, they must nevertheless be borne in mind. Despite the uncertain uniformity imposed under French rule, the existence of societies with considerable economic and political differences once again meant that the various measures taken had different effects.

From 1795 to 1814 in particular, sections of the Italian bourgeoisie sought to gain control over the peninsula with French support. To a great extent they succeeded in doing so, even if this involved a certain amount of bargaining with the old feudal or aristocratic forces and took very different forms in the north and in the south of the country.[101] This led above all to the multiplication, and in many cases the sharpening, of processes and phenomena which had already been set in motion during the eighteenth century. An impressive amount of legislation was passed with the twin aims of subverting the economic and political power of feudalism and the church and of laying the basis of and strengthening the new bourgeois state built on the Napoleonic model. The anti-feudal laws of the South,[102] the introduction of conscription and an oppressive tax system based mainly on indirect taxation, contributed to considerable confusion in the countryside, frequently causing sections of the peasantry, align themselves with reactionary forces.[103] Such sections, very much under the ideological domination of the church, felt, especially in the North, that they were being attacked from all sides by the changes taking place. The pillage and destruction wreaked both by French and, on their brief return, Austrian troops, the oppressive new military levies, and a whole series of exorbitant taxes hastened the process of primitive accumulation in the countryside. This was to reach its peak half way through the century and especially after unification. A major redistribution of capital and labour was forced through either by fiscal methods and debt or by confiscating land which the exhausted peasants could no longer work. At the same time, the question of land reform, of the spread of capitalist methods of production, was considered for the first time. In this way, the basis was laid for future productive development and opened up possibilities for rural labourers to organise themselves. But in the meantime, the Po Valley area was plagued by one famine after another, by a growth in the number of brigands, their ranks swelled by deserters and expropriated peasants, by bands of unemployed folk and vagabonds who committed a whole series of typical crimes as an expression both of their need to survive and their willingness to rebel against the *status quo*.

In any one year, brigandage rose and fell depending on the size of the harvest and therefore on the extent of hunger, then on the general political-military situation, on the degree of repression to which they were subjected and so forth. Nevertheless, as we have seen, it had been a constant feature of Southern Italy for some centuries and essentially expressed an autonomy and a peasant tradition in a quite complex relationship with other social forces and their ideologies. In fact, E. J. Hobsbawm has observed in his book *Bandits*,[104] what he calls *social banditry* tends to occur in any country at the point at which it undertakes that long and painful process which is, to quote Marx, the birth of the new society of capital from peasant society.[105] In this way, it was easy for bandit rebellion, which is objectively class rebellion and which is moved and moves itself both against the old feudal lords and the new bourgeois authorities (often the same thing, as, for example in Southern Italy), to place itself at the disposal of the most reactionary forces who knew how to rally support around the only ideological structure which they felt was really theirs – that of religion. This was the case for the *lazzaroni* (Neapolitan lumpen- proletariat) and for Cardinal Ruffo's bands in 1799 and it was also to be (in part) the case for the post-unification peasant guerrillas. But this alignment also happened because the mass of peasants never found revolutionary-democratic political forces capable of representing their real interests – at least, not until sometime after unification.[106]

How far this was possible within the context of a bourgeois revolution and how much more by contrast the bourgeoisie needed the economic, cultural and often physical destruction of the peasantry[107] is not something we can consider here. Suffice it to note, however, that, especially in Northern Italy, the rural masses and the most advanced forces in the towns were pushed back by an alliance between the big landowners and the moderate bourgeoisie. This was sanctioned by Napoleon in the course of his authoritarian and anti-Jacobin operations which corresponded to the stabilisation of bourgeois power and the emergence of the conflict between the bourgeoisie and the proletariat as the primary contradiction. At any rate, the forces of reaction, especially amongst the clergy, confined themselves, at least in the north, to exploiting peasant anger without ever giving it a decisive lead. Thus the peasants remained without political direction until the 1880s and 1890s, when further capitalist development in the Po Valley area resulted in socialist hegemony over the mass of *braccianti* and sharecroppers.[108]

Taking Romagna as an example, we can see quite clearly how brigandage is essentially a struggle against the bourgeoisie and its drive for accumulation. This area was overrun with bandits throughout the period of French rule. In the face of the depredations of French rule, brigandage had a markedly patriotic and municipalist character, as a result of which it was frequently allied with popular uprisings of local citizens and democrats.[109] Moreover, it was also directed against the new institutions of bourgeois rule, above all, against conscription, which tore peasants away from the land often causing their ruin and thus adding another contributory factor to the flight from the countryside.[110] During this period, the Napoleonic authorities made continual pleas to deserters, often making generous promises which revealed their own weakness and impotence in the face of this phenomenon.[111] Moreover, attacks by brigands were almost always selective: they hit those with property, never the poor. This is no obvious comment; in many cases it was quite clear that robbery was not simply motivated by gain in that much contempt and brutality was displayed towards wealthy victims. A whole series of crimes frequently involved warnings and blackmail: farmsteads were burnt down, cattle killed, vines and fruit trees cut down. All this revealed a desire to strike the owner where it hurt most – in his property. Before common rights were usurped by the propertied class, it had been possible freely to collect wood, glean, make fires, pick fruit, graze animals and so on. Another symptom of this attitude was the fact that a brutal end was usually reserved for any 'spies' or persons collaborating in one way or another with the authorities against the brigands.

Documents cited in Manzoni's richly informative book report dozens of thefts, clashes, arrests, executions, robberies and mutilations, at times gruesome and ironic. No distinction was made between thefts committed by poor peasants, who in the coldest winters struggled to survive, by the unemployed who wandered through the countryside, by deserters or by authentic brigands who usually met their end in the umpteenth brawl. This lack of differentiation obviously implied a great deal of *class* solidarity between the various categories. Bandits were looked after, lodged and fed by peasants whom they paid. This is why there were invincible, why they were for years the *signori* as the poet Pascoli was to say 'of the roads and forests'. They were bound to their communities and to the local priesthood in common cause in the struggle against the lords, 'the Jacobins' and the 'French'. And the clearest demonstration of this – a passing mention should suffice since so much is written on this subject[112] – is the myth built up by the lower classes around the bandit, their true hero and representative: one who has found the courage to stand up to years of subjection, suffering and poverty in violent opposition to his rulers. Somewhere in brigandage lies the matrix and the remote memory of the modern popular guerrilla.

But in the face of these phenomena, indeed, at their roots, was the slow, gradual organisation of the modern state. The highest authorities in the Kingdom of Italy continually sought to enlist parish priests as agents of surveillance and control.[113] The first police measures were taken: they made registration of hotel guests compulsory,[114] prohibited the carrying of arms without a special licence,[115] introduced the census and made the reporting of violent deaths and their causes compulsory.[116] They sought to discourage brigands by terrorising those who gave them shelter – in brief, they invented all the classic forms of prevention and repression which were to become the patrimony of police practice in all bourgeois states.

In this context, the last of the various French codes introduced in Italy, the French penal code of 1810, was extended in 1811 to all Italian regions under French rule (and most of them were).[117] We have already seen how this was designed to defend state authority and to protect the form of property most under attack, that is, agrarian property. This involved the extension of punishments in the two forms of the house of force and the workhouse, which had in any case been instituted for vagabonds as early as 1802.[118] On the other hand, interest in prison reform, already lively during the Enlightenment, grew at a remarkable rate in the great material and moral ferment brought on by the bourgeois revolution. The principles of detentive punishment and prison labour, though already present, as we have seen, in a considerable number of eighteenth-century Italian states, were spread uniformly throughout the country by French troops and became part of the Italian legal framework (at least in principle). Once more, as we have seen in other European countries, and earlier on in Italy, the social relations of the capitalist mode of production generated the problem and its solution (from the point of view of these relations), creating simultaneously the crime and the punishment: vagabonds, brigands, deserters; labour in houses of correction, forced public works and execution squads.

Apart from an initial shock reaction, the period following the defeat of the French did not seriously delay the inevitable process that had been set in motion. If anything, it endorsed the *status quo*, especially, as far as Italy was concerned, between the old aristocratic forces and the bourgeoisie. The latter made every effort to assert itself under the aegis of moderation and compromise in order to accomplish the first stage of Italian capitalist development: the achievement of national unity. In the nineteenth century, as opposed to the prerevolutionary period, the various states underwent little change with the possible exception of Piedmont, where a greater level of development ultimately enabled it to accommodate the process of unification. As in other fields, Piedmont became the guiding light with respect to the penitentiary; its prison system was the prototype for the whole of Italy.

With the edict of March 1814, Vittorio Emanuele I, King of the Sardinian states, instituted a direct reversion to the period before the French Revolution.[119] He reintroduced a range of punishments and tortures which were considered barbaric even by earlier standards. Only with the accession to the throne of Carlo Alberto was there renewed talk of reform, including the penal question.[120] A new code was brought out in October 1839. The government did not confine its interest to legislation alone: it also sought to reform the material conditions of prisons (thanks above all to the work of Count Ilarione Petitti di Roreto). Between 1830 and 1840, particularly due to the influx of foreign works, the debate between the 'two schools' of Auburn and Philadelphia reached its height. Piedmont chose the former (nightly segregation and communal work in silence during the day) and built two new penitentiaries at Alessandria and Oneglia on the basis of this system.[121] This debate will be dealt with later. However, it is opportune at this point to stress that according to Petitti himself, the Auburn system, which permitted collective and thus productive work, was considered particularly suitable in Piedmont where industry was still very much in its infancy.[122] Up until 1848, this system continued without much innovation. However, a speech by Cavour in Parliament in 1849 revived the debate. As a partisan of the Philadelphian system, he called for a reassessment of the question.[123] There then followed a report in which the minister announced various new regulations in which basic assumptions remained unchanged. Changes were not brought about until the question was taken up again with regard to legislative proposals on the reform of *carcere giudizaria* (custodial prisons) made by the Minister of the Interior to whom responsibility for penitentiary administration had passed.[124] These proposals, which in truth merely presented minor difficulties, envisaged the adoption of a system of solitary confinement. Finally, despite much opposition, they were passed with the support of Cavour who had now become Prime Minister. Opposition had been particularly concerned with two points: the criticism the system had aroused in practice on account of its inhumanity and the difficulty of raising the necessary funds for the general reorganisation of buildings required. The Sardinian-Italian penal code of 1859 (so called because it was to become the code for the new Kingdom of Italy) anticipated as its main component at least six different types of detentive punishment, divided into *criminal penalties* (forced labour for life or for a certain period, confinement) and *corrective penalties* (prison and custody) all of which, with the exception of custody, were envisaged to include the compulsion or possibility of serving one's time in labour. However, there was nothing in the code about the particular regime to which the prisoner would be subjected: whether it was to be solitary confinement with work in one's own cell or with communal labour as in the Auburn system, or whether it was to be along the lines of a *mixed system* then being developed theoretically and finally adopted in 1889.

After the brilliant rebirth of the eighteenth century and Napoleonic periods, Lombardy underwent a definite decline (which affected the field of penal reform) under the Austrian domination which followed the Restoration.[125] The Austrian code of 1803 was introduced; it defined prison penalties as 'harsh' or 'very harsh'. Rossi said that the latter was really a kind of 'slow death'.[126] However, at least according to the regulations, prison labour continued to be encouraged. Indeed, prisoners would not have been able to survive on their rations, which were well below the minimum for subsistence, had it not been for the small earnings derived from labour which allowed them to make extra purchases.[127] In 1847 there was a call, among other things, for penitentiary reform. The *durissimo* (very harsh) prison penalties were scrapped under the new penal code of 1852.[128] But little if anything changed before unification.

The Grand Duchy of Tuscany was notable for the enormous amount of reform activity which took place there, both with regard to prison regulations and the very buildings themselves.[129] Here too, once a pre-revolutionary situation had been called into existence, reform began around 1840. First, the house of *Volterra* was set aside for forced labour; then the *Stinche* prison in Florence was closed down and, while the women were moved to San Gimignano, the new *Carcere delle Murate* was opened. At the beginning of the 1840s the *Maschio* of *Volterra* and *Murate* were transformed into cellular prisons. In 1845 a general provision was adopted which radically reformed the Tuscan prison system.[130] It established nightly separation but retained the principle of association for school and work. This regulation forbade a number of practices which dated back to medieval times, such as the low windows permitting continual outside contact,[131] the sumptuous banquets at festivals, etc. In other words, a true and proper *bourgeois* prison regime was introduced. It is noteworthy that though this reform was passed off as being humanitarian, in the knowledge of the increased harshness of the punishments it involved, it was not made retroactive: it affected only those sentenced after it came into operation.[132]

In 1848, Peri, the great artificer of all Tuscan penal reform between the middle of the 1840s and unification, published a book – *Cenni sulla riforma del sistema penitenziario in Toscana* (Notes on the Reform of the Penitentiary System in Tuscany) which was for its time an extremely thorough and detailed examination of prison conditions containing many interesting statistics. He brought together the history of each establishment, the movement of prisoners, maintenance costs and production, the *moral register* (rewards and punishments) and the illnesses suffered by the prisoners every year plus a blueprint of each building. It is not possible here to examine this data in detail even though it would be extremely significant if it could be verified in comparative terms. Suffice it to note that there were six penal establishments in Tuscany at the time: the *Bagni* at Livorno and Portoferraio for forced labour in public works, the penal establishment at Volterra, the penal and corrective establishment at Florence, the house of correction at Piombino and the penal and corrective establishment for women at San Gimignano. The total number of prisoners at the end of 1844, 1845, 1846 and 1847 was 672, 658, 759 and 770 respectively.

In 1849, the adoption of the Philadelphian system of solitary confinement became widespread. Peri ardently supported this system which was definitively sanctioned by a general regulation of 1850 and then by the new penal code of 1853 which remained in effect even after unification. The introduction of the Philadelphian system corresponded to a further devaluation of prison labour, now mainly concerned with the internal needs of the prison (furniture, clothes, etc.); the explicit reason for this was the threat of competition to outside enterprises.[133] However, it was not long before solitary confinement met with opposition: a so-called 'party of philanthropists' was formed. This group strongly criticised the damaging consequences such a regime had on the health of the prisoners. Of particular effectiveness was the work of Morelli, a doctor: *Saggio di studi igienici sul regime penale della segregazione fra i reclusi* (A collection of studies of the health of prisoners under the penal regime of segregation).[134] A commission was set up to study the problem. It concluded that the benefits of the fine principle of separation were indisputable but that the rigidity of the Philadelphian system was unacceptable, especially 'in the southern countries of Europe' (this was a common argument at the time).[135]

The whole debate resulted in the reform which came into effect on 10 January 1860, in the pre-unification period. It abolished the death penalty and reduced the length of almost all sentences. Above all, it introduced the *mixed* principle under which the first part of the sentence was generally served in solitary confinement while the second part – at least in longer sentences – involved communal work in silence. This seems to me to be particularly important not just because the Tuscan penal legislation remained in effect up to the Zanardelli code (1889 Italian penal code) but because, as we have already observed, the latter was itself to adopt a similar system of discipline in detentive punishment.

There is nothing particularly innovative to note with regard to the Duchies or the Papal States. Suffice it to observe that the processes of social change, already described for the preceding period, proceeded with ever-greater velocity, paving the way for the explosion of the post-unification decades and thereby resulting in an intensification of the various phenomena of rural theft, vagabondage, etc.

During the 1840s and 1850s the general economic revival in the Po Valley saw the creation of police preventive institutions in Piedmont – which were later to pass into the legislation of the new state. This related precisely to those categories of 'the idle and vagabonds' to which we have more than once referred; to rural theft; and to workers – a novelty at the time.[136] At the same time, brigandage persisted in Romagna and gave rise to such legendary figures as *Il Passatore*.[137] This was symptomatic of the economic stagnation of the Papal States, although the stagnation concealed a ferment affecting the entire fabric of social relations, here much more in crisis than in Tuscany or the South.[138] In fact, only a few years later, the young lawyer Enrico Ferri could claim for the socialist movement, in front of the jury at the Venetian court of assize, the merit of having transformed masses of impoverished *braccianti*, who lived by rural theft, into combatants for the proletarian cause.[139] However stagnation manifested itself chiefly in institutions. And for those in the prisons, run by the 'foul priestly tribe',[140] there was an abominable state of confusion and corruption – at least according to Beltrani, who was highly critical of the Papal States. He reports one item of news, among others, according to which the instruments of torture were still in use at Bologna prison as late as 1838.[141] Prison conditions in the Kingdom of the Two Sicilies were not much better despite some reformist activity above all on the part of Mancini and Volpicella.[142] Suffice it to add that on their defeat, the Pontiffs and the Bourbons magnanimously opened all prisons in their kingdoms!

The role which had already been played by bourgeois *culture* between Enlightenment and Restoration in European countries where the industrial revolution had taken place, notably England, was now tackled in Italy in the 1840s and even more so after unification. In this period, Italian culture took upon itself the task of providing the ruling class with both practical and theoretical guidance – and at the same time, of course, an *ideology* – in the process of structuring Italian capitalism, or at least providing directions as to the *conditions* which would allow such a process to take place.

In this connection, a fundamental task was the elaboration of a social policy geared towards assisting an inevitable development: *the formation of the proletariat*. It was a question of the conscious and carefully cultivated formation of a mass of expropriated peasants and artisans who had to become a modern industrial proletariat. That is to say: education of the workforce was necessary in order to ensure its transformation from the old social context to the new in the most ordered and productive way so as to maximise its value. This may not have concerned the first generation, which was brutally uprooted from one set of conditions to another, but was certainly a problem for the following generations and therefore for the *education of the young*.

As we have seen, it was no coincidence that a series of corrective measures, which anticipated those of true and proper prisons, were instituted in the eighteenth century specifically for young criminals or juvenile delinquents. Such a social policy, which historically was none other than *the* social policy, was articulated in various stages: school, in its various grades and differentiations; social assistance; the multiform variety of segregated institutions: prisons, colleges, juvenile institutions, psychiatric hospitals, homes for the poor and the old; hospitals; conscription (the barracks); and so on. The philosophers, the men of science who studied these mechanisms had the task of identifying problems and formulating solutions often in collaboration with governments.[143] Naturally, the *science* was neutral and objective – the great age of positivism was around the corner! It would demonstrate the objectivity of *facts* and the objectivity of solutions. But a science which was still influenced by enlightened universalism (for it was still dominated by the same people in the same places[144]) was as yet too uncertain and insufficiently specialised and refined to grapple with the vast range of the *Encyclopedie*. It was also a *bourgeois* science not only in its conclusions, of course, but in its deepest assumptions and in its definition of the problems that were being thrown up. In the various *Riunione degli scienziati* (conferences organised by Italian men of science) in the 1840s, philanthropists met to discuss everything that had to be faced and overcome by a country that was poor and still hardly developed but already well on the way to the establishment of capitalist hegemony. In among these problems, therefore, in among the discussions on agricultural techniques and the factory system, on the problem of finance and that of religion, on medicine and the natural science, were the questions of social policy and the penitentiary.

They continued to subscribe to the theory advanced by Muratori, which was seen to have triumphed at this time in England, to argue that the 'non-industrious' poor must be deprived of assistance, and to propose forms of forced labour, beyond which no help should be given. But it was symptomatic of the Italian situation, of its poor industrial development in this period, that what was being proposed was not so much workhouses as agricultural colonies which would reclaim land that was uncultivated, malarial, etc. This gave rise to that strange association, still very much in vogue long after unification, between the *social reclamation* of pauperism and criminality and the *agricultural reclamation* of uncultivated land.[145] Perhaps this vision reflected the indisputable supremacy of the agrarian capitalistic sectors. The fact was that the intention of these proposals was not so much to benefit the peasant driven into the town but to force him to return to what he had left, to put him back to work on the land. In any case, these proposals expressed a continuing unease so well described by Dal Pane for the eighteenth century: peasant proletarianisation and a flight from the countryside which industry was too small to accommodate. The way was being paved for that immense deportation of millions of Italian workers throughout the nineteenth and twentieth centuries: capital accumulation does not recognise national boundaries and a free workforce produced in Italy was destined for industries in other countries.

As we have seen, the beginning of the 1840s was a time of intense activity in the field of prison reform in those Italian states where the problem was most threatening – particularly in Piedmont, Lombardy – Venetia and Tuscany (which were, moreover the most advanced regions in every field). This provided the basis for the intensive use of the institution which was to follow unification. The *Riunione degli scienziati* also took up this question, in particular those at Florence (1841), Padua (1842) and Lucca (1843).[146] At Florence the problem was discussed, thanks largely to Petitti, but no solutions were proposed. In the interval between this congress and the congress at Padua in the following year, a series of papers on the subject appeared which included contributions from Petitti himself and from Carlo Cattaneo. These were sequels to the works of 1840 in which the two authors had taken up authoritative positions on the subject.[147] A typical representative of a culture firmly welded to practical and governmental activity, Petitti was in touch with the most distinguished European writers on penitentiary reform. He was deeply involved in the lively debate on the 'two systems' in America.[148] Having described the 'actual conditions of prisons'[149] and the 'history of corrective education'[150] in various European countries and in Italy, Petitti goes on to take up the fundamental theme of his work: *Del sistema di educazione correttiva che sembra degno di preferenza*[151] (On which system of corrective education seems worthy of preference). This essentially concerned the merits and defects of the various systems: communal life, the Philadelphian and Auburn systems and the mixed system which combined other systems in various ways. The first thing that strikes the modern reader is his absolute indifference to the choice between the two systems in comparison with the importance he gives to the basic principle of isolation. The thing that clearly appears in Petitti as in all other contemporary writers is extreme hostility towards communal life. All these studies, statements and writings contribute to a kind of anthology of the 'Scottish' School *Weltanschauung*. To support this, I will cite from Petitti's work, *Regioni addotte degli aderenti alla scuola detta della segregazione notturna e della riunione silenziosa diurna col. lavoro* (Reasons adopted by adherents of the school of nightly segregation and daily silent reunion for labour.)[152] The fact of citing from this particular study rather than, say, a study supporting the Philadelphian system makes little difference since, as we have said, with regard to the fundamental question, divergences are minimal. Note particularly the very close correlation between sexual phobia, productivity of labour and the spirit of obedience and discipline:

> The adherents of the said school of *nightly segregation and daily reunion in silence for labour*, hold:
>
> 1. That thanks to *nightly separation* the most serious problems caused by bad habits, commonly found in dormitories, are avoided.
> 2. That, shut away in a cell, and once fatigued by long and hard work, the danger of the vices to which a man *alone* can still abandon himself must be minimal.
> 3. That the rule of silence, *strictly observed*, prevents corrupting relations and, instead *accustoms the inmate to reflection as to a moral compulsion on the will*; this compulsion effectively renders formerly undisciplined and rebellious souls obedient and submissive.
> 4. That while work carried out communally *tempers the overwhelming effects of solitude* with the sight of companions, their work at once becomes *more diligent, more productive* and *more efficient* with the continual material fatigue to which they are constrained ...
> 5. This state of material and moral compulsion succeeds in achieving the necessary amount of intimidation produced by the rigour of the punishment, so that once they see this kind of punishment for themselves, and despite the better food provided, those inmates who are recidivists, would wish to return to prisons managed differently with communal life, not excluding the *Bagni* where they are made to do the heaviest work, where flogging occurs and food and beds are far worse.

This last point, which Petitti cites in praise of the system of isolation, is by far the most chilling and is evidence of what the much- praised prison *civilisation* actually meant. Better the beatings, the dirt, the degradation, the fatigue of the old *bagno* than the health and order which constitute a far worse torture![153] Finally, Petitti expresses his own feelings;

he declares himself a supporter in general of the Auburn school in the case of longer sentences, in that it permits higher industrial output and the chance to take part communally in the rites of the Catholic religion, whilst for short sentences, in which it is only possible to intimidate rather than reform, solitary confinement is acceptable.[154]

Cattaneo, however, declared himself completely in favour of the Philadelphian system, insisting on the psychological effectiveness of solitary confinement.[155] Such a stand was, in fact, nearly taken by the Padua Congress of 1842,[156] despite the fact that reports were submitted from various groups (particularly from physicians) on the results of research carried out abroad on the effects of the two systems which demonstrated a higher rate of mortality (*also* of suicide) and of mental alienation (psychological effectiveness!) where solitary confinement was in use.[157] However, the Commission which was to report to the congress at Lucca split over the issue: there was severe criticism of the physicians' reaction since it was felt that they had failed to assume a neutral role as health 'technicians' to entangle themselves in the politics of the issue.[158] But this criticism overlooked the fact that the doctors were actually called upon to take precisely that role; they were required to provide scientific backing for political measures which had apparently already been taken.[159] The contradiction was however resolved at the congress, which passed the solution proposed by Petitti: the Philadelphian system for short sentences and the silent system for longer sentences. Thus he was the real victor in the whole dispute, not merely because his was the final hypothesis but above all because, as we have seen, the most advanced experiments on the eve of unification tended towards a mixed system, which came to be established, in one form or another, both in the new Kingdom of Italy and in other European states. On the other hand, Marino rightly points out the substantially false philanthropy of the Auburnians. They were motivated not so much by the health needs of the inmates as by the concern of the various governments with the excessive expenditure the introduction of an entirely cellular system would involve.[160]

Thus in Italy, too, both the debate on and the practical solution to the prison question went in a direction dictated by particular social circumstances and yet both were substantially similar to those in the rest of Europe. Genuinely reformist initiatives, such as those in Lombardy,

Tuscany and Savoy, arose and developed for limited periods when the 'corrective' reorientation of a still sparse and reluctant labour force effectively became a necessity for the mode of production. But as early as the 1840s, the whole debate was quite close to what was happening in England and France (and it is significant that this literature pervaded much of Italian culture). The introduction of machinery and the rapid production of a large surplus population following the industrial revolution drove any theory about the productive and resocialising aspects of prison (according to capitalist criteria) further and further into the background. Diatribes on the various systems had a particularly ideological, 'spiritual' flavour.

In such a situation (that is, with the institution assuming an increasingly symbolic and representative significance), the only value faithfully retained was isolation, whether by solitary confinement or by silence. This value had but one basic exigency, that of intimidation[161] and control, as is apparent in the analysis carried out by the most politically aware man of the period, Petitti. He is largely indifferent to whatever 'system' has been chosen. The decision in favour of the Auburn system for long sentences derived from the need to limit expenditure on prisons; amongst those who defended the system, not one voice was raised in support of what would be its most salient feature: communal and thus productive industrial work. At the same time, the conception of prison as an instrument of intimidation and general prevention was masked by the emphasis everyone put on the need for isolation according to the formula of penitence and by the 'spiritualistic' polemic against the excessive attention paid by Enlightenment philanthropists to the material condition of the inmates. Over and above the fine words about the 'psychological effectiveness' of isolation, even a prison system such as that in use after unification, which retained the overcrowded institutions at Naples, Rome and Palermo described by Howard, was extremely effective in this respect. The principle of 'less eligibility' in relation to the lowest standard of living outside the penitentiary was safeguarded at all costs. The *spirituality* of the nineteenth century was realised, in the case of prisons, in the attempt to worsen prison conditions and in the impact that the institution was designed to produce on the 'spirit' of offenders and above all, potential offenders.

In this way, pre-unification activity prepared the ground for wide use of the institution immediately after unification, not only because it set up (a few) new prisons and introduced corresponding penal legislation, but also because it pointed to a trend which was literally to explode with the conquest of the Southern Provinces by Savoy. This resulted in the creation of an enormous industrial reserve army which neither the chronic hunger of southern capital nor the moderate level of industrial development in the North was capable of channelling into the factories. The chronic 'crisis' of the Italian prison system followed from this. The reasons for such a crisis were not so much due to the institution itself as to the persistence of pre-capitalist relations, particularly in the South, and thus to the particular use which came to be made of the southern working class. It became an industrial reserve army for the north (and later, with the start of emigration, for other countries) and provided a mass for manipulation by the ruling political forces. In Italy, as elsewhere, the prison system was an essentially bourgeois creation and had as its basic aim education in discipline and obedience. However, more than in other nations, contempt for a perennially excessive workforce rendered it a deterrent instrument of social control.

On the one hand, therefore, the revolution in punitive forms, which had slowly developed out of the origins of the capitalist mode of production up to the developed liberal capitalism of the nineteenth century meant that, in Italy as elsewhere, prison was defined as the dominant form of punishment, bourgeois punishment *par excellence*. On the other hand, the particular features of the institutions reflected individual national circumstances at particular times. And if the basic structure, everywhere the same, was modelled on the *ideological* needs of a particular mode of production (therefore, on the factory), the ancillary nature of the institution was further affected by a specific set of class relations.

As Italy moved towards unification, the existence of a vast number of unemployed workers – as in Britain and France in the first half of the century – prevented prison from pursuing directly resocialising aims (as would have been and was the case in societies with a limited supply of industrial labour). Instead, it was geared towards the ideological-deterrent control of those sections of the population excluded from production. The debates of the 1840s between social scientists, philanthropists, penologists and doctors (as those of the years following unification and long after) concealed this simple truth under the ideological trappings of their sciences.

Notes

1. M. Dobb, *Studies in the Development of Capitalism* (London, 1963) p. 151.
2. Regarding social relations in the Italian countryside, we use here (and subsequently) in particular studies by E. Sereni; cf. *Agricoltura e mondo rurale*, in *Storia d'Italia*, I (Torino: 1972) p. 133, which summarises the theses advanced in other basic texts. In particular, see pp. 185 ff. for a study of the role played by the *Mezzadria* system in central-northern Italy.
3. On the Florentine *Ciompi*, protagonists of an intense round of class struggles in the second half of the fourteenth century, see Dobb, *Studies in the Development of Capitalism*, p. 158; N. Rodolico, *I ciompi* (Firenze, 1965); V. Rutemberg, *Popolo e movimenti popolari nell'Italia del '300 e '400* (Bologna, 1971) pp. 157–329.
4. Dobb, *Studies in the Development of Capitalism*, p. 119. On these themes see K. Marx, *Capital* (London: Lawrence & Wishart, 1977), vol. I, p. 258 ff. and 688 ff.
5. *See Dobb,* Studies in the Development of Capitalism, *p. 160.*
6. Ibid., p. 158.
7. Cf. A. Fanfani, *Storia del lavoro in Italia (Dalla fine del secolo XV agli inizi del XVIII)* (*Milano, 1959*) pp. 1–59.
8. Ibid.
9. Ibid., pp. 51, 52; for a very specific but important discussion demonstrating this kind of productive development, see C. Poni's essay: 'Archéologie de la fabrique: la diffusion des moulins à soie "alla bolognese" dans les Etats Venitiens du XVIeme au XVIIIeme siecles,' *Annales* (1972) p. 1475.
10. See Fanfani, *Storia del lavoro*, pp. 113–17.
11. Ibid., p. 114.
12. Ibid., pp. 118–19.
13. See B. Geremek, *Il pauperismo nell'età preindustriale (secoli XIV–XVIII)*, in *Storia d'Italia*, vol. v, no. 1 (Torino, 1973) pp. 677 ff. On the conception of charity in Luther, see pp. 24 ff. and in Muratori, pp. 77 ff.

14. Geremek, *Il pauperismo*, pp. 678–83.
15. Ibid., pp. 686–7.
16. Ibid., pp. 689–91.
17. Ibid., pp. 691–2. On the origins of *ospedali* in Italy (and Europe) between the late medieval period and the Renaissance cf. the ample documentation in *Atti del Primo Congresso Italiano di Storia Ospitaliera* (Reggio Emilia, 1957) and the *Primo Congresso Europeo di Storia Ospitaliera* (Reggio Emilia, 1962) ed. Centro Italiano di Storia Ospitaliera.
18. From the preface to the 'Statuti' of *Opera medicanti* (Bologna: 1574). In G. Calori, *Una iniziativa sociale nella Bologna del '500 – L'Opera Medicanti* (Bologna, 1972) p. 17.
19. Calori shows how in Bologna, between the sixteenth and seventeenth centuries, a continual flux of paupers from the countryside was accompanied by the unproductive immobilisation of capital characteristic of the political economy of the Counter-Reformation. Even though Bologna enjoyed a relatively developed manufacturing industry, it was typical of the Italian situation during this period.
20. The small treatise *La Mendicità proveduta nella città di Roma coll'Ospizio pubblico*, dated 1639, was written at the express wish of Innocent XI in support of the practice of internment and it also served to spread the conviction that *Hôpitaux* were necessary in France. In Geremek, *Il pauperismo*, pp. 692–3.
21. Cf. A Guevarre's position in Geremek, *Il pauperismo*, p. 693.
22. Calori, *Una iniziativa*, p. 45.
23. See T. Sellin, 'Filippo Franci. A Precursor of Modern Penology,' *Journal of American Institute of Criminal Law and Criminology*, XVII (1926–7) p. 104. Also on this see, M. Beltrani-Scalia, *Sul governo e sulla riforma delle carceri in Italia, saggio storico e teorico* (Torino: 1867) p. 359; D. Izzo, 'Da Filippo Franci alla riforma Doria (1667–1907),' *Rassegna di studi penitenziari* (1956) p. 293. For documentation and bibl. see Sellin's essay cited above.
24. See Sellin, *Filippo Franci*, p. 108.
25. See Dal Pane, *Storia del lavoro in Italia (dagli inizi del secolo XVIII al 1815)* (Milano, 1958).
26. Ibid., pp. 1–5.
27. Ibid., p. 6; cf. on Italian demographic situation, A. Bellettini's essay, 'La popolazione italiana dall'inizio dell'era volgare ai giorni nostri. Valutazioni e tendenze,' *Storia d'italä* vol. v, no. 1 (Torino: 1973) p. 489. It should be borne in mind that during the preceding century,

population growth did not reach half of that reached in the eighteenth century. In any event, population growth in Italy was lower than that of Europe in general.

28. See Dal Pane, *Storia del lavoro in Italia*, pp. 84–6.
29. Ibid., pp. 202–17.
30. Ibid., p. 221.
31. Ibid., pp. 240 ff.
32. Ibid., pp. 309 ff.
33. Ibid., pp. 313, 314.
34. See B. Caizzi, *Storia dell'industria italiana* (Torino: 1965) pp. 31–3. See how at the end of the eighteenth century charitable institutions furnished work to master craftsmen who were thrown out of work in Piedmont, Lombardy and the centres of the silk industry (Bologna, Florence, Veneto) in L. Dal Pane, *Storia del lavoro in Italia*, pp. 384, 385 (and bibl. Therein).
35. See G. Candeloro, *Storia dell'Italia moderna, I: Le origini del Risorgimento* (Milano, 1959) pp. 90 ff.
36. See Dal Pane, *Storia del lavoro in Italia*, pp. 309–11.
37. See Beltrani-Scalia, *Sul governo e sulla riforma*, pp. 372, 373; A. Bernabo-Silorata, *Case penali*, in *Digesto italiano*, vol. VI (Torino: 1891) pp. 307 ff.
38. See Beltrani-Scalia, *Sul governo e sulla riforma* (1867) from which information on this topic hereafter is taken.
39. Ibid., pp. 389–90.
40. See pp. 79 ff.
41. *See J. Howard, Prisons and Lazarettos, I: The State of the Prisons in England and Wales (1792)* (Montclair, NJ, 1973) p. 122.
42. Ibid., p. 123. On prisons in the Savoy States at the end of the eighteenth century, also see Beltrani-Scalia, *Sul governo e sulla riforma*, pp. 402 ff.
43. C. A. Vianello, Introduction to *Relazioni sull'industria, il commercio e l'agricoltura lombardi del '700,* ed. C. A. Vianello (Milano, 1941) p. XIII; and generally cf. Candeloro, *Storia Dell'Italia moderna*, pp. 78 ff.
44. Vianello, *Relazioni sull'industria*, p. XIII
45. Ibid., p. XVI. The different forms of punishment which came to be created in correlation to class differences with respect to the two typical participants of this offence is exemplary; one should remember that precisely in these years the *Casa di correzione* was set up in Milan (see below). On this edict see also Dal Pane, *Storia del lavoro in Italia*, p. 295.

46. Vianello, *Relazioni sull'industria*, p. XXVI.
47. See Beccaria, *Dei delitti e delle pene* (Milano, 1964), Eng. trans. *Crimes and Punishments*, J. A. Farrer, (London: Chatto, 1880).
48. See my observations on pp. 47 ff.
49. Beccaria, *Dei delitti e delle pene*, p. 97 (my emphasis); Eng. trans., p. 213. Here Beccaria formulates what is probably the clearest and most explicit definition of the meaning of detentive punishment in a society wherein this can take root, that is, in a classic bourgeois society based on free competition. Cf. also G. Rusche and O. Kirchheimer, *Punishment and Social Structure* (New York, 1968), p. 76.
50. See above p. 49.
51. See Beltrani-Scalia, *Sul governo e sulla riforma*, pp. 385, 386; C. Cattaneo, 'Delle carceri' (1840) in *Scritti politici*, vol. I (Firenze, 1964) pp. 292–5.
52. Cf. besides Beltrani-Scalia and Cattaneo, ibid. Howard, *Prisons and Lazarettos*, pp. 121, 122 where a plan of the *Casa di Correzione* can also be found. Though Howard states that in 1778 the *Casa* is incomplete it was functioning. Beltrani-Scalia reports in this case of a *Progetto per un Albergo de' Poveri e Casa di correzione* (project for a paupers' hostel and house of correction) by Count P. Verri (on p. 386). Cf. also on the *casa* at Milan C. I. Petitti di Roreto, *Della condizione attuale delle carceri e dei mezzi di migliorarla*, in *Opere scelte* (Torino, 1969) p. 370; Comoli-Mandracci, *Il carcere per la società del Sette-Ottocento* (Torino, 1974) pp. 33–4.
53. C. Cantù, *Baccaria e il diritto penale* (Firenze, 1862) p. 11.
54. The fact that one day in the house of correction counted for two days' punishment came to be represented by Cantù and Cattaneo, supporters of absolute segregation during the debate in the 1840s, so as to give the impression that in the *casa* such a principle was already being applied. But this is drastically excluded from Howard's eye-witness account. Howard speaks in *Prisons and Lazarettos* (p. 121), of a dormitory and large work-rooms. Moreover, looking at the relationship between the actual number of prisoners and the number of cells (300/140), it seems doubtful that nightly separation was maintained. This may have been a practical expedient arising from the impossibility of implementing the original plan. But in view of the presence of rooms adapted for common labour, it would seem that even in terms of intention, the principle of nightly and daily segregation was not contemplated. Large common dormitories were envisaged for women – it was

typical to allot different sections of the institution to men, women and vagabonds. Single cells were allocated to male criminals alone. See for example, the *Maison de force* at Ghent which, as we have said, was very similar to the Milanese *casa*, in Howard, *Prisons and Lazarettos*, pp. 145 ff. (cf. the plan).

55. See Howard, *Prisons and Lazarettos*, p. 122.

56. Cattaneo makes the same observation in *Delle carceri*, p. 295.

57. See Howard, *Prisons and Lazarettos*, pp. 121, 122.

58. Ibid., pp. 120, 121.

59. Ibid., p. 106.

60. Cf. generally Candeloro, *Storia dell'Italia moderna*, pp. 98 ff; Beltrani-Scalia, *Sul governo e sulla riforma*, p. 374; Bernabò-Silorata, *Case penali*, ch. 6.

61. See Beltrani-Scalia, *Sul governo e sulla riforma*, pp. 400–1.

62. See Candeloro, *Storia dell'Italia moderna*, pp. 111 ff.

63. Ibid., p. 121; Beltrani-Scalia, *Sul governo e sulla riforma*, p. 374; D. Palazzo, 'Appunti di storia del carcere', in *Rassegna di Studi Penitenziari* (1967) p. 20; Bernabò-Silorata, *Case penali*, ch. 6.

64. See Candeloro, *Storia dell'Italia moderna*, p. 125; cf. also P. Nocito, *I reati di Stato* (Torino, 1893) pp. 202 ff. See essay cited by E. Sereni, *Agricoltura e mondo rurale*, in relation to social relations in the countryside.

65. See Howard, *Prisons and Lazarettos*, p. 107.

66. Ibid., pp. 108–10.

67. Ibid., p. 110.

68. See Candeloro, *Storia dell'Italia moderna*, pp. 136 ff.

69. Ibid., p. 150.

70. See Beltrani-Scalia, *Sul governo e sulla riforma*, pp. 401, 402; Bernabò-Silorata, *Case penali*, chs. 5, 6.

71. G. M. Galanti, *Nuova descrizione storica e geografica delle Sicilie* (Napoli: 1787–90) vol. iii, pp. 68–9; cf. on Galanti's work, Dal Pane, *Storia del lavoro in Italia*, pp. 420 ff. but cf. in general the whole of ch. xiii, 'Le questioni sociali negli scrittori italiani del Settecento', p. 389.

72. Howard, *Prisons and Lazarettos*, p. 117. The *Vicaria* was the court and custodial prison of Naples. In the thirteenth century, Charles i of Anjou turned it into a supreme court and seat of the King's vicariate with judicial responsibility. (A similar prison with the same name could be found at Palermo). The Vicaria was infamous amongst the southern

masses; in the nineteenth century a song ran: 'I raised my eyes and saw the Vicaria where I heard my punishment'; and another, 'My heart sinks when I see the Vicaria'. (See the introductory note to *Canti e racconti di prigione*, ed. S. Boldini, *I dischi del sole*, DS 185/87/CL, 1969, pp. 31 ff. to which we refer the reader for other lively expressions of popular feeling towards prison although most of these are dated later than the period examined here.)

73. *Howard, Prisons and Lazarettos,* p. 290.
74. See C. Poni, *Aspetti e problemi dell'agricoltura modenese dall'età delle riforme alla fine della restaurazione, in Aspetti e problemi del Risorgimento a Modena* (Modena, 1964) p. 123.
75. See L. A. Muratori, 'Della carità cristiana in quanto essa è amore del prossimo' (1723), in *Opere*, vol. I (Milano-Napoli: 1964); Candeloro in *Storia dell'Italia moderna* stresses the great contribution Muratori made to the political and cultural life of the Duchy, pp. 110–11.
76. See Poni, *Aspetti e problemi dell'agricoltura modenese*, pp. 123 ff.
77. Ibid., p. 130.
78. Ibid., p. 131.
79. Ibid., p. 170; this also happened for the great part of the following century.
80. Ibid., p. 134.
81. Muratori, *Della carità cristiana*, p. 397.
82. Ibid., p. 397.
83. Ibid., p. 398.
84. Ibid., p. 401.
85. Ibid., pp. 402–3: the emphasis on *honourable prison* is mine.
86. See above p. 37.
87. See Poni, *Aspetti e problemi dell'agricoltura modenese*, pp. 140–1. See ibid. for how the constitution of *Opera Pia Generale dei Poveri* to which the construction of the *albergo* was assigned brings with it the secularisation of charity and the confiscation of ecclesiastical property; cf. again on Muratori's work on this theme: Dal Pane, *Storia del lavoro in Italia,* p. 398; Geremek, *Il pauperismo*, pp. 693 ff.
88. See L. A. Muratori, *Dei difetti della giurisprudenza* (1742) (Roma, 1933); cf. B. Veratti, *Intorno al trattato di L. A. Muratori sopra i difetti della giurisprudenza riguardato come uno dei fonti del Codice estense* (Modena, 1859). The new code was published in 1771.
89. Dal Pane, *Storia del lavoro in Italia*, p. 311.

90. Ibid., p. 312.
91. For the general situation in the Papal states, Candeloro, *Storia dell'Italia moderna*, pp. 693 ff. On the Civitavecchia galleys, cf. Howard, *Prisons and Lazarettos*, pp. 115, 116; on Bologna, p. 107 and on the prisons and *ospedali* at Rome, pp. 111–15.
92. See Candeloro, *Storia dell'Italia moderna*, pp. 131 ff.
93. See above p. 65.
94. The two *moto proprio* are dated 1693 and 1790. See Sellin, 'The House of Correction for Boys in the Hospice of Saint Michael in Rome', *Journal of American Institute of Criminal Law and Criminology*, vol. xx (1929–30), p. 533; Geremek, *Il pauperismo*, p. 691.
95. See Sellin, *The House of Correction*, pp. 539 ff.; cf. also Beltrani-Scalia, *Sul governo e sulla riforma*, pp. 384 ff.; Petitti di Roreto, *Della condizione attuale*, p. 368; Cattaneo, *Delle carceri*, p. 293; Izzo, *Da Filippo Franci alla riforma Doria*, pp. 290, 298; G. Minozzi, 'Il trattamento del detenuto nella storia dell'edilizia carceraria italiana', *Rassegna di studi penitenziari*, (1958) p. 696; Palazzo, *Appunti di storia del carcere*, vol. I p. 20; and finally, Howard, *Prisons and Lazarettos*, pp. 113–14 (with plan and elevation). For recent bibl. see Sellin above. We should however cite the work of C. L. Morichini, *Degli istituti di pubblica carità ed istruzione primaria e delle prigioni di Roma* (Roma, 1842).
96. See Sellin, *The House of Correction*, illustration on pp. 548–9.
97. Ibid., p. 547.
98. Howard, *Prisons and Lazarettos*, p. 114. Howard took the second motto for his *Prisons and Lazarettos*.
99. See Sellin, *The House of Correction*, p. 550.
100. Ibid., pp. 552–3.
101. Cf. Candeloro, *Storia dell'Italia moderna*, chs. III and IV.
102. Ibid., pp. 329 ff.
103. Suffice to record the famous essay by V. Cuoco on the failure of the Neopolitan Jacobin revolution in 1799 and on the subsequent use which came to be made of the 'lazzaroni' V. Cuoco, *Saggio storico sulla rivoluzione di Napoli del 1799* (Bari, 1929); Candeloro, *Storia dell'Italia moderna*, p. 273.
104. See E. J. Hobsbawm, *Bandits* (Harmondsworth: Penguin, 1969).
105. Ibid., pp. 19 ff.
106. Cf. for this thesis, A Gramsci, *Selections from the Prison Notebooks* (London: Lawrence & Wishart, 1971) pp. 55 ff. Gramsci's thesis is

harshly criticised by R. Romeo in his essay *Lo sviluppo del capitalismo in Italia*, in the second part of his *Risorgimento e capitalismo* (Bari, 1959). The polemic arising therefrom can be followed in the anthology edited by A. Caracciolo, *La formazione dell'Italia industriale* (Bari, 1973). In particular see essays by A. Caracciolo, L. Dal Pane and D. Tosi. The basic theme of the polemic substantially coincides with the question of primitive accumulation in Italy, particularly in the post-unification period. In fact, it was only after unitification in conjunction with the industrial revolution and the economic 'take-off' that the fundamental elements of primitive accumulation in Italy became quite evident. This also applies to the central question of this research, the formation of a factory proletariat and the prison question.

107. This is precisely one of the central questions raised in the debate referred to in the preceding note.

108. Cf. E. Sereni, *Il capitalismo nelle campagne* (Torino, 1948) pp. 355 ff. Sereni was one of the chief artificers of a political-theoretical elaboration of the question inspired by Gramsci's remarks on the matter.

109. For example, on the uprisings in Bologna in 1802, see Candeloro, *Storia dell' Italia moderna*, p. 307. Cf. on the general theme of the conquest and organisation of Napoleonic power in Northern Italy, pp. 289–322.

110. Ibid., p. 318.

111. What follows here on the topic of brigandage in Romagna under Napoleonic domination is taken from G. Manzoni, *Briganti in Romagna, 1800–1848* (Ravenna) which largely comprises a reproduction of documents. On the question of deserters, notices and warnings are reproduced on pp. 173 ff.

112. This is Hobsbawm's thesis (cf. *The Bandit as Symbol*, p. 127). Suffice to record the abundance of folklore inspired by the figure of the *social bandit*.

113. Cf. the numerous documents reproduced by Manzoni, *Briganti in Romagna*, pp. 165 ff. The persistence of attempts to do this was also due, of course, to the ambiguous attitude particularly on the part of the lower clergy which was more closely tied to the people in the face of Napoleonic authority.

114. See Manzoni, *Briganti in Romagna*, p. 94, warning of 7 June 1805.

115. Ibid., p. 119, decree of 21 Nov 1806.

116. Ibid., pp. 153, 194.

117. See above p. 58. It is worth reproducing the letter which the Prefect of the Department of Rubicone used to notify his priests about the new code:

> It would please our most Learned Majesty to give to his people of the Kingdom of Italy a penal code. Every parish priest must be provided with a book necessary for the instruction of his parishioners. This is something which conforms to their holy office. On feastdays after a commentary on the Gospel which enlightens men on offences against God and their neighbour and on eternal punishment, they will also be enlightened on crime and its temporal punishments.
>
> Thus the clergy are invited to explain from the altar those penalties threatened by the Code so that everyone is encouraged to avoid the deeds which incur them. The people's attention must be directed especially to the fourth book, which lists contraventions and police measures. When dealing with a felony or a crime, the inner prompting of conscience shows men the gravity of the evil and the voice of nature calls upon them to abstain therefrom; this does not occur if some contravention is dealt with simply as a police measure. The notion of evil, perceived not intrinsically but with regard to the social order, is directly related to our education and culture. Now, the lower orders do not often recognise this kind of contravention except in terms of the threatened penalties...
>
> I shall watch over those who are mindful of my suggestions and who wish to distinguish themselves by their zeal just as I will take note and inform the Government of those who, by chance, fail to heed so important a suggestion. (Manzoni, *Briganti in Romagna*, p. 196, 197)

118. See Beltrani-Scalia, *Sul governo e sulla riforma*, pp. 412 ff. Bernabò-Silorata, *Case penali*, ch. 7.
119. See Beltrani-Scalia, *Sul governo e sulla riforma*, p. 416; Bernabò-Silorata, *Case penali*, ch. 9.
120. See Beltrani-Scalia, *Sul governo e sulla riforma*, p. 420; Bernabò-Silorata, *Case penali*, ch. 9.
121. Cf. particularly Petitti di Roreto, *Della condizione attuale*, pp. 423–34; Beltrani-Scalia, *Sul governo e sulla riforma*, p. 422; Bernabò-Silorata, *Case penali*, ch. 9. Comoli Mandracci, *Il carcere per la società del Sette-Ottocento*, pp. 41–52.
122. As in Izzo, *Da Filippo Franci alla riforma Doria*, p. 303.
123. See Beltrani Scalia, *Sul governo e sulla riforma*, p. 424.

124. Ibid., pp. 430 ff.
125. Ibid., pp. 414 ff.; Bernabò-Silorata, *Case penali*, ch. 8.
126. See Beltrani-Scalia, *Sul governo e sulla riforma*, p. 413.
127. Ibid., p. 414.
128. Ibid., p. 416.
129. Ibid., pp. 435 ff; Petitti di Roreto, *Della condizione attuale*, p. 421; Bernabò-Silorata, *Case penali*, ch. 10.
130. See Beltrani-Scalia, *Sul governo e sulla riforma*, p. 441; Bernabò-Silorata, *Case penali*, ch. 10; C. Peri, *Cenni sulla riforma del sistema penitenziario in Toscana* (Firenze, 1848) reports on this regulation on pp. 15 ff.
131. See Beltrani-Scalia, *Sul governo e sulla riforma*, p. 440.
132. Ibid., p. 441; Bernabò-Silorata, *Case penali*, ch. 10.
133. See Beltrani-Scalia, *Sul governo e sulla riforma*, p. 445.
134. See Firenze, 1859. Peri published a *Risposta del cav. Carlo Peri all'opuscolo del dottor Carlo Morelli* (Reply by Cavalier Carlo Peri to Dr. Carlo Morelli's pamphlet) (Firenze, 1860).
135. Beltrani-Scalia, *Sul governo e sulla riforma*, p. 449.
136. On the 'idle and vagabond' at the origins of preventive measures in Italian society, cf. M. Pavarini, 'Il "socialmente pericoloso" nell'attività di prevenzione', *Rivista italiana di diritto e procedura penale* (1975) p. 396.
137. See F. Serantini, *Fatti memorabili della banda del Passatore in terra di Romagna* (Ravenna, 1973).
138. See Sereni, *Il capitalismo nelle campagne*, pp. 216–21.
139. See E. Ferri, 'I contadini mantovani all'Assise di Venezia (1886)', *Difese penali e studi di giurisprudenza* (Torino, 1899).
140. See M. Beltrani-Scalia, *Sul governo e sulla riforma*, p. 464.
141. Ibid., p. 466.
142. Ibid., pp. 467 ff.; C.I. Petitti di Roreto, *Della condizione attuale*, p. 420; from F. Volpicella his *Delle prigioni e del loro ordinamento* (Napoli, 1837); On Volpicella's work, see D. Palazzo, 'A proposito di "riforma delle prigioni" nella prima metà del sècolo scorso', *Rassegna di Studi Penitenziari* (1970) p. 677; 'Su alcune speciali prigioni del secolo scorso', *Rassegna di Studi Penitenziari* (1971) p. 591.
143. In practice, this whole process developed after unification. But the way was paved beforehand – in this connection the question of prison is exemplary–particularly in Piedmont in its role of guiding state for the ranks of the Italian bourgeoisie which it assumed in the process of uni-

fication. What we give here is merely some indication on this. As in the case of penal reform, it would be necessary to proceed to a determinate scientific reconstruction of the way in which the various other institutions connect to the central question of the formation and control of the proletariat. At the moment of unification, the cultural, scientific and ideological patrimony which was to be supportive of the subsequent construction of a capitalist society in Italy had largely been elaborated. Most interesting in this relation is the volume by G. C. Marino *La formazione dello spirito borghese in Italia* (Firenze, 1974) which is above all based on an analysis of the proceedings of the various *Riunioni degli scienziati italiani* held during the 1840s.

144. This is exactly what happened in the case of the *riunione degli scienziati* which Marino above examines.

145. Ibid., pp. 330 ff.

146. Ibid., pp. 345 ff.

147. This relates to the studies by Petitti which we have frequently cited: *Della condizione attuale*; on the other hand, here Petitti resumed a theme which he dealt with in one of his writings dated 1837 in which he devoted many pages to the question of prisons, *Saggio sul buon governo \ della mendicità, degli istituti di beneficienza e delle carceri* (*Torino, 1837*). The work of Cattaneo, *Delle carceri* was published in *Il Politecnico* (*1840*).

148. See Petitti di Roreto, *Della condizione attuale*, pp. 448 ff. Petitti was an intellectual of European stature in contact with all the best-known theorists and men of government in the field of prison. Moreover, he applied his interest to socio-economic themes of a wide nature: all his work is collected in the *Opere scelte*, already cited. Though these studies are wide ranging, they always relate to the concrete organisational needs of the Piedmont state.

149. See Petitti di Roreto, *Della condizione attuale*, pp. 327 ff.

150. Ibid., pp. 361 ff.

151. Ibid., pp. 448 ff.

152. Ibid., pp. 450 ff.

153. In note c. on p. 451, ibid., Petitti reports on a talk he had with a prisoner at a prison run on Auburnian lines in Geneva. This prisoner had previously served a sentence at the *bagno penale* at Tolone: 'He said that once he returned to a more moral way of thinking he understood that the rigour of the discipline at the Geneva prison was for his own good; but at first he regretted that he had not committed the second crime in

France because in that event he would have been sent to the *bagno* where, despite the apparent hard life therein, *for most it was easier to endure*, due to the fresh air one could enjoy, the freer association, the attraction of possible escape, the possibility to consume spirits and the like. He added that, even after he had reformed, he sometimes recalled to mind the *better life* at the *bagno* and this *stimulated an abhorrence for the prison he now found himself in.*

154. Ibid., pp. 455 ff.
155. See Cattaneo, *Delle carceri*, pp. 302 ff.
156. See Marino, *La forurazione dello spirito borghese*, p. 351.
157. In n. 199 on p. 94 above, I cite the passage from Marx in which he makes the connection between solitary confinement and the creation by the isolated individual 'of perceptible, sensible ghosts' which represent both 'the mystery of all pious visions' and 'the general form of insanity' (K. Marx and F. Engels, *The Holy Family* (Moscow: 1956) p. 245). This looks like the process Cattaneo describes in *Delle carceri*, p. 239, when he refers to the psychological effectiveness produced by solitary confinement: 'in the silence men undergo and in the sleep of their passions, advices which have been much derided in the past, words which seem remote from the memory are recalled, religious terror, all the images and memories of good and evil, surge forth before the guilty conscience and become increasingly potent and irresistible each day' (p. 304). Both Petitti, p. 462 and Marino on pp. 355–6, relate the results of contemporary enquiries into the disastrous effects of the Philadelphian system (suicide and cases of insanity).
158. See Marino, *La formazione dello spirito borghese*, pp. 362, 363.
159. In this respect, Marino, ibid.
160. Ibid., pp. 364–5.
161. Clearly expressed by Cattaneo thus: 'unfortunately, the incomplete reforms which modern humanity introduced into prison had deprived this unique penal instrument of any terror. There, the evil loafer found shelter, bed, guaranteed food, light work and whatever company he desired; for many honest workers, burdened with children and for many day labourers, famished amid the fertile countryside, a stay in prison was, unfortunately, a seductive prospect. But the genuine evildoer will always prefer the filth and discomfort of a promiscuous dungeon, bare floor, chains, whip and all, to strict confinement even if the cell is spacious, bright, well-lit, aired, heated and equipped with all that industrious poverty could desire; for the former leaves him in full possession of his wickedness' (p. 305).

Part 2

The Penitentiary Invention: The US Experience of the First Half of the Nineteenth Century
Massimo Pavarini

The Jacksonian Era: Economic Development, Marginality and Social Control Policy

Massimo Pavarini

Labour is the fate of the modern peoples … Labour must become the religion of the prisons. A society-machine requires purely mechanical means of reform. (L. Faucher, De la reforme des prisons, Paris, 1838, p. 64)

Real Estate and the Family: The Basis of Social Control in the Colonial Period

The originality and truly revolutionary nature of social control characterising the United States of America from the early part of the nineteenth century is fully intelligible if we bear in mind social attitudes towards deviant phenomena in the colonial period preceding the birth of the new republic.

In particular, we want here to trace in a synthetic manner the general co-ordinating factors from which we may grasp how colonial society both evaluated and reacted to processes of social disintegration.

Within the confines of that 'suffocated economy' which was the United States of America of the eighteenth century, neither poverty nor crime were afforded the political attention they were to receive in the

© The Author(s) 2018
D. Melossi, M. Pavarini, *The Prison and the Factory (40ᵗʰ Anniversary Edition)*,
Palgrave Studies in Prisons and Penology, DOI 10.1057/978-1-137-56590-7_4

post-revolutionary period. The existence of the vagabond, the insane and the criminal were not taken as evidence of a crisis in society. In consequence, there was no formulation of any real social policy to deal with these problems – let alone in a consciously political way.

Instead, the approach to the problem of pauperism was essentially religious. This went hand in hand with a rigid belief in a fixed social order (a typical reflection of an exclusively agricultural economy) and a pronounced and specific sense of community originating from the first colonial settlements.[1]

The Protestant church was one of the most influential agents in the forming of public opinion on pauperism. In fact poverty was seen as something natural, inevitable and fair. In exactly the same way, giving alms to the distressed was considered to be right as long as it was a question of individual charity. At the root of this religious view lies the clear conviction that the existing stratification of society reflects a divine order in which the status of the poor is not determined by accident or chance but by fate. Poverty so determined held out opportunities for human charity. According to a Boston vicar named Cooper, the giving of relief to the poor: 'ennobles our nature, by conforming us to the best, the most glorious betters ... Charity conforms us to the Son of God himself.'[2]

This approach allowed few exceptions. Interestingly enough, classifications such as deserving and undeserving poor or voluntary and involuntary unemployment did not develop. Had they done so, it would have been a direct reflection of a political concern which would have denoted a perception of pauperism as a social problem.

The persistence of an unpolitical evaluation of pauperism can be explained in terms of the particular economic circumstances – and even more significantly, the particular social circumstances – of the time. Even if recent historiography[3] has clarified the existence of marginal classes in some colonies of eighteenth century America, it is nevertheless necessary to highlight the ability of the original settlements to absorb politically as much as economically the socially marginal, provided they were local residents, that is, provided they were inside the community itself.

Reactions to vagabondage (or so-called fluctuating pauperism) and more generally, the social view of social mobility, were quite different. In other words, the obsession which conditioned the thinking of the epoch did not so much centre on the question of marginality as on that of the mobility of the distressed sections of the population. This emphasis reveals the existence of stability as a firm underlying ideal in the dominant ideology.

This last observation needs to be developed. The forms of social aggregation of the original colonial settlements were certainly very marked; the points of real cohesion and the close-knit web of mutual relationships between various members were bound firmly to cement the small agricultural community. This process of cultural homogenisation was accentuated by the natural difficulties colonists had to face and endure on the one hand and by the relative isolation of the community on the other.[4] Social impermeability was certainly one result; on the other hand, the existence of vast and as yet uncolonised territories (that is, the existence of that 'expanding frontier' responsible for shaping so much of American socio-political thought)[5] discouraged new immigrants from moving into areas which were already occupied until, of course, the emergence of a manufacturing economy made massive and dramatic urban concentration a necessity.

If we then bear in mind that in certain territories the fertile lands had already been divided up among the first three generations of colonists and that this offered little incentive for new settlement as a result, it also partially motivated the prejudice against outsiders, especially those without means.[6] This situation also explains the phenomenon (mentioned earlier) of the marked presence of static elements in the small communities[7] which were ideologically coupled both with a strong conception of social hierarchy and with a deep sense of community.[8] This was reflected in attitudes towards pauperism–provided it was endemic (that is, inside the community): there was no concern to eliminate the pauper since, on the one hand, he was a 'natural' phenomenon and, on the other, there was a moral duty to assist him as a member of the community. In this sense, the great colonial family was able to accommodate the weaker sections of society inside its own productive process (though still only within the limits of private charity) through a form of poor relief based mainly on hospitality and on the commission of agricultural and seasonal work.[9] The use of non-institutional, non-segregational methods, for example, the so-called household help to distressed residents, therefore, emerged as the main feature of poor relief.[10]

But attitudes towards non-resident paupers – needy new immigrants – were quite different. These newcomers bore the brunt of the stubborn conviction that residential stability was the main foundation of social order,[11] an outlook closely linked to the dominance of private real estate.

However, we cannot generalise from this without qualification. In the frontier colonial settlements, for example, discrimination between now and established arrivals clearly did not take place. In Carolina and Pennsylvania – two large areas of constant immigration – hostility towards new colonists was less marked. Even so, the ideal American farmer of the eighteenth century lived in an economically self-sufficient community; the residential population (townsmen) were privileged as against the migrant and needy (dependent outsiders). Thus colonial society introduced strict legislation to limit the phenomenon of vagabondage; though particularly severe, this legislation was not as bloody as that operated in some European countries, especially England. As early as 1683, the first New York code took a line on the questions of vagabondage and pauperism which was to remain a constant feature of colonial legislation for more than a century: assistance to the local, residential needy and opposition to the immigration of the poor.[12] In fact the relevant law obliged the officer in command of disembarkation to register the names of passengers and forcibly to accompany those unable to demonstrate possession of property or a place of destination back to the port; similarly, police agents were to accompany vagabonds and beggars back to the frontier if they had no legal authorisation to enter.[13]

The New York legislation of 1721 tightened up sanctions on clandestine immigration; it laid down fines and corporal punishment and even introduced the first forms of forced confinement in jails (the original preventive prisons) for a fixed period in the case of recidivists.[14] In 1773, the legislative Assembly of the New York colony introduced certificates of residence; by means of this administrative authority, a strict control on social mobility was enforced both inside and outside the colony's boundaries.[15]

This legislative model was quickly copied. For example, by 1748, Rhode Island compelled new immigrants to own a minimal amount of land on pain of expulsion.[16] The same thing happened in the southern colonies: the Assembly of Delaware in 1741 promulgated laws similar to those in New York[17]; likewise North Carolina settled the question in 1754 with a law emphasising the difference in the treatment of the *local poor* and *strangers*.[18]

The situation changed considerably – especially with regard to controls on non-residents – in the more densely populated colonies where immigration was high; here we can detect the (somewhat limited) growth of traditional European institutions for the control and repression of vagabondage: the workhouse, the almshouse and the house of correction.

The introduction of these institutions in colonial America probably goes back to the legislative period of William Penn in 1683; the subsequent vicissitudes these institutions experienced highlight the contradictory nature of policies of social control in eighteenth- century America.

Even a brief chronology of the evolution of these institutions can provide us with a general picture of the complexity of legislation aimed at the social control of the marginal classes in colonial America; this analysis in turn introduces the more specific theme of the prevention–repression of criminality.

Pennsylvania was the theatre of the first social policy[19]; its principal actors were drawn from the Quaker community.[20] Before the 1682 legislation the only institution known in Pennsylvania was the country jail. This had originally been a military fort which came to be used for preventive imprisonment[21]; in fact in this period the laws of the mother country held sway (Anglo-Saxon penal legislation to be precise); first capital punishment and then corporal punishment dominated the system of sanctions.

William Penn, the inspirer of the initial legislation of 1682, abolished the death penalty for all crimes with the exception of wilful and premeditated homicide and high treason[22]; this great reformer would have retained the county jail as a detentive prison whilst the introduction of a new institution – the house of correction on the Dutch model – would have served to confine *felons* (transgressors of laws for which neither corporal nor capital punishment were appropriate) and forcibly put them to work. By law in 1718, it was decided to construct a new jail for debtors, for absconding apprentices and, of course, for those awaiting trial, as well as a workhouse for criminals.[23] For the time, the project was both utopian and ineffective even if it had some political importance. Various factors contributed to this revolutionary legislative reform: in the first place, there was a political desire to 'emancipate' America from dependence on the mother country even with regard to legislation; further, the need for a punitive hypothesis which would somehow be in keeping with the intense Quaker emphasis on ethics and morals; and finally, the fascination that a cosmopolitan 'intelligentsia' still culturally linked to Europe felt for the latest forms of social policy.

In this light, we can see how the plan for a house of correction proposed by Penn (sometimes defined as a workhouse) already contemplated the isolation and division of inmates according to an articulated typology and envisaged forced confinement for vagabonds and the idle; once again, inmates were forced into paid labour.[24]

In effect, this initiative collapsed and with the death of Penn, the reintroduction of English legislation brought back corporal punishment and, above all, the death sentence. Significantly, however, capital punishment for theft was abolished (crimes against property came to account for two-thirds of all crime). In this respect, the reform of 1682 remained unaltered, that is to say, theft was punishable by confinement in a workhouse for a fixed period. Thus the penal set-up in colonial Pennsylvania can be defined as follows:

1. The jail kept its original function as a 'preventive prison'. Here the Anglo-Saxon fee system prevailed; prisoners had to pay for their keep and give a fee to the jailer. Since the latter was not paid out of public funds, he was able to use his superior position to exploit inmates. It was only in 1736 that the obligation to maintain detainees on public funds was introduced.[25]

    Conditions in the jails were described as deplorable; here the critical pen of Quaker moralism could find ground for invective and denunciation as to the dangerous promiscuity in which inmates lived:

    What a spectacle [wrote Robert Vaux] must this abode of guilt and wretchedness have presented, when in one common herd were kept, by day and by night, prisoners of all ages, colours, and sexes! No separation was made of the most flagrant offender and convict, from the prisoners who might perhaps be falsely suspected of some trifling misdemeanor; none of the old and hardened culprit, from the youthful and trembling novice in crime.[26]

The diary of a defaulting Quaker jailed during the revolution (S. R. Fisher) illustrates the abuses practised by jailers on prisoners, the violence and corporal punishment inflicted on inmates for disciplinary infractions and the brutal relationships amongst prisoners themselves, etc.[27]

2. Houses of correction or workhouses began as architectural appendages to jails and it was envisaged that the disciplinary regime in both institutions would not substantially differ. However, the internal population of workhouses was different: the majority were petty offenders for whom corporal punishment was not contemplated; then there were those who had violated immigration controls; and more generally, there were vagrants and vagabonds; finally, there were paupers not in receipt of home-relief.[28]

We can now go beyond Pennsylvania and analyse the whole position concerning the system of social control in colonial America.

From available data,[29] it is difficult to give an exact account of how many individuals were subjected to these various forms of control- assistance in the colonial period. Certainly, in regard to the numbers interned in institutions (workhouse, almshouse, poorhouse) it is reasonable to assume that numbers were more contained than was the case in Europe.[30] In fact, it should be remembered that at that time, the total population of all the colonies was fewer than four million, about half of whom were black slaves (for whom these institutions were generally inappropriate).[31]

The whole situation is readily intelligible when one considers that the dominant system of relief for the distressed sections of the population (particularly if they were local) was that of household and neighbour relief (community assistance of a charitable nature).[32] Moreover, it is interesting to note how – even within a framework of assistance through enforced confinement – the paradigmatic model is still of a domestic, family nature. Even in architectural terms, the almshouse or poorhouse was built on the same model as the colonial household. In fact, no specific building or specification was designed for this institution, use being made of existing farmhouses.[33] Similarly, institutional rules and practices were drawn from a model of domestic life. In fact, staff and officers lived in the poorhouse with their families; the inmates did not wear uniforms and the only known form of segregation – although it is impossible to determine how far it was applied-was that between the sexes; meals were taken together with the staff and inmates had free access to all rooms.[34]

In other words the poorhouse – in which the majority were poor residents, orphans and distressed widows – functioned on the lines of a household; thus it was not – as Rothman observes[35] – a true and proper asylum; in fact, whoever lived in these places formed part of a family rather than of a community of inmates. In time, this model of the poorhouse came to 'contaminate' more general institutional practices.

For example, the social question of lunatics was normally resolved by means of domestic relief; only when a mental illness was considered socially dangerous was an insane person forcibly confined in a special section of an almshouse or, in some cases, in rooms set aside in a house of correction.[36]

Hospitals originated in a specific service provided by the poorhouse; in fact, in many cases, the poorhouse was gradually transformed into an infirmary. At the end of the colonial period and with the advent of specialised private and public places for hospital assistance, the poorhouse tended to function as a bona fide hospital for the infirm poor.[37]

The structure for the social control of criminal deviancy was less well defined. We have already spoken of the essentially procedural nature of the jail and of the predominant role played by various forms of corporal punishment. These punishments included the gallows: as we can see from statistics, particularly in periods of serious social tension, North American colonies made very ready use of this last resort.[38]

Interestingly enough, the best-known form of corporal punishment next to flogging was probably the stocks; by virtue of its essentially public nature, this kind of penal sanction was charged with moral importance as opposed to the mere infliction of physical suffering; in other words, it reflected a social structure in which reputation and a sense of honour were basic values[39] and which therefore indirectly reaffirmed in cultural terms an agrarian socioeconomic system profoundly linked to real estate.

Bearing in mind the weight of biblical-religious traditions amongst the first colonial communities we must view branding in the same light; here the condemned were stamped with the initial letter of the crime committed.[40] We have also mentioned the sanctions typically applied to those transgressing immigration regulations; apart from being confined in houses of correction, these people were more easily expelled from colony and town alike; this kind of sanction was also used against petty offenders especially if they were non-residents.

There were still wide areas of uncertainty and ambiguity as to the nature and function of houses of correction and workhouses; certainly the two terms were used to mean the same thing. Originally the work-house, which grew from a model analogous to European institutions, was supposed to serve as a form of punishment for petty offenders (*felons*) to whom corporal punishments were not applicable. In time, in fact, the workhouse was filled with beggars and vagrants, that is, non-residents violating immigration norms. Later, the institution was used as a com-pulsory refuge for the residential poor and in some cases it also served as a prison for debtors. In this heterogeneous world, characterised by social precariousness and marginality, institutional discipline was supposed to impose that re- educative process which was considered socially expedi-ent – on a purely ideological level and imitative of dominant practices in the mother countries.

In colonial practice, this aim was never achieved. In fact the institu-tional structure of the workhouse or the house of correction rarely dif-fered from that of the poorhouse or almshouse and, in reality, the latter was organised along the lines of household relief. The very same compul-sion to work which should have – at least according to its declared prin-ciples – characterised the execution of the punishment in workhouses in no way differed from the use of forced labour in poorhouses; in other words, it was work which followed the productive model of the large colonial family.[41]

To conclude this summary of pre-revolutionary America, we can state that the principal mechanisms of social control were in practice totally based on the institution fundamental to the epoch: the *colonial family*.[42] It is probably reasonable to assume that the colonial family did not pro-vide a model for the social control of the dangerous or marginal classes; rather it had the institutional role of educating and repressing juvenile delinquency. Evidence of this particular view of the family is furnished by numerous testimonies of the time, in which it is stressed that by its con-trol of the young, the family unit becomes the agent of control of the whole of society.

The civil and religious preachings and sermons frequently published in cheap editions and distributed amongst loyal members of the community strengthened this viewpoint[43]: As Wadsworth warned his readers:

> When children are disobedient to parents, God is often provoked to leave them to those sins which bring them to the greatest shame and misery ... When persons have been brought to die at the gallows, how often have they confessed that disobedience to parents led them to those crimes?[44]

The educative role of the family, the duty of parents to repress their children's deviant behaviour is thus projected onto the problem of juvenile delinquency and 'errors in family education' come to be interpreted as the main cause of social pathology as a whole:

> Let all children ... beware of disobedience ... Appetites and passions unrestricted in childhood become furious in youth; and ensure *dishonor, disease,* and an *untimely death.*[45]

It is useful to remember that the educative role of the family for infants is not just confined to an ethical-ideological level but takes place through a normative-institutional structure, concretising for example, the obligation on parents to impart a rigid discipline to their children. In the absence of familial influence in the educative process, the authorities are quick to intervene, for example, by forcibly withdrawing natural parental powers and taking over the control of the child – either by handing it over to another family or, if this is not possible, by taking the child into public care. And this is why, as early as the colonial period, it was possible to suggest confinement in workhouses for juveniles who had not yet violated the penal law but who were shown to be lacking suitable upbringing.[46] Thus, at the risk of excessive schematism, we can state that in a territorially stable agricultural community, the family tended, by means of a process of progressive growth, to reproduce itself almost by segmentation in a web of analogous structures of social control. The process was thus symmetrical: just as the situation of the marginal classes (paupers, lunatics, criminals, etc.) was seen as being similar to that of the juvenile, so the family – originally simply responsible for control of infancy – became the paradigmatic term for the social control of all other forms of deviancy (household and neighbour relief, almshouse, workhouse, etc.).

The Structural Framework: From an Agricultural Society to an Industrial Economy

The Post-revolutionary Period: Process of Accumulation and Mercantile Economy

In 1790 the United States was still a country with fewer than four million inhabitants; there was no town with more than 50,000 inhabitants; only seven towns centres with a population of more than 5000 and twelve with more than 2500; the rest of the population (3.7 million) lived in the countryside.[47] In 1820, the rural population more than doubled whilst the urban population (accounting for 700,000 in total) more than tripled.[48] In 1791, there was just one textile plant, two in 1795, another two were set up in 1803 and ten between 1804 and 1808; by the end of 1809,[49] there were eighty-seven plants; the productive capacity of the textile industry grew from 8000 spindles in 1808 to 31,000 at the end of 1809; by 1811 there was a total of 80,000 spindles.[50]

Not one bank existed in the whole of the country at the time of the Declaration of Independence. The first to be established was the North American Bank, founded at a citizens' meeting at Philadelphia in 1780 to finance army provisions. The bank began with only $3,000,000 capital. By 1789, two other banks began operations at Boston, Mass. and New York.[51]

Even if these figures are not uniform, they undoubtedly point to a rapid and violent process of economic change in the post-revolutionary American economy. In fact – as we will try to show – the break from the mother country, to which the colonies had been deeply tied, brought about an economic transformation (necessitated by the new autarchic regime that automatically followed independence from England). Even if one can only talk of a true and proper take-off after 1820, the thirty preceding years were marked by those economic and social processes which constitute the necessary structural premise for industrial revolution. In other words, throughout the nineteenth century and in the space of a relatively short time, the United States underwent a marked and rapid process of capitalistic accumulation with consequent socio-cultural changes.

One of the first and most significant results of the new socioeconomic order was that landed property took on a different form. Although not altering the central role of agriculture in American political economy, the years immediately preceding and following the revolution witnessed both the dissolution of large estates and the slackening of the ties which had bound the day-labouring workforce to them.

In fact, we should stress that in colonial America landed property was based on large estates just as in England. In the states of New York, Pennsylvania, Maryland, Virginia and the Southern colonies, one could find properties comprising thousands of acres; in the state of New York, for example, more than $2\frac{1}{2}$ million acres belonged to a small number of families. In 1769, at least five-sixths of the inhabitants of Westchester County lived on great manors. The Fairfax estate in Virginia at one time embraced six million acres whilst the property of Lord Granville in North Carolina comprised at least one third of the whole of the colony.[52] These vast properties were largely cultivated by the labour of wage-earners or slaves.

Various factors contributed to the sharp alteration of this economic order. First, royal restrictions on the acquisition of new land fell into abeyance; in fact the King's proclamation of 1763 forbidding the settling and patenting of lands beyond the Alleghenies and the provisions of the Quebec Act of 1774 restricting westward expansion were both abrogated. In the second place, in the majority of the colonies, the laws under which every acre of land was taxed for the benefit of the Crown or of the proprietary of the Province were also abrogated.[53] However, the most important inroad into the old property order was made by the great confiscations (usually of Tory estates) by the various state legislatures at the height of the war. Purely by way of example, as early as 1782, the state of New York had confiscated royalist landed property valued at about $2,500,000. In Pennsylvania, the largest estate confiscated was that of the Penn family estimated to be worth a million pounds.[54]

The expropriated lands were then sold to small proprietors in lots which did not usually exceed 500 acres. At the same time, and still with an eye to coping with rising war debts, the various states also sold the vast domains of the Crown to small-holders.

Abrogation of the old medieval institutions which had been forcibly imposed from England, including the right of primogeniture and limitations on the breaking up of landed property, accentuated processes described above by modifying the social geography of property. Jefferson's Act of 1776 should be seen as relevant in this context. It released from entail at least half and possibly three- quarters of the property in Virginia.[55] If these interacting factors had the main effect of a more democratic redistribution of landed property (remember that franchise went with land ownership), it also brought about a process of social mobility. On the one hand the various redistributions gave some the chance to be small-holders; on the other, vast numbers of ex-colonists, originally employed as farmhands on the large estates, were forced or induced to abandon their original places of residence and move to new uncultivated territories.

In fact, in the older states, there was extensive migration to the western uplands; this was, as a rule, an intermediary stage towards trans-Allegheny migration. By about 1791, the regions west of the mountains already had a sizeable population; the conditions had been realised for the great 'westward movement'.[56] In this period, the old colonial legislation against migration was almost entirely dropped; the primitive ideal of the territorially stable community was definitively smashed.

Concomitantly with the disintegration of the old economic property order, the post-revolutionary period was also characterised by the rapid accumulation of large private fortunes no longer based on real estate but on the very high profits from certain commercial activities. The mainstays of this lucrative activity were, on the one hand, the slave trade and, on the other, the importing of manufactured goods from the Orient, with which the American colonies had formerly enjoyed only indirect links. The slave trade, particularly in the Southern states, was an economic necessity linked to the constant and almost endemic scarcity of labour and its consequent high cost.[57] During the revolution, navigation restrictions and the repeated incursions from invading armies, reduced or indeed interrupted the 'migration' of coloured peoples; with the advent of peace, the great need for labour again boosted the slave trade.

Profits from the Orient – particularly those derived from luxury goods which had become hard to obtain on the market once links were broken with England-were immense. Jameson tells how a shipment of plain glass tumblers worth less than $1000 imported from Mauritius were sold in America for $12,000. And 300–400 per cent profit could be made on coffee imported from the Indies.[58]

Under the impulse of the revolution, the various Navigation Acts were abrogated. These had permitted the mother country to monopolise trade with the colonies and open up new avenues for itself. Now, for example, tobacco was either exported directly to France, Spain and Holland or channelled via their West Indian dominions. Thus a true and proper mercantile class emerged along with the large capitalistic concentrations of this period. And even if this mercantile class still lacked entrepreneurial qualities or bourgeois habits, it was certainly endowed with a healthy open mind and sensitivity when it came to trade.

In this period, manufacturing activity was essentially of a domestic-craft nature. There was in the small isolated communities scattered throughout the hinterland, a rudimentary division of labour in which a number of local producers made goods for tiny self- sufficient markets. This activity was necessitated by an autarchic economy in which a good part of the population was not affected by the existence of a market.[59] As Jameson records:

> The spinning-wheel came into renewed use in every household, and home-spun was worn by the wealthiest. Spinning matches at neighbors' houses became a common occurrence, and an excellent outlet for patriotic ardor. Imports from England into the northern colonies went down in 1769 to not much more than a third of what they were in 1768. Hence the repeal of all taxes save that on tea. A Harvard commencement in 1770, the graduating class appeared in black cloth entirely of American manufacture.[60]

Thus large-scale manufacture was still a marginal phenomenon. Even as early as this period, however, a limited number of exceptions could be found, particularly in the processing of locally accessible raw materials.

Resource-oriented production was therefore the most important aspect of manufacture: a good example was shipbuilding which owed its existence to the dense forests, as did the milling and timber industries.[61]

The explanation for the delay in real industrial take-off is essentially located in the scarcity of labour and its consequent high cost; and it was for this reason that the limited capital available was channelled into commerce and speculation connected with maritime trade.

The situation partly changed with the embargo limiting trade with foreign countries established in 1807 by Jefferson, who feared involvement in the European war; in fact this provision was followed by a serious depression, particularly in the commercial sector. The heavy reduction in the export trade was accompanied by a consequent depression in imports, particularly in textiles. New possibilities were opened up in the American market by the inevitable price rises, in so far as the textile industry began to look to those resources which in the past had been used by the export trade.

Arising from the same political contingency, other sectors of manufacture developed with similar rapidity; they all sought to profit from the hiatus in the import of manufactured goods. The economic crisis after 1814 – a result of tough foreign competition once the trade embargo had been lifted – forced the central US government to implement a *protectionist policy* of high tariffs on imported goods. In any case, the crisis had a salutary effect: the tariff restrictions provided effective protection in the face of a fall in the price of the coarsest textiles. As North observes:

> The early, and for the most part aborted, efforts of American manufacturing came to a close with the depression of 1818. Once revival got under way in the early 1820s, the manufacturing which did survive this period became the base for the gradual pattern of development which ultimately resulted in the industrialised economy of 1860.[62]

We would add – in summarising our present discussion – that the basis of future industrial development must be most precisely located in the emergence of certain structural constants in the post-revolutionary period:

1. A change in the distribution of landed property resulting in social mobility on a massive scale.

2. The endemic scarcity of labour which pushed up wages; this was why future industrial organisation had to use comparatively more capital for the same level of production as in contemporary Europe.
3. The vast amount of capital amassed in a short time through maritime trade.
4. The presence of considerable natural wealth and the generally low cost of the provision of raw materials.

Industrial Take-Off (1820–60)

In the decade 1820–30 manufacturing enterprise in the Eastern United States developed in a wide range of sectors; in the following decade economic growth, still protected by tariffs, accelerated. As early as 1845, the industrial census of Massachusetts valued total production at $124,749,457 as against $86,282,616 in 1837.[63] In the five years 1844–9 the rate of growth of American production – at constant prices – was 68.3 per cent.[64] In 1860, the United States of America was already the second most industrialised country in the world.

In 1820, the urban population was a little over half a million; by 1830 it had already tripled[65] and by 1860 it had increased more than tenfold (6,216,518 inhabitants), whilst the rural population only trebled in the same forty years. The phenomenon of urban concentration was immense. Industry based on the available resources influenced the kind of urbanisation taking shape: the North-east, including the mid-Atlantic states, accounted for more than half of the industrial employees in 1850; in 1860, the figure rose to 71 per cent.[66]

The motive force behind the exceptional economic growth lay in the textile industry. In 1831, there were 795 cotton mills and the total value of their product was around 32 million dollars; in 1860 there were 1991 cotton mills capable of producing goods to the value of $115,700,000.[67]

The importance of the textile industry for production in general can be demonstrated in economic terms; this area of production played a strategic role in 'upstream' and 'downstream' links with other kinds of manufacture: on the one hand, the clothing industry and, on the other hand, the tool-making industry.[68]

In 1860, cotton was the main industrial sector. It employed 114,955 operatives and boasted the highest productivity in the country; it accounted for 50 per cent of total production[69]; as far as employment was concerned, the clothing sector followed with 114,800 operatives and finally, the tool-making sector and wool production together furnished work for more than 80,000 workers.[70]

As we have indicated, the vast growth of textile production and its related activities was partly determined by the employment of large sums of capital and the increasing use of machinery (especially the power loom). This process – dependent also upon technological innovation – only developed on a large scale after 1830. It was then that the 'upstream' links (between the textile industry itself and the production of machinery for textiles) played an essential role in manufacturing activity, raising the American economy to first rank in world production. In fact, as one author observes:

> The manufacture of cloth was America's greatest industry. For a considerable part of the 1813–53 period the manufacture of textile machinery appears to have been America's greatest heavy goods industry, occupying the primary position in point of size and value of product among all industries which fabricated metal. Size, however, is not the most critical measure of importance. From the textile mills and the textile machine shops came the men who supplied most of the tools for the American Industrial Revolution. From these mills and shops sprang directly the machine tool and locomotive industries together with a host of less basic metal fabricating trades.[71]

Thus the development of factories for textile machinery had a positive effect on American industry in two ways: on the one hand, it produced a process of industrial specialisation by separating the construction of machines from the making of textiles, resulting in a reduction in costs; on the other hand, it constituted an important pool of experience which was to influence other kinds of machine enterprises.[72]

The wool and shoe industries can be seen to have undergone the same course of development as the cotton industry though in an even more accentuated form. Thus at the end of 1860, the United States had more than $1\frac{1}{2}$ million operatives in manufacture.[73]

This rapid process of industrialisation characterised by the high cost of labour led to a steady rise in living standards; this is particularly discernible in the more industrialised regions of the North-east. One of the most significant effects of this economic situation was the remarkable growth of internal demand; in the long run, this expansion of the market stimulated the production of manufactured goods. In fact, to meet the growth in demand, the development of the specialisation of functions led to the birth of the standardised product.

An English commission closely analysing US manufacture in the 1850s studied this economically favourable situation[74]; the main cause of this widening in the market was located in the development of regional specialisations together with the growth of inter-regional trade. For this reason the textile and clothing industries and the production of high consumption goods in general assumed a national character.[75]

As we have said more than once, if on the one hand the reduced dimensions of the labour market encouraged the employment of large sums of capital in production, on the other hand, it increasingly acted as a brake on productive potential. In other words, even the extremely high rate of immigration from Europe and the notable level of social mobility could not keep pace with the speed of industrialisation. If this situation remained unchanged in the period here examined, it is also true that around the 1830s it is possible to detect the beginnings of processes in the labour market which were to swell the supply of labour and therefore subsequently to boost productive capacity. In fact, the process of regional specialisation we have mentioned deepened the socio-economic fracture between the states of the North-east and those of the South.[76]

The cotton trade contributed to this phenomenon. The constant specialisation in cotton production in the South brought about a situation in which the Southern states only produced modest amounts of other consumer goods, particularly machine tools, auxiliary to their economy and thus came to rely increasingly on the manufacturing economy of the North and the agricultural economy of the Western states. In consequence, the rising profits which the Southern economy derived from the export of cotton drained away again through the acquisition of goods and services. If this process accentuated overall demand and thus the productive capacity of agricultural and industrialised regions, at the same time, it also rendered the Southern slave economy more and more dependent.[77]

In the middle of the nineteenth century, the territory of the United States could thus be divided into three parts, each of which had its own kind of society: the landowning and slave-trading South, where cotton was the main product; the agricultural West dominated by small independent farmers; and the heavily industrialised regions of the North-east. The peasant class living on the fertile land of the West tended both economically and culturally to be most tied to the political interests of the South upon which it largely relied for its agricultural trade.[78] On the other hand, the uncultivated lands of the West attracted most of the immigrant labour, leaving the demand for labour in the North-east still unsatisfied. It was therefore northern capital's political attempt to break the economic barriers which hemmed it in that caused deep social changes and intensified that political-economic conflict between South and North which was to lead to the Civil War.[79]

Between the end of the Napoleonic wars and the outbreak of the Civil War, the West developed from a land of pioneers into a land of commercial agriculture. Up to the end of the 1830s most of the surplus from agricultural production went to nourish the more specialised economy of the South. This situation changed with the development of manufacture in the East and the consequent rise in the demand for the agricultural products of the West. This specialisation in the western economy, and its reversion to the North, meant that the produce of these states had to come onto the new northern market at prices competitive with those of the agricultural economy still thriving in these industrial areas. The produce of the West gradually increased its competitiveness to the detriment of New England agriculture largely due to the reduction in transport costs. This in turn caused a constant flow of peasants from farm to factory, considerably increasing the supply of wage labour.[80]

This situation was to the considerable advantage of industrial capital but it did not solve the crucial problem of the high cost of labour, especially in comparison with that in the industrialised countries of the old world during this period.

The comparative density of the old and the new countries, differing as they do, will account for the very different feelings with which the increase of machinery has been regarded in many parts of this country [England] and the United States, where the workmen hail with satisfaction all mechanical improvements, the importance and value of which, as releasing them from the drudgery of unskilled labour, they are enabled by education to understand and appreciate.[81]

Processes of Disintegration and a New Policy of Social Control: The Institutional Hypothesis

Amongst the most important effects of the profound economic transformation the United States underwent during the first half of the nineteenth century, we must highlight the emergence of a new composition of social classes and the extensive breakdown of the old colonial sociocultural order; in the face of these changes, a different evaluation of the social order, together with what was now a political consideration of the problem of control of the marginal classes, became evident.

A deep and widespread conviction as to the structural peculiarity of the economic processes lay at the basis of this new approach to social problems. This conception – nourished by a large dose of optimism as to the future course of the new republic – firmly negated the notion that the experiences of the past or of other countries could somehow resolve emerging problems, in so far as it underlined the uniqueness of its own social universe.

The euphoria borne of the knowledge that one was 'living in a different world', the polemical willingness to highlight the new, and the immeasurable horizons still open to the young country, sharpened the critical faculty of American culture in its analysis of its own social reality. In this light, both the struggle against pauperism and the desire to defeat criminality were, on the one hand, seen as rightful movements in opposition to legacies from the old colonial period, that is, they opposed the reality linked to the old world; on the other hand, these problems were seen as being, in any event, capable of resolution within the new economic context.

The change is significant and radical: the phenomenon connected to processes of social emargination, no longer seen as the inevitable effects of human society, now came to be interpreted as a political problem, that is, as a problem for which a positive solution could – indeed should – be found. What grew with this heartfelt and widespread conviction was the knowledge – as we have already stressed – that people were in a favourable and perhaps unique economic position: well-being and prosperity could come to all.

> In this country [it was enthusiastically proclaimed] the labour of three days will readily supply the wants of seven, while in Europe the labour of the whole week will barely suffice for the maintenance and support of the family of an industrious labourer or peasant.[82]

The following necessarily followed from this premise:

> ... in a country where labour is paid for in a ration double to that of any other, where all the necessaries of life are so abundant and cheap ... there can be no danger of a meritorious individual being allowed to suffer.[83]

The abundance of uncultivated, fertile lands supported contemporary opinions as to the possibilities of finally defeating pauperism. In 1819, Cadwalleder Colden, the Mayor of New York, could state that:

> Our situation is not, and cannot be for ages, similar to that of England ... while we have so many millions of acres of uncultivated land; it is impossible that any portion of our population should want employment.[84]

The optimistic vision of an imminently bright future full of wealth and prosperity for all suffered no exceptions; this ideal tension thus cemented political commitment to the struggle against distress and poverty fought in the unwavering certainty of sure victory. 'The people of the United States', it was declared, 'escaped from the poverty of Europe; now it is high time to inquire how they can, as far as may be, escape from their own poverty.'[85]

The Commission of Inquiry set up in 1820s for the study (and subsequent legislative recommendation) of the true extent of pauperism in the

United States was inspired by the above ideals even though the Commission had to tackle a real situation considerably removed from its assumptions – despite everything, the United States was still a country with a relatively large number of poor people.

The Commission, headed by Yates, calculated that in 1822 in the state of New York – with about 1,300,000 people – a good 22,111 poor were assisted in one way or another at a cost of over $250,000.[86] Similarly, the Quincy Commission reported that the town of Boston alone gave assistance to 6000 people a year.[87] Small towns and country areas painted a similar picture.

At least up to the end of the 1830s, there is a ready explanation as to the cause of this phenomenon: the high rate of internal social mobility, the mass desertions of rural workers from landed estates to the west, and the rising levels of immigration did not succeed in providing labour for industry in a short space of time. In other words, manufacture and factories could not completely absorb the workforce available, at least to begin with. It has thus been calculated that in the Jacksonian era, the stable labour force employed in industry was never more than 5 per cent of the whole working population.[88] On the other hand, in the initial period of accumulation, the US economy was essentially agricultural and wage levels among rural workers were very much lower than those among industrial employees.

Certainly these were not the conclusions arrived at by the Commissions of Inquiry concerned with the problem of pauperism at that time. The analytical efforts to locate the causal factor of a problem prevailing in a country both wealthy and needy of labour bore a striking resemblance to the earlier European approaches in countries flooded by members of marginal classes. In fact, they arrived at the same conclusion: if the economic situation effectively permits full employment, the principal cause of pauperism must lie within the individual. Thus the old social view of the poor typical of the colonial period was finally overthrown; now discussion focused on the undeserving poor ('pauper') and the deserving ('poor'): in general, the needy and distressed were considered to be personally responsible for their status.

But even at this stage of accepting a voluntaristic explanation of 'being poor' – conducive to a 'punitive' approach – we must bear in mind that the analysis at that time (even if only unconsciously) took account of the social processes of disintegration caused by economic factors; that is, there was an awareness of the effects of a rapid process of industrialisation and of the demolition of the old political-cultural order on the social behaviour of growing sections of the population. Thus the theme of pauperism came to be intimately connected with the problem of deviant and criminal behaviour; a connection which tended to remain constant in the future. The Association for Improving the Condition of the Poor concluded:

> Official data show how a large part of the pauperism of this city and State is occasioned by indolence, intemperance, and other vices ... There is little pauperism among us not directly or indirectly traceable to these and kindred sources.[89]

Contemporary documents frequently recorded alcoholism as the primary cause of social breakdown; its connection with a state of economic distress (or rather the total absence of an 'enthusiasm' and 'love' for work) is stubbornly stressed. Certainly, however, the immoderate use of alcohol reached very high levels, particularly amongst those residents in the great urban centres. The Association for Improving the Condition of the Poor noted:

> The careful inquires on this subject, show that the mechanics of this city expend a large a sum for strong drink ... In the whole of New York City, there is one tavern for every eighteen families; but in the precincts of the lower classes ... there is one grog shop for every five or ten families.[90]

A doctor using statistics at hand follows this observation with the comment that 90 per cent of those in almshouses must be considered as alcoholics.[91]

Moral invective against the vice of drinking – a genuine scourge of the lower classes – was accompanied by the observation that the pauperisation of the urban proletariat was rooted in a lack of personal care and attention and the absence of thrifty habits.[92] In this light, the problem presented by the existence of marginal sections amongst the lower classes came to be directly or indirectly traced back to a question of culpable and thus reprehensible behaviour. The diffusion of these new ways of looking at the problem overturned the colonial view of pauperism. In fact, the whole pre-revolutionary system of poor relief lacked both a political perception of poverty and a moralistic evaluation of the question; the deep-rooted conviction that the existence of the needy was a natural phenomenon and thus a necessary feature of social life had brought about the development of a system of assistance based on charitable and private relief (household and neighbour relief). It is clear therefore that as soon as poverty began to be attributed to 'vice' (unwillingness to work) the colonial system of assistance was automatically thrown into crisis.

In fact, from the 1820s onwards, the colonial system of assistance increasingly became the target of energetic and violent criticism. Given its premises, the reasoning behind the attacks was as follows: if those social strata debilitated by alcohol and laziness fall into a state of distress, then charitable relief can only exacerbate the problem by producing an assisted population which is more dependent on collective generosity and benevolence than on its own resources and working potential.

In this context, any practical alternative could only lead in one direction: progressive abolition of the original system of private assistance and strengthening of public relief through forced labour. The 'old' poor-houses, workhouses and almshouses were thus revitalised; there was new interest in these institutions, which hitherto had not represented a real alternative to the existing system of social control. The institutional hypothesis, that is, the hypothesis that the mass of the poor, the idle and vagabonds should be forcibly confined and that public administration would provide education through work, was progressively put into practice. Thus in the United States of America during the first half of the nineteenth century, the institutional hypothesis – the preference for confinement – was placed at the centre of the whole policy of social control; the segregational choice, initially restricted to the problem of pauperism, progressively expanded, almost by osmosis alone, until it assumed the role of a paradigmatic model of the struggle against different forms of social deviancy.

The problem of vagrant children and destitute orphans was one of the first to be confronted in the clear knowledge of its causal dependence on the state of social disintegration of the lower classes and, in particular, on the profound crisis which faced the patriarchal family.[93] The risk that today's mass of abandoned young might become tomorrow's criminals was also taken seriously. The response to this danger was again forced confinement: the farm-school modelled on the workhouse provided an appropriate institution for juveniles.[94]

The new approach towards mental illnesses was similar even if it had many specific features of its own. The pivot around which the whole political-scientific debate on the origins of insanity revolved in the Jacksonian era in fact presents interesting analogies with the then dominant interest in locating the various forms of 'social disorders' – in this case mental illness – inside the economic processes of the new state. Now that the original explanation of 'psychic disturbance' as a demonic phenomenon, or in its most refined form, as an inevitable aspect of an anatomically perceptible pathology of the mind had been critically superseded, insanity was clearly related to the greater process of erosion of primitive social cohesion.[95] Mental disorder – explained Javis[96] – is part of the price we pay for civilisation; whilst Earle added that it was possible to demonstrate a parallel between the progress of society and the rise of insanity.[97] And this, he stated, was the main reason for the relatively high rate of insanity in the New World.[98] As Javis explained to a Massachusetts medical society meeting:

In this country where no son is necessarily confined to the work or employment of his father, but all the fields of labor, of profit, or of honor are open to whomsoever will put on the harness ... [and where] all are invited to join the strife for that which may be gained in each [it is inevitable that] the ambition of some leads them to aim at that which they cannot reach, to strive for more than they can grasp ... [as a result] their mental powers are strained to their utmost tension, their labour in agitation ... their minds struggle under the disproportionate burden.[99]

Thus the analysis of the remote cause of mental deviancy became more and more precise: in so far as the cycles of inflation, speculation and technical innovation in both commerce and industry render economic life precarious, they induce moments of tension, the social impact of which inevitably rebounds on the psychic level, particularly amongst the more 'exposed' and 'fragile' individuals.[100] On the other hand, it was claimed[101] that the traditional mechanisms which seek to contain conflict were now obsolete; one could not longer place one's trust in religious institutions and the family. Like the family, religious confession suffered a deep crisis of authority, particularly amongst the urban proletariat. There was no guarantee that these institutions could provide an efficient means of socialisation and social control. This breakdown prevented these institutions from playing their former role in the assistance and care of the mentally ill.

As we can see, the line of argument in this case is analogous to that of the contemporary critique of the colonial system of charitable and private 'relief' to the poor and to the abandoned or stray young. Moreover, the solution put forward is no different from those we have already looked at: the need for public authority to take exclusive responsibility for the problem of mental deviancy. In point of fact, the final conclusion is the same: segregation and confinement in a special institution.[102] The solution has an irreproachable ideological justification: if insanity is the result of a specific social contradiction, it is unreasonable to think of eliminating it or even of merely containing it as long as the sufferer remains in the environment which undoubtedly caused the problem in the first place.[103] The basic intention is thus explicit: only by tearing the unwitting victims of the 'disorder' (the insane) out of the social fabric and by segregating them in a concentrated universe where the best regulations for social life (hierarchy, discipline, work and worship) can ultimately rule is it possible to 'cure' and 're-educate'.

Despite its particular characteristics, the history of the new forms of struggle against criminal deviance, particularly the 'invention' of the prison, was not substantially different.

The Birth of the Penitentiary: From Walnut Street Jail to Auburn Prison

The social control of criminal deviancy at the end of the eighteenth century was similar in some respects to that of the colonial period, despite the fact that the new socio-economic situation had radically altered the old repressive system.

If the jail retained its original purpose as a preventive prison, things were different when it came to the system of social control based on the institutional hypothesis of the house of correction – or workhouse (given the terminological inexactitude with which this institution came to be designated). We have already stressed how workhouses or houses of correction, originally modelled on the European institution, were for the punishment of petty criminals (*felons*); in time, they also came to house the idle and vagabonds; later, they were used as compulsory homes for the 'residential poor'; and, in some cases, they served as a prison for debtors.

From a theoretical point of view, the *discipline of work* should have operated inside this institution with the aim of forcibly imposing that re-educative process fitting to a future proletariat – purely in imitation of prevailing European practices. In colonial practice – as we have seen – this aim was totally neglected; we know that workhouse sentences, which should have been characterised by forced labour (at least according to their declared intentions), did not substantially differ from the organisation of labour in poorhouses: that is, the form of labour adopted was modelled on the large colonial family.

With the advent of manufacturing and with the vast processes of social transformation which accompanied capitalist accumulation, agricultural forced labour, which prevailed in this institution, came to seem increasingly anachronistic. The basic reason for this was that since a number of technical and economic difficulties impeded the use in the workhouse of a system based on machinery which could compete with the outside world, the house of correction increasingly functioned in a manner typical of prison institutions, that is, it assumed the role of a segregated universe – now confined to purely punitive aims – for those to whom other kinds of sanction were not appropriate. As a direct consequence of this change in the role of the house of correction, there was a gradual departure from the original aim of re-education through work, even if this effectively continued to survive in the uneconomic forms of repetitive manual work without the aid of machines. In this way, the institution came to lose its economic dimension, its existence becoming a heavy burden to the authorities; the administrators of the New World were particularly concerned with financial order.[104]

On the other hand, the original colonial system of assistance based on charitable relief (household and neighbour relief) now entered a definitive crisis. With the progressive abolition of the private and non-segregational system of assistance and the strengthening of public relief by means of compulsory labour, the institutional hypothesis – that is, the preference for confinement – emerged as the central feature of policies of social control. The scope of segregation, originally limited to pauperism, steadily grew. The immediate and direct effect was an uncontrollable rise in the institutional population.

By the end of the eighteenth century, the system was plainly contradictory and it was actually similar to that described by Howard in England at the time of his survey: the true and proper prisons – we refer here to jails as institutions of preventive custody – were empty or half-empty, while the houses of correction or workhouses overflowed with a population that was more heterogeneous than ever (petty offenders, authentic criminals to whom corporal punishment did not apply, illegal immigrants, non-resident poor, local needy, etc.)

The central contradiction is brought out in the following paradox: the more institutionalisation became the instrument of social control, the more compulsory and productive labour as a means of resocialisation disappeared from the institutions themselves for objective economic reasons. Inevitably, at this stage, institutionalisation was transformed into a legitimate punishment in which repressive and deterrent functions triumphed over the original aim of reeducation. It was in the attempt to resolve this problem that the United States, through its reforming fantasies about social control, arrived at its most original 'invention': the penitentiary system.

In the last decade of the eighteenth century, the endemic scarcity of labour produced a singularly favourable situation; the violent redistribution of landed property had caused a vast process of internal social mobility which, coupled with growing levels of immigration from Europe and the low cost of raw materials, permitted the profitable use of capital in nascent manufacture. This is probably what gave the solution to the problem of the uneconomical nature of the workhouse system its quite particular shape. The chronic deficit which local authorities incurred in running these institutions resulted, as we have seen, essentially from two causes: the high cost of supervision and the non-productiveness of institutional labour. Thus, in abstract terms, there were two possible solutions: to find a system which was more economic to run or to raise the productivity of institutional labour.

In the period we are examining, preference was given to the first option.[105] As a matter of fact, boosting labour productivity would have necessitated the expenditure of large amounts of capital (private or public) in order to introduce industrial techniques. This solution was not viewed favourably for the simple reason that the relative availability of labour meant that capital investment on the free market was more profitable.

This simple economic evaluation – undoubtedly explicitly present on more than one occasion in the minds of the protagonists of penitentiary reform themselves – was then accompanied by a whole range of other considerations of an essentially ethical-social nature.

Once more the Quaker Sects were the protagonists of a significant 'revolution' in the sphere of criminal policy. In 1787, the 'Philadelphia Society for Alleviating the Miseries of Public Prisons', was founded; the moral tone and the declared philanthropic aims of the society are clear from the following preamble to its constitution:

When we consider that the obligations of benevolence, which are founded on the precepts and example of the Author of Christianity, are not cancelled by the follies or crimes of our fellow creatures ... it becomes us to extend our compassion to that part of mankind who are the subjects of these miseries ... By the aids of humanity, their undue and illegal sufferings may prevented; ... and prevented ... and such degrees and modes of punishment may be discovered and suggested, as may, instead of containing habits of vice, become the means of restoring our fellow creatures to virtue and happiness.[106]

It was due to this philanthropic society's incisive and constant appeals to the public that legislation was drawn up in 1790 to establish an institution in which 'solitary confinement to hard labour and a total abstinence from spirituous liquors, will prove the most effectual means of reforming these unhappy creatures'.[107] By legislative order, work was begun in the garden of the Walnut Street (preventive) jail on the construction of a cellular building providing for the solitary confinement of those condemned to detentive punishments. The pre-existing construction was to remain as a preventive prison.[108]

Under the same legislative provision, it was laid down that the Walnut Street prison authorities would also use the new building to house inmates from workhouses in other Pennsylvanian towns until similar institutions were built elsewhere. In fact, this never happened and the Philadelphian penitentiary system functioned from the outset as the 'state penitentiary' rather than as a town penitentiary; the situation remained unchanged and this example came to be copied in other states: in 1796 at Newgate in the state of New York, in 1804 at Charleston, Massachusetts and Baltimore, Maryland and in 1803 at Windsor, Vermont.[109]

This form of penitentiary punishment was based on the solitary confinement of inmates, the rule of silence, meditation and worship. In the first place, the system drastically cut the cost of supervision and in the second place, the rigid segregation of each individual denied a priori the possibility of introducing any form of industrial organisation into the prison.[110]

It must be stressed that this punitive hypothesis was not wholly original: the Belgian *Maison de Force* and Bentham's Panopticon,[111] which was put into limited practice in England, were clear precursors of cellular prisons. It is easy enough to identify the ideology behind this hypothesis: the structure of this building was able to satisfy the needs of any institution in which 'people must be kept under surveillance'[112] – not just prisons but also workhouses, factories, hospitals, *lazzarettos* and schools.

The problem of high running costs was thus partially resolved: this was one of the reasons for the rapid diffusion of this model of punishment in the various American states.

Certainly the economic preoccupations we have stressed were sublimated on an ideological level in the most extreme formulations of Protestant thought; a fact which is reasonably comprehensible from a Weberian analysis. This point has some importance; in fact, it assists in an understanding of the assumed good faith which characterised the fanaticism with which specific religious beliefs were directly and ruthlessly applied to the organisation of prisons of the Philadelphian kind. There was no confusion in the minds of these reformers, who were convinced that solitary confinement was capable of resolving every penitentiary problem: it prevented the disastrous spread of criminality that was thought to occur when inmates were allowed to mix freely; and it promoted, through isolation and silence, that psychological process of introspection considered to be the most efficient means of obtaining repentance.[113] Apart from these reasons, the overall solution to the problem of labour should not be underestimated: in a system of solitary confinement, labour could not be economical since it was of an artisan nature. On the other hand, in the conception of the penitentiary, work, even in ideal terms, was not endowed with any economic function; on the contrary, it was seen as a purely therapeutic instrument. Thus the report of the Board of Inspectors in 1837 in the state of New Jersey came to the conclusion that the Philadelphian system was undoubtedly the most humane and civilised system known, even though the facts revealed an increase in the incidence of suicide and insanity as the direct result of this system of punishment.

But the definitive crisis of the Philadelphian conception was not so much due to humanitarian considerations (which were certainly not lacking) as to an important change on the labour market; at the beginning of the nineteenth century, as we have already seen, there was a considerable rise in the demand for labour, which was more intensive, for example, than in mercantilist Europe. Slave trading became increasingly difficult to operate in the light of new legislation whilst the labour market lagged behind the demand for labour created by the conquest of new territories and rapid industrialisation, even though the birth-rate and immigration levels were growing: the immediate effect of this economic situation was the remarkable rise in wage levels, already quite high by other standards.

Amongst its more significant social consequences, the scarcity of labour resulted in that new political consideration of the marginal classes we have already noted. The underlying causes of the 'criminal question' were now seen as being essentially 'different' in the United States, compared to the Old World: for example, the lower level of crime. It was felt that the real possibilities of finding well-paid work in America would quickly reduce the need to commit crimes against property while the availability of work, even to the ex-convict, as a result of the economic situation was an incentive not to repeat offences. Thus it can be readily understood that what came to the fore in this debate, particularly from administrators of penal justice, were the following accusations against the existing penitentiary system: that solitary confinement not only deprived the market of labour but also, through the uneconomic nature of the work they were forced to do, diseducated the inmates, thus reducing their original working capacities. These criticisms of and deep reservations about the cellular penitentiary system did not differ, therefore, from those formulated and championed by Europeans who had, in their time, opposed the policy of exterminating workers, that is, the 'bloody legislation' against the idle and vagabonds.

For these reasons productive work was introduced – or rather reintroduced – in prisons: at first the fact that the system of solitary confinement continued unchanged undermined the whole initiative.[114] Compulsory labour in the cells was still an insuperable obstacle to the introduction of industrial organisation – the introduction of machinery and common work. In other words, the attempt to change the content of the punishment did no more than reimpose the economic contradiction which had been the chief cause of the gradual disappearance of work in workhouses or houses of correction in the first place. To compel prisoners to carry out work in which physical effort played a fundamental part could not overcome the diagnosed difficulties: prisons remained an unproductive investment since they could not compete with the productivity of the so-called free labourer and since, at the same time, inmates could not be educated to the skills and abilities required of a modern worker.

The first rational attempt to arrive at a form of punishment capable of overcoming these contradictions was made at the Auburn penitentiary (from which the term Auburn system derives). In time, the widespread adoption of this system made it synonymous in practice with American penitentiary administration.

This new 'penitentiary system' was based on two fundamental criteria: solitary confinement by night and communal work by day.[115] The principle of solitary confinement was to a significant extent retained in the rule of absolute silence (at times the Auburn system was called the silent system) which prevented contact between inmates and forced them to meditate, so reinforcing the functions of both discipline and general education.

Thus the originality of this new system lay essentially in the introduction of work structured in the same way as the dominant form of factory work. A number of developments gradually took shape: first (as we shall see in detail in the next paragraph), the individual capitalist could be granted a concession under which he could transform the prison institution itself into a factory at his own expense; secondly, a contractual scheme was adopted whereby the institutional organisation was run by the administration but the direction of work and the sale of goods was handled and controlled by a contractor. At a later stage, the private contractor simply distributed the product on the market. This last phase signalled the final form of prison industrialisation.[116] But the peculiarity of this form of prison sentence was not just in its economic content but more specifically in its inclusion of factors such as education, discipline and the form of treatment itself, all of which are directly traceable to the existence of 'productive work' in the punishment.

For example, the form of discipline was radically changed; the reasons are obvious. In the first place, productive work itself – as it imposes regulations necessary for the interaction of the convicts which dictate the form and timing of their activity – replaces discipline based simply on supervision by the internal discipline of labour organisation. Secondarily, it was recognised that workers were much more motivated into working by the prospect of 'reward' rather than under the threat of 'punishment'.

And it is precisely on the basis of this second point that a form of prison sentence was structured: going beyond the ideological screen which purported that treatment was of a re-educative nature, the real judgement of good conduct was based on working ability.[117] For example, this criterion inspired the idea of commuting sentences which exceeded five years; these could be reduced by up to one quarter for good behaviour. On the same fundamental level, in terms of learning new work techniques, inmates 'condemned to short sentences' and those subject 'to long sentences' were separated. The latter group was assigned to special institutions in which work organisation was more productive, requiring a higher grade of ability and thus a longer period of confinement.[118] For the same reason, even if from a different angle, short sentences were criticised as diseducative and above all, unproductive.

But the most important objective achieved by the introduction of productive work in prison was the possibility (exploited for the whole of the nineteenth century) of lowering the cost of production in certain industrial sectors and of restraining rising wage levels through competition.

Forms of Exploitation and Convict Labour Policy

Throughout the period spanned by this study, the American penitentiary system developed – even if only superficially in some respects – those different forms of exploitation/utilisation of convict labour which were to constitute the economic guidelines of penitentiary policy right up to this day.[119] The central core of this policy could only be fully implemented in the first decades of the twentieth century. This was due to programmatic state intervention in the economy together with working-class opposition to the private use of convict labour. However, it is important to underline that even before the Civil War, that is, during the birth and formation of the capitalist state, the theme of convict employment was at the centre of a heated debate.

As we seek to give a critical view of political-economic perspectives on convict labour emerging at that time, we think it useful to make some general observations with a view to evaluating the structural constants which, in an historic analysis, identify the real basis of the problem rather than the ideological aspect.

We will leave aside the fact that many reformers wanted to transform the penitentiary into a productive enterprise, to make convict labour into an economic business, since this was rarely realised in the period under examination here. The various systems of production, together with the different legal forms of convict labour employment, must be carefully interpreted as 'planning attempts' to modify (re-define) the institutional world on the current economic- productive model of the free market (manufacture, factory).

If these various institutions – true juridical 'inventions' – did not achieve their hoped-for success from a productivist point of view, they still succeeded in radically changing penitentiary practices, thereby effectively transforming the model of the prison sentence. Thus penitentiary labour invented *models* which were aimed much more at the *creation* of that 'virtual subject' from time to time imposed by the free market than to the economically meaningful production of goods.

In this period, the question of *remuneration*, of wages for the convict labourer, remained profoundly ambiguous. These terms were used and thus understood in a juridically inappropriate sense, in that they bore no proportional relationship either to the inmate's working performance or to the wage levels on the free market. Clearly, the introduction of this variant of economic participation of the convict labourer had the indirect aim of imposing on the prisoner the moral form of wages as the condition of his own existence.

> Prison wages are not a reward for effort; they function instead as a device for transforming individual people; a juridical fiction, as wages here do not represent 'freely given' labour power but are an artifice making the technique of correction effective.[120]

The main systems of prison labour in America were as follows: 1. *public account*; 2. *contract*; 3. *piece-price*; 4. *lease*; 5. *state-use*; and 6. *public works*. These 'models' (each one appearing in a wide variety of forms and combinations) are easier to understand if we bear in mind that each one represented at different times a compromise, sometimes even between opposing approaches, in the existing juridical system depending on the external economic- political situation. The principal variables conditioning the dominance of one system over another were:

1. Pressure from the entrepreneurial class (in the face of a fluctuation in the demand for labour) to use convict labour to regulate wage spirals.
2. Organised working-class resistance against the competitive use of prison labour in production.
3. Economic difficulties faced by the administrators in the industrialisation of the productive process inside the penitentiary.
4. The predominance of agriculture or industry, depending on the economic and geographical situation.

5. In a dependent relationship with these 'objective' reasons: the issuing from time to time of 'humanitarian' and 'philanthropic' appeals which were falsely progressive, were concerned with affirming the essentially re-educative and remedial nature of prison punishment and were thus strongly opposed to the exploitation of convict labour by private enterprise.

The normative systems above came to prevail at one time or another to varying degrees; they were spread along a 'range of positions' which are easily identified. At either end of this range, there were two completely opposed 'positions':

1. *Convict labour completely organised and run by the prison administration.* From this it usually followed that: (i) the penitentiary staff were in charge of discipline; (ii) goods were not manufactured for the free market but were 'absorbed' by the state; (iii) there was no 'remuneration' for the labourers employed; (iv) the productive process was backward, rarely industrialised and essentially manual.
2. *Convict labour organised by a private contractor, sometimes 'outside' the prison institution.* The characteristics of this system were: (i) the private contractor had complete responsibility for the maintenance and discipline of the prison population; (ii) the goods were sold on the free market; (iii) the convict-labourer was partially 'remunerated'; (iv) production was economically efficient and frequently industrialised.

The rest of the 'models' are in intermediary positions between these two extremes. In looking schematically at the various systems of prison labour, we will first follow the logical-systematic order listed below; this order partially contradicts chronological order; in dealing with an historic analysis, we will then readjust the 'real order' we have momentarily disturbed.

1. The 'model' of the state-use system,[121] introduced in penitentiary practice relatively late on, is an attempt at obviating the disadvantages of the private exploitation of prison labour, above all else, the 'inconveniences' attendant on competition between free and prison labour.

The penitentiary produces goods but instead of selling them on the market, they are 'consumed' by the prison or by other state authorities. Though this system was more favourably received by trade unionists and 'moralists' who were against private exploitation, it unavoidably tends to reduce work to a barely productive process when the demand for goods and services by the administration is lower than the supply.

2. A particular variant of the state-use system is the public works system.[122] Here inmates are employed by the prison administration for public works outside the penitentiary, for example, in road and railway building or the construction of other prisons.

3. One of the first juridical forms of convict labour was the public account system.[123] Here the prison institution is transformed into a company: it acquires raw materials, organises production and finally sells goods on the free market at the best possible prices. In this way, all profits belong to the state and the imposition of discipline falls completely on the penitentiary authorities.

   This system was strongly opposed by the working class; the inmates received no pay for their work and this permitted the administration to place goods on the market at extremely competitive prices. Also, the absence of wages from production costs permitted such high profit margins that the administration had no incentive to increase capital investment (buildings, machines, etc.). Thus the form of production adopted in the public account system was 'backward' (usually shoes, scarves, cord, boots and brushes, etc.).

4. One model of convict labour rarely employed was that of the piece-price system.[124] Here the prison authorities attempted to reconcile the use of a private contractor with its own right to handle production and discipline. In fact the contractor is completely excluded from penitentiary 'life'; he simply furnishes raw materials, and in rare cases, the tools and machinery. He then receives the finished product for which the administration pays him a fixed price by the piece. The products are finally placed on the market and the convict-labourer is 'paid' on piece- rate.

5. The contract system was the most widely adopted model of convict labour.[125] Here the prisoners worked inside the prison but they were not dependent on or controlled by the penitentiary authorities.

In fact, it was the private contractor (who paid the state a contractually fixed price for every working day and for every prisoner employed) who with his own staff ran and supervised the labourers in the prison workshops. Hence the inmates were subject to two kinds of authority: to work discipline under the supervision of the contractor and to prison discipline during the times they were not engaged in work.

Under this regime, there was daily 'remuneration'. The tools and machinery were usually furnished by the administration, whereas the raw materials were the contractor's responsibility; just as the whole organisation of work was his responsibility so was the handling of goods on the free market. This practice also gave undeniable economic advantage to the administration: (a) prison labour was profitably employed; (b) benefits to the state were guaranteed without risk. Prisons adopting this system made up to 65 per cent of their running costs as against a maximum of 32 per cent in penitentiaries adopting the public account system.[126] However, inevitably, the prison labourer tended to be exploited to an intolerable extent; at the same time, the competition between free and convict labour led to organised working-class struggles for the abolition of this system, which was rightly seen as a means by which wage spirals could be regulated.

Again, the re-educative dimension of this hypothesis tended to be subordinated to the needs of production pure and simple, even to the point of the physical destruction of the labour force.

6. The last, most important and most widespread system was called the leasing system.[127] In this case, the state temporarily abdicated all direction and control of the institution; inmates were actually 'hired out' to a contractor for a fixed period and for a fixed sum. The contractor had to provide for the maintenance of the prison population and was responsible for its discipline. The advantages for the penitentiary administration were undeniable; as a matter of fact, this system proved the most 'remunerative': however low the price paid by the contractor, the proceeds of the contract were always net of costs.

This system, which was widely adopted in the South for plantation work, not only worsened the level of exploitation (the most brutal forms of corporal punishment were meted out to convict labourers who resisted discipline and the pace of work), but gave rise to a dangerous compromise between the judiciary and business interests with the result that small sentences were transformed into medium and long ones.[128]

In reconstructing the history of convict labour systems in the United States in the first half of the nineteenth century, we find ourselves running alongside, in the specifics of the organisation of work, the evolution of the penitentiary system itself. That is to say, the history of the penitentiary system follows the lines of development of penitentiary labour. Or even better: *the history of the rise of the American prison is* (also) *the history of models of prison employment* (with the caution that the term 'model of employment' is not intended in an exclusively economic sense but also in the sense of 'model of education in a particular form of subordinated work'). In this way, the close dependence between those 'outside' and those 'inside' is reaffirmed not just generally but also in a more qualified and qualifying sense: to be precise: between economic process of/in the free labour market and the penitentiary. If the counterposition between solitary confinement and the silent system (Philadelphian and Auburnian) finds its economic-social justification in the predominance of manufacture or industrial production, in the same way, it reaffirms its structurally antinomic nature in the employment of its prison labour. In fact, the penitentiary system inspired by the principle of solitary confinement actually adopts the criterion of the public account; that organised around the principle of the silent system adopts the contract system. Two radically different penitentiary systems; two modes of exploitation of the labour force diametrically opposed to each other.

The contrast between the two models of penitentiary punishment – initially proposed here purely for reasons of exposition – thus finds further confirmation in this particular area:

1. The cellular prison at Philadelphia presents on a miniature scale *the ideal model* of bourgeois society and early capitalism (that is, the abstract idea of how class and production relations ought to be organised on the 'free market'). Thus work need not necessarily be productive so much as instrumental to the designs of the ruling class at that time – the desire to 'transform' the criminal into a 'subordinate being'; the virtual model of 'subordinate' which prison punishment based on

solitary confinement proposes is that of the worker still employed in production of a craft nature in the workshop. To this end, education for labour must pass through a productive process which is essentially manual and where fixed capital is practically non-existent.

The public account system satisfies this necessity: the organisation of production is the complete responsibility of the penitentiary administration and, as we have seen, since this is unpaid work, goods can be placed on the market at extremely competitive terms without the necessity of 'industrialising' the productive process.

2. The Auburn penitentiary theory, however, puts forward a model of labour subordinated on industrial lines. Where the silent system prevails, labour-saving machines and communal work are introduced along with factory discipline. The contract system thus provides the best model to accommodate this. The contractor enters the prison, efficiently organises production, industrialises the workshops, partially pays for work done, manufactures noncraft goods and personally handles the distribution of these goods on the free market.

Historically, it was only in 1796 at Newgate prison (New York) – built on the principle of solitary confinement – that convict labour in the form of the public account system was introduced for the first time; in 1797 the state of Virginia introduced the same system in the Richmond penitentiary; in both cases shoes and boots were produced.[129] Later, in New Jersey (1799) and Massachusetts (1802) old legislation which made relations and guardians responsible for the provision of work to minors and imprisoned dependents in houses of correction[130] were abrogated; at the same time new prisons for preventive custody and some state penitentiaries were built – there labour was organised along the lines of the public account system.

This original system also initially prevailed in the Auburn penitentiary, whilst the Sing-Sing penitentiary was built in 1825 by 100 prison workers under the public works system.[131] Following this example, in 1844, New York State erected Donnemora prison. It was only in 1807 that Massachusetts introduced the contract system in its penitentiary. In time, this became the prevalent model for prison labour: in 1824 it was adopted at the Auburn penitentiary, in 1828 at Connecticut and finally in 1835 at Ohio.[132]

It was due to exclusively economic reasons that the public account system was progressively abandoned and replaced by the contract system. Production under the public account system was inferior in quality to that obtained from free labour and therefore was confined to a restricted market resulting in heavy debt for the penitentiary administrations.

The already precarious financial situation of prison labour was worsened by the rapid process of industrialisation in the realm of 'free' production at that time: among other things, massive investment in the renewal of fixed capital and the introduction of new and more efficient machinery considerably reduced production costs and therefore the price of goods; thus the administration's profits from the use of prison labour were ultimately reduced. The immediate and direct effect of this 'external' situation was a growth in 'unemployment' levels amongst convict labourers.[133]

These economic processes affecting the penitentiaries were accompanied by a more general deterioration. The penitentiary administrations responded to mounting deficits by progressively reducing their own running costs; the prisoners' standard of living fell to subsistence level; they were made to pay the price of economic contradictions. Automatically 'penitentiary reform' backtracked: punishment again became a 'way of destroying' the workforce.[134]

If the phenomena we have summarised here aroused the concern of enlightened reformers, it also stimulated the interest of the employing class, which was seriously concerned at the scarcity of labour as a result of new industrial production. Thus if the reformers pleaded for a different economic use of the mass of prisoners, whilst administrations complained that convict labour did not pay, the employers, on their part, offered an alternative which would definitively resolve the problem: the conditions for the adoption of the contract system had been realised.[135]

The entrance of capitalist employers into the penitentiary and the consequent transformation of prison into factory – by means of a violent process of industrialisation in the workshops – reversed the chronic situation in which 'penitentiary reform' found itself; the model based on the principle of the silent system came to define the new contract system, that is, intensive and private exploitation of prison labour. Or rather, the need to use convict labour economically took private capital into the prison under the juridical form of the contract; private capital transformed prison into factory; it imposed the discipline of labour on the institutionalised population; thus the silent system emerged as a model of 'penitentiary pedagogy' for an industrialised prison, for a prison-factory.

The effects of this transformation will be examined when we come to describe the Auburn penitentiary model; suffice it to note here that according to this new hypothesis, the *virtual man* (or ideal man, product of the re-educative process) which came to be imposed through subordinate work was no longer a *dependent-artisan*, a worker of/for manufacture and the workshop, but a *worker*, a disciplined operative, subordinated by/ to the factory.

This radical change in penitentiary practice, this succession of different models of education of the criminal into a subordinate being met with much resistance in the nineteenth-century United States of America, both on the part of influential public opinion and on the part of working-class organisations. Although these social forces frequently found themselves struggling side by side for the abolition of the contract system, however, their reasons for opposing this new mode of exploitation were different and, at times, antithetical.

The first objections were raised by those who feared that the new form of punishment would slacken or totally thwart the punitive content of sanctions. This position was later cloaked by humanitarian and philanthropic sentiments; the fear was hypocritically raised that private exploitation would 'brutalise' the prisoner and therefore reduce his chances of moral 'education'. The preference for a moral-religious orientation reaffirms the superiority of the Philadelphian model and hence the superiority of unproductive work.[136] This conservative standpoint was expressed by many influential voices. For example, E. Lynds, director of Sing-Sing, interviewed on the subject by de Beaumont and de Tocqueville, stated that the presence of contractors inside the prison would sooner or later totally destroy all attempts at discipline.[137] And G. Powers stated in the New York legislature in 1828:

> This mode of employing convicts is attended with considerable danger to the discipline of the prison, by bringing the convicts into contact with contractors and their agents, unless very strict rules are rigidly enforced.[138]

Finally A. Pilsbury of Connecticut came to the conclusion in 1838 that the contract system should be seen as 'Destructive to everything which may be called good, both as it relates to the institution and the prisoners'.[139]

However, these protests did not in themselves provoke any crisis in the contract system on the contrary, by the end of the 1850s this form of employment was widespread throughout practically all the American states[140] with the exception of the Southern states, where restrictions on the African slave trade led to the employment of convicts on plantation work under the leasing system.[141] However, the increasingly widespread use of the contract system led to the first organised protests by the trade union movement.[142] As early as 1823 an ad hoc Workers Commission which met at New York expressed its opposition to the threat to their organisation caused by the appearance on the market of goods manufactured in prison.[143] In the same year, engineering workers handed a petition to the authorities demanding the abolition of competing prison labour; their demands were summarised in the following terms:

> Your memorialists have seen the convicts … hired out to individuals, in some instances at reduced compensation, and in others employed for the benefit of the state, and the products of their labor thrown into market and disposed of at prices very little above the cost of materials of which they were manufactured, to the ruin of workers.[144]

In this document, it was humbly requested that if prisoners were to work, it should at least be in public works at marble quarries. This was tried out at Sing-Sing in 1825 but the experiment was unsatisfactory and was very quickly abandoned.[145] Later, at a Workers Conference in Utica in 1834, engineering workers reaffirmed their position on the contract system in the following manner:

> Mechanics are not called upon to pay in the form of taxes for the support of the prisoners only, but for the products sold that are manufactured in the prison from 40 % to 60 % less than the goods manufactured by free labor. Thus the wages are driven down to a point where a free laborer cannot live and support his family; and the consequence is that hundreds of mechanics are thrown out of employment and, in many cases, their families are reduced to beggary.[146]

Trade union opposition became more energetic in the face of mounting unemployment during the economic depression of 1834. In the same year, the New York trade unions turned to legislative powers in seeking the establishment of a special commission to examine the general situation of prison labour in the whole of the United States.[147] The commission was vested with wide powers and in its conclusion it reaffirmed the need for inmates to be set to work in some way, not just for humanitarian reasons but also in the general interests of production. Work, then, must be necessarily productive since this would assist the problem of finance. In this light the trade unions sought a compromise. They asked that prisoners should be used only for public works in the construction of roads and railways.[148] The commission responded that this suggestion would not resolve the problem of competition with free labour in so far as the job situation in this area was also 'problematic'. Instead, it proposed certain standard restrictions on contracts: (a) they should be of limited duration; (b) no new enterprise should be encouraged to use prison labour; (c) the contract should stipulate that the employer should not sell goods on the free market at a lower price than those produced by free labour. The trade unions judged the conclusion of this report to be 'deceptive'[149] and gave evidence that prison labour goods were still being sold at lower prices.[150]

A further indication of the high profitability of prison labour for the contractor, and the economic gains to the penitentiary administration, can be seen in the growing trend towards the depreciation of running costs and in the net gains for the state. For example, the Auburn Penitentiary balanced its books in 1829 and by 1830 could boast a credit of $25 and later in 1831 of at least $1800; in the same way, Wethersfield Prison went from a $1000 credit in 1828 to $3200 in 1829 and to $800 in 1831; and the Baltimore administration went from $11,500 in 1828 to about $20,000 in 1829; finally in 1835 Sing-Sing prison could count a net gain of $29,000.[151]

The energetic opposition of trade union organisations did have a partial success – even if it was only temporary – in the period immediately preceding the Civil War, partly due to a slackening of industrial development. In this period we thus witness the growth of certain alternative systems to the contract.[152] However, in the face of a considerable expansion of industries geared towards war production during the Civil War, there was again a rise in the exploitation of convict labour by means of the contract system[153]; as a result, the workers' movement toughened its stand on this form of labour. In 1864, members of the Chicago Typographical Union voted for a resolution against convict labour and asked for the speedy passage of laws prohibiting the contract system which they considered to be most prejudicial to their interests.[154]

Further, in 1878 a Milliners' Convention issued an official document in which the union's position on convict labour was reaffirmed in the following terms:

> The convention expressed its unalterable opposition to the system of hiring out to favoured contractors the labor of criminals; and adopted a resolution that it protest against turning the prisons into private workshops; that the government had no right to tax business when that government is at the same time lending its authority to destroy the business; that the chief purpose of imprisonment should be the reformation of a criminal; that his earnings should be removed from party politics; and that the convention urge in all states:
>
> 1. The abolition of the contract system.
> 2. The removal of machinery from prisons and employments of prisoners at hard labor only.
> 3. Employment of prisoners at public-works carried out by the state and for the manufacture of articles needed in prisons.
> 4. The instruction of prisoners in common educational branches.
> 5. That no merchant who deals in any manner whatever in prison-made articles be patronised directly or indirectly.
> 6. That mechanics refuse to work for or with 'any man who has been so base as to go to a state prison and instruct convicts in any branch of skilled labor'.[155]

Protests and agitation in the labour movement against penitentiary production continued right up to 1930, even if the question of competition between the two could be considered as effectively resolved by the end of the century. The official figures around the end of the nineteenth century and the beginning of the twentieth century are significant in this respect. In 1885, for example, 26 per cent of all prisoners employed in productive work were under the leasing system; in 1895, 19 percent; in 1905, 9 percent; in 1914, 4 per cent; by 1923, one could consider the system as having been completely done away with.[156] We can see the same thing occurring in relation to the contract system: in 1885, 40 per cent of prisoners worked for private contractors; in 1923, this was down to 12 per cent.[157] There were other, even more important changes: in 1885, 75 per cent of prisoners were employed in productive labour, whilst in 1923, the so-called productive prison population amounted to 61 per cent. This last factor must then be related to the following: the public account system together with the state-use and public-works systems employed just 26 per cent of prison labour in 1885, whilst by 1923 the percentage had risen to 81 per cent.[158]

Clearly the private exploitation of convict labour became obsolete as against the increasingly massive adoption of those systems of convict labour which did not compete with free labour. On the one hand, the basic reason can be traced back to the difficulties encountered by private capital when it came to industrialising the penitentiary productive process in forms which would still be competitive with technological innovations in the outside world. On the other hand, it was also located in the growing strength of the union organisations in the economic and political life of the United States. Thus at the beginning of the new century, the penitentiary ceased to be a 'productive concern': in fact budgets once again began to show growing deficits.[159]

Notes

1. This thesis is largely agreed upon by the main authors concerned with the question of poor relief during the colonial period. Among the best documented and interesting are: D. M. Schneider, *The History of Public Welfare in New York, 1609–1866* (Chicago, 1938); M. Creech, *Three Centuries of Poor Law Administration* (Chicago, 1942); J. Leiby, *Charity and Corrections in New Jersey* (New Brunswick, N J, 1967); and finally, the first chapter ('The Foundaries of Colonial Society') by D. J. Rothman, *The Discovery of the Asylum, Social Order and Disorder in the New Republic* (Boston-Toronto, 1971).

2. S. Cooper, *A Sermon Preached in Boston, New England, Before the Society for Encouraging Industry and Employing the Poor* (Boston, 1753) p. 20.
3. Besides the authors already cited in note 1, on the theme of social mobility in eighteenth-century America, see specifically: R. W. Romsey, *Carolina Cradle: Settlement of the Northwest Carolina Frontier, 1747 – 1762* (Chapel Hill, N C, 1964).
4. Besides works already cited, see: S. V. James, *A People Among People: Quaker Benevolence in Eighteenth-Century America* (Cambridge, Mass., 1963) particularly the second and third chapters.
5. See the classic (even if it is criticised by many): F. J. Turner, *The Frontier in American History* (New York, 1920).
6. Rothman, *The Discovery of the Asylum*, p. 12.
7. For an analysis of the first urban settlements in the colonial period, see: M. Zuckerman, *Peaceable Kingdoms: New England in Eighteenth Century* (New York, 1970); P. J. Grevin, Jnr., *Four Generations: Population, Land and Family in Colonial Andover, Massachusetts* (Ithaca, New York, 1970).
8. Besides Romsey already cited, for an analysis of the culture of the community of settlers, see: C. Bridenbaugh, *Cities in Revolt* (New York, 1955); H. Adams, *The United States in 1800* (Ithaca: New York, 1955).
9. Besides the authors cited in note 1, see: S. Riesenfeld, 'The Formative Era of American Assistance Law', *California Law Review* (1955) n. 43, pp. 175–223.
10. The most reliable sources on the colonial American relief system – plus some figures and statistics on the phenomenon – can be found in: C. G. Chamberlayne (ed.), *Vestry Book of St Paul's Parish, Hanover County, 1706 – 1786* (Richmond, Va., 1940); Chamberlayne (ed.), *Vestry Book and Register of St Peter's Parish, New Kent and James City Counties, Virginia, 1684–1786* (Richmond, Va., 1937); Chamberlayne (ed.), *The Vestry Book of Blisland Parish, New Kent and James City Counties, Virginia, 1721–1786* (Richmond, Va., 1935).
11. The most revealing sources which bear witness to the fact that social order was seen as being ideally based on residential stability and landed property is provided by the prolific production of preachings and sermons published in cheap editions, amongst which see: B. Colman, *The Unspeakable Gift of God: A Right Charitable and Bountiful Spirit to the Poor and Needy Members of Jesus Christ* (Boston, 1739); C. Chauncy, *The Idle Poor Secluded from the Bread of Charity by Christian Law* (Boston, 1752). A. Heimert, P. Miller (eds), *The Great Awakening* (Indianapolis, 1967).

12. In *Colonial Laws of New York from the Year 1664 to the Revolution* (Albany, 1894).

13. D. M. Schneider, *The history of Public Welfare in New York State, 1609–1866* (Chicago, 1938) ch. 2.

14. In *Laws of New York from the Year 1691 to 1751, inclusive*, (New York, 1752) pp. 143–5.

15. In *Colonial Laws of New York*, pp. 513–17.

16. In *Acts and Laws of the English Colony of Rhode-Island and Providence Plantations, in New England, in America* (New Port, R. I., 1767) pp. 228–32.

17. In *Laws of the Government of New Castle, Kent and Sussex upon Delaware* (Philadelphia, 1741) pp. 208–15.

18. In *A Complete Record of all the Acts of the Assembly of the Province of North Carolina Now in Force and Use* (Newbern, N. C., 1773) pp. 172–4.

19. Amongst the many essays on the most advanced positions on general social policy and penitentiary reform, particularly in Pennsylvania, for the moment see: T. Sellin, 'Philadelphia Prisons of the Eighteenth Century', *Transactions of the American Philosophical Society*, vol. 43, part I (1953) pp. 326–30; H. E. Barnes, *The Evolution of Penology in Pennsylvania* (Indianapolis, 1927); H. E. Barnes, N. K. Teeters, *New Horizons in Criminology* (New York, 1943) pp. 490 ff.; N. K. Teeters, *The Cradle of the Penitentiary* (Philadelphia, 1955) ch. 1; O. F. Lewis, *The Development of American Prisons and Prison Customs, 1776–1845* (Albany, 1922); B. McKelvey, *American Prisons. A History of Good Intentions* (Montclair, N J, 1977) ch. 1.

20. On the social implications of religious feeling in pre-revolutionary policy, see: Haimert, Miller (ed.), *The Great Awakening*; A. Haimert, *Religion and the American Mind: From the Great Awakening to the Revolution* (Cambridge, Mass., 1966). More particularly, on the role of the Quakers in American Colonies, see: J. Sykes, *The Quakers. A New Look at Their Place in Society* (New York, 1958).

21. The legal corpus, approved by the Assembly of Chester, 4 December 1682 was called *The Great Law or Body of Laws*.

22. This legal corpus begins with an unusual (for the time) declaration which guarantees freedom of conscience and belief thereby abolishing the side range of religious crimes. Teeters deals with this point in *The Cradle of the Penitentiary*, p. 3.

23. Taken from Teeters, ibid., p. 3.

24. Ibid., p. 3.
25. Again from Teeters, ibid., p. 4.
26. This testimony from R. Vaux on the internal regime of the gaol – in this case the Old Stone Prison – is taken from his work, *Notices of the Original and Successive Efforts to Improve the Discipline of the Prison of Philadelphia* (1826) p. 14.
27. The diary of S. R. Fisher (1745–1834) in which he describes his experience as an inmate (1779–81) was published after his death by his niece, Anna Wharton Morris, at Philadelphia, precise date unknown.
28. Sellin, *Philadelphia Prisons of the Eighteenth Century*, p. 326.
29. See Rothman, *The Discovery of the Asylum*, pp. 30–1.
30. For a description of the prevention-repression of vagabondage and pauperism in the mother country and for figures on internment in poorhouses and workhouses, see Sidney and Beatrice Webb, *English Local Government: English Poor Law History:* Part I, *The Old Poor Law* (London, 1927); M. Blaug 'The Myth of the Old Poor Law and the Making of the New', *Journal of Economic History*, no. 23 (1967) pp. 151–84.
31. Population figures are taken from: U S Census Bureau, *Historical Statistics of the United States, Colonial Times to 1957* (Washington, 1960) p. 14.
32. Precise information on this typical form of poor relief during the colonial era is found in the volumes edited by Chamberlayne, cited in note 10.
33. D. Carrol, 'History of the Baltimore City Hospitals', *Maryland State Medical Journal* (1966) p. 15.
34. Rothman, *The Discovery of the Asylum*, p. 43.
35. Ibid.
36. H. M. Hurd, *The Institutional Care of the Insane in the United States and Canada*, vol. III (Baltimore, 1916) p. 380.
37. R. H. Shryock, *Medicine and Society in America: 1660–1860* (New York, 1960).
38. Between 1693 and 1776, amongst the 446 cases brought before the Supreme Court of New York, at least 87 were sentenced to death (from J. Goebel, T. R. Naughton, *Law Enforcement in Colonial New York* (1944) p. 702, note 139). On the role of capital punishment in the colonial period, see also L. H. Gipson, 'Crime and Punishment in Provincial Pennsylvania', in *Lehigh University Publications*, no. 9 (1935) pp. 11–12; H. F. Rankin, *Criminal Trial Proceedings in the General Court of Virginia* (Charlottesville, Va., 1965) pp. 121–2.

39. On this see: Goebel and Naughton, *Law Enforcement*, p. 707, note 151.

40. Rothman, *The Discovery of the Asylum*, p. 50.

41. Ibid., p. 55.

42. Ibid., p. 55.

43. See note 11.

44. B. Wadsworth, *The Well-Ordered Family or Relative Duties: Being the Substance of Several Sermons* (Boston, 1712) p. 90.

45. S. Willard, *Impenitent Sinners Warned of their Misery and Summoned to Judgment* (Boston, 1698) p. 26

46. As we will see, the phenomenon of the institutionalisation of stray and abandoned children will only become dominant from the nineteenth century.

47. US Census Bureau, *Historical Statistics* (1960) p. 14.

48. Ibid.

49. D. North, 'Industrialization in the United States', *The Cambridge Economic History*, vol. VI, part II (Cambridge; 1965) p. 678.

50. F. W. Taussig, *The Tariff History of the United States*, (New York, 1914) p. 28.

51. J. F. Jameson, *The American Revolution Considered as a Social Movement*, (Princeton, 1926) pp. 100, 101.

52. Ibid., pp. 46, 47.

53. Ibid., p. 49.

54. Ibid., p. 52.

55. Ibid., p. 58.

56. Ibid., p. 66.

57. H. Conrad, J. R. Meyer, 'The Economics of Slavery in the Antebellum South', *Journal of Political Economy*, vol. LXVI, no. 2 (1958) pp. 95–130; P. S. Foner, *Business and Slavery: The New York Merchants and the Irrepressible Conflict* (Chapel Hill, 1941).

58. Jameson, *The American Revolution*, p. 108.

59. North, *Industrialization in the U S*, p. 678.

60. Jameson, *The American Revolution*, pp. 85, 86.

61. North, *Industrialization in the US*, p. 678.

62. Ibid., p. 739.

63. J. P. Bigelow, *Statistical Tables: Exhibiting the condition and products of certain branches of Industry in Massachusetts, for year Ending April 1, 1837* (Boston, 1838); D. Francis, *Statistical Information Relating to*

Certain Branches of Industry in Manufactures for the Year Ending June 1,1855 (Boston, 1856).

64. R. Gallman, 'Commodity Output, 1839–99', *Trends in the American Economy in the Nineteenth Century, Studies in Income and Wealth*, vol. XXIV (Princeton, 1960) table A-5, p. 56.

65. US Census Bureau, *Historical Statistics*, p. 14.

66. North, *Industrialization in the US*, p. 683.

67. M. T. Copeland, *The Cotton Manufacturing Industry of the United States* (Cambridge, Mass., 1912) p. 6.

68. V. S. Clark, *The History of Manufactures in the United States, 1860-1914*, vol. II (New York) p. 452.

69. US Census Office, *The Eighth Census: Manufactures of the United States in 1860* (Washington, 1965) pp. 733–42.

70. Ibid., pp. 733–42.

71. G. S. Gibbs, 'The Saco-Lowell Shops', *Textile machinery Building in New England, 1813–1849* (Cambridge, 1950) p. 179.

72. A. H. Cole, *The American Wool Manufacture* (Cambridge, 1926) vol. I, p. 276.

73. US Census Office, *The Eighth Census: Manufactures of the United States in 1860* (1865) pp. 733–42.

74. The English Commissions which investigated United States manufacturing in the 1850s, whose reports represent the most careful evaluation of American manufacture progress prior to the Civil War, placed first emphasis upon the size and composition of the market. They noted not only the absolute size and rate of growth of the population but also the high average wealth of the people. The two investigations were: The official reports presented to the British Parliament by Sir Joseph Whitworth and George Wallis, later published separately as: J. Whitworth, G. Wallis, *The Industry of the United States in Machinery, Manufactures and Useful and Ornamental Arts* (London, 1854); and *Report of the Commission of the Machinery of the United States*, in *Parliamentary Papers 1854–55*, L.

75. D. North, *The Economic Growth of the United States, 1790—1860* (Englewood Cliffs, 1961).

76. B. Moore, Jr., *Social Origins of Dictatorship and Democracy: Lord and Peasant in the Making of the Modern World* (London, 1967), ch. III, 'The American Civil War: The Last Capitalist Revolution', p. 111.

77. Moore, Jr., ibid., p. 14.

78. P. W. Gates, *The Farmer's Age: Agriculture 1815–1860* (New York, 1962) p. 143; North, *Economic Growth*, pp. 67–8.

79. Moore, Jr., *Social Origins of Dictatorship*, p. 132.

80. North, *Industrialization in the US*, p. 690.

81. Whitworth, Wallis, *Industry of the United States*, preface, p. *viii*.

82. This observation is taken from the famous report of Yates (1824) to the Parliament of New York. The full text of his report can be found in *New York Senate Journal* (1824).

83. Again in Yates's report, above.

84. NYSPP, *Second Annual Report* (New York, 1819) Appendix, p. 6.

85. T. Sedgwick, *Public and Private Economy*, Part I (New York, 1836) p. 95.

86. See note 82.

87. From the report of Quincy to the Parliament of Massachusetts, in Massachusetts General Committee Pauper Laws, *Report of the Committee* (1821).

88. S. Lebergott, *Manpower in Economic Growth: The American Record Since 1800* (New York, 1964) p. 188.

89. New York Association for Improving the Condition of the Poor, *Thirteenth Annual Report* (New York, 1857) p. 16.

90. New York Association for Improving the Condition of the Poor, *Fourteenth Annual Report* (New York, 1857) p. 16.

91. New York Almshouse Commissioner, *Annual Report for 1848* (New York, 1849) p. 86.

92. Rothman, *The Discovery of the Asylum*, p. 164.

93. Writings on the historical origins of American childcare are particularly prolific: amongst the many essays, see: H. Folks, *The Care of Destitute, Neglected, and Delinquent Children* (Albany, 1900): H. Thurston, *The Dependent Child* (New York, 1930); R. S. Pickett, *House of Refuge: Origins of Juvenile Reform in New York State, 1815 – 1857* (Syracuse, N.Y., 1969); M. Katz, *The Irony of Early School Reform* (Cambridge, Mass., 1968); R. Bremner (ed.), *Children and Youth in America* (Cambridge, Mass., 1970) vol. 1.

94. Rothman, *The Discovery of the Asylum*, p. 170.

95. On the specific theme of the interpretation of insanity in the new republic and more generally, on the historic reconstruction of social reaction of an institutional and segregational form to the world of the insane, see: A. Deutsch, *The Mentally Ill in America: A History of their Care and Treatment* (New York, 1949); N. Dain, *Concepts of Insanity in*

the United States, 1789–1865 (New Brunswick, 1964); R. Caplan, *Psychiatry and the Community in Nineteenth Century America* (New York, 1969); M. D. Altschule, *Roots of Modern Psychiatry: Essays in the History of Psychiatry* (New York, 1957).

96. E. Javis, *Causes of Insanity: An Address Delivered Before the Norfolk, Massachusetts, District Medical Society* (Boston, 1851) p. 17.

97. P. Earle, *An Address on Psychologic Medicine* (Utica, New York, 1867) p. 18.

98. G. Howe, 'Insanity in Massachusetts', *North American Review*, no. 56 (1843) p. 6.

99. E. Javis, *Causes of Insanity*, p. 14.

100. E. Javis, 'On the Supposed Increase of Insanity', *American Journal of Insanity* (1852) p. 34.

101. I. Ray, *Mental Hygiene* (Boston, 1863) pp. 259–61.

102. See note 95.

103. Rothman, *The Discovery of the Asylum*, p. 129.

104. H. E. Barnes, *The Evolution of Penology in Pennsylvania* (Indianapolis, 1927) pp. 63 ff.; F. Lewis, *The Development of American Prisons and Prison Customs* (Albany, 1922) pp. 51 ff.

105. G. Rusche and O. Kirchheimer, *Punishment and Social Structure* (New York, 1968) pp. 127 ff.

106. Related in Barnes, *The Evolution of Penology in Pennsylvania*, p. 82.

107. Ibid., p. 90.

108. B. McKelvey, *American Prisons. A History of Good Intentions*, pp. 6 ff.

109. Ibid., p. 7.

110. H. E. Barnes, *The Repression of Crime* (New York, 1926) pp. 29 ff. Lewis, *The Development of American Prisons and Prison Customs, 1776–1845*, pp. 43 ff: McKelvey, *American Prisons, A History of Good Intentions*, pp. 6 ff.

111. J. Bentham, *Panopticon* (1787), in *The Works of J. Bentham*, vol. IV (New York, 1962).

112. Bentham, *Panopticon* from the 'subtitle'. In an interview with the journal *Pro Justitia*, Foucault sharply observed: 'Le rêve de Bentham, le Panopticon, ou un seul individu pourrait surveiller tout le monde, c'est, du fond, le rêve, ou plutôt, un des rêves de la bourgeoisie (parce qu'elle a beaucoup rêves)' (1973) no. 3 and 4, p. 7.

113. For an analysis of penitentiary organisation of the Philadelphian type, also see pp. 212 ff.

114. McKelvey, *American Prisons*, ch. 1; Lewis, *The Development of American Prisons and Prison Customs*, p. 77.

115. Regarding the internal organisations of prisons of this kind, see pp. 218 ff.

116. See, in particular, pp. 180 ff.

117. See: T. Sellin, 'Commutation of Sentence', *Encyclopedia of Social Sciences*, IV, pp. 108–9.

118. Barnes, *The Repression of Crime*, pp. 272–3.

119. The most informed studies in terms of documentation and full treatment of the topic of convict labour policies in nineteenth century America are: H. C. Mohler, 'Convict Labor Policies', *Journal of American Institute of Criminal Law and Criminology*, vol. 15 (1924–5) pp. 530–97; H. T. Jackson, 'Prison Labor', *Journal of American Institute of Criminal Law and Criminology*, vol. 15 (1927–8) pp. 218–68.

120. M. Foucault, *Surveiller et punir, Naissance de la prison*, (Paris, 1975) p. 246, English Trans., *Discipline and Punish. The Birth of the Prison* (London, 1977).

121. Besides authors cited in note 119, see: L. Collins, 'The State-Use System', *Annals of the American Academy of Political and Social Science*, vol. XLVI (1913) pp. 138–41; H. Frayne, 'The State-Use System', *Journal of Criminal Law and Criminology* (1921) pp. 330–8.

122. S. J. Barrows, 'Convict Road Building', *Charities*, vol. XXI (1908–9) pp. 1879 ff; Idem, 'Roadmaking as a Reform Measure', *The Survey*, vol. XXVI (1911) pp. 157 ff; H. R. Cooley, 'The Out Door Treatment of Crime', *The Outlook*, vol. XCVII (1911) pp. 403–11; O. R. Geyer, 'Making Roads and Men', *Scientific American*, vol. lxxxi (1916) supplement no. 2112, pp. 408 ff.; S. Hill, 'Convict Labour in the Road Building', *Town Development* (1913) pp. 119 ff.

123. E. H. Sutherland, *Criminology* (New York, 1926) pp. 456–7; Jackson, *Prison Labor*, pp. 225–6; Mohler, *Convict Labor Policies*, p. 548.

124. L. N. Robinson, *Penology in the United States* (Philadelphia) pp. 159 ff.; Mohler, *Convict Labour Policies*, p. 551.

125. Robinson, *Penology in the United States*, pp. 164 ff; Jackson, *Prison Labor*, 26 ff.

126. Mohler, *Convict Labour Policies*, p. 548.

127. M. N. Goodnow, 'Turpentine-Impressions of the Convict Camps of Florida', *The Survey*, vol. XXXIV (1915) pp. 103–8. O. F. Lewis, The Bright Side of Florida's Penal Methods', *Literary Digest*, vol. lxxvii (1923) pp. 210 ff; idem., 'The Spirit of Railford–Florida's Substitution for the Convict Lease-System', *The Survey*, (1921) pp. 45–8; P. S.

J. Wilson, 'Convict Camps in South', *Proceedings of the National Conference of Charities and Corrections* (Baltimore: 1915) pp. 378 ff.

128. Jackson, *Prison Labor*, p. 230.
129. G. Ives, *A History of Penal Methods* (London, 1914) p. 174.
130. Mohler, *Convict Labor Policies*, p. 556.
131. J. B. McMaster, *A History of the People of the United States, from the Revolution to the Civil War*, vol. VI (New York, 1920) *p.* 101.
132. Mohler, *Convict Labor Policies*, p. 557.
133. Ibid., p. 557.
134. 'Its dealings with the criminal mark, one may say, the zero point in the scale of treatment which society conceives to be due to its various members. If we raise this point we raise the standard all along the scale. The pauper may justly expect something better than the criminal, the self-supporting poor man or woman than the pauper' (L. T. Hobhouse, Morals in Evolution', *Law and Justice* (London, 1951) p. 125).
135. E. T. Hiller, 'Development of the System of Control of Convict Labor in the United States', *Journal of Criminal Law and Criminology*, vol. v (1915) p. 243.
136. Mohler, *Convict Labor Policies*, p. 558.
137. G. de Beaumont, A. de Tocqueville, *On Penitentiary System in the United States and Its Application in France* (Southern Illinois University Press, 1964) p. 36.
138. In E. C. Wines, *The State of Prisons and of Child-Saving Institutions in the Civilized World* (Cambridge, 1880) p. 109.
139. In Wines, ibid., p. 109.
140. Mohler, *Convict Labor Policies*, p. 558.
141. See authors cited in note 127. On the employment of the leasing system in the Southern States of America, see: H. Alexander, 'The Convict Lease and the System of Contract Labor. Their Place in History', *The South Mobilizing for Social Service* (1913) p. 167; G. W. Cable, 'The Convict Lease System in the Southern States', *Proceedings of National Conference of Charities and Corrections* (1883) pp. 296–7; C. E. Russell, 'A Burglar in the Making', *Everybody's Magazine*, vol. 28 (1908) pp. 753–60.
142. J. R. Simonds, J. T. McEnnis, *The Story of Manual Labor in All Lands and Ages* (Chicago, 1886) pp. 486–94.
143. J. R. Commons et al., *History of Labor in the United States* (New York, 1921) vol. *I*, p. 155.

144. Ibid., p. 155.

145. Mohler, *Convict Labour*, p. 559.

146. Commons et al., *History of Labor in the United States*, vol. I, p. 347.

147. J. P. Tracy, 'The Trade Unions' Attitude toward Prison Labor', *Annals of the American Academy of Political and Social Science*, vol. xlvi (1913) pp. 132–8.

148. Jackson, *Prison Labor*, p. 245.

149. Commons et al., *History of Labor in the United States*, vol. I, p. 369.

150. Mohler, *Convict Labor*, p. 560.

151. Commons et al., *History of Labor in the United States*, vol. I, p. 347.

152. Mohler, *Convict Labor*, p. 561.

153. Ibid., p. 561.

154. Commons et al., *History of Labor in the United States*, vol. II, p. 37.

155. In Hiller, *Development of the Systems of Control of Convict Labor in the United States*, p. 256.

156. United States Bureau of Labor, *Convict Labor*, *Bulletin* no. 372 (1923) p. 18.

157. Ibid., p. 18.

158. Ibid.

159. See *Twenty-Seventh Annual Report of the State Commission of Prisons, State of New York* (New York, 1921), *Proceedings of the National Prison Association* (1870, 1873, 1874, 1883–1921); vol. 40 (New York, 1871–1921).

The Penitentiary as a Model of the Ideal Society

Massimo Pavarini

Man in prison is the virtual image of the bourgeois type which he still is to become in reality ….

The prison is the image of the bourgeois world of labour taken to its logical conclusion; hatred felt by men for everything that they would themselves wish to become but is beyond their reach, is placed as the symbol in the world ….

Since de Tocqueville the bourgeois republics have attacked men's souls whereas the monarchies attacked his body; similarly, the penalties inflicted in these republics also attacked man's soul. The new martyrs do not die a slow death in the torture chamber but instead waste away spiritually as invisible victims in the great prison buildings which differ in little but name from madhouses (M. Horkheimer, T. W. Adorno, *Dialectic of the Enlightenment*, New York, 1972, pp. 226–8).

Prison as 'Factory of Men'

The preceding thesis dealing with the penitentiary as a factory could be taken to mean that the penitentiary was in reality a unit of production; or rather, that prison labour had effectively attained the goal of 'creating

© The Author(s) 2018
D. Melossi, M. Pavarini, *The Prison and the Factory (40ʰ Anniversary Edition)*,
Palgrave Studies in Prisons and Penology, DOI 10.1057/978-1-137-56590-7_5

economic utility'. But as we have seen, even where historically authorities sought to render convict labour productive, in the event this desire was always frustrated: in economic terms it was difficult for prisons to become purely 'marginal enterprises'. Thus the concept of the penitentiary as a focus of economic activity has never been useful and in this sense it would be incorrect to talk of prison as a manufactory or as a factory (of commodities). It would be more correct to say that the first historic instances of prisons were modelled (as far as their internal structure was concerned) on the factory. However, an atypical productive aim (the transformation into something more useful) was pursued with some success at least in the early history of prison: namely, the transformation of the criminal into proletarian. The object was thus not so much the production of commodities as the production of men. From this point we can see the real dimensions of the 'penitentiary invention': a 'prison as a machine' capable of transforming, after close observation of the deviant phenomenon (prison as a place specifically reserved for the observation of criminals), the violent, troublesome and impulsive criminal (real subject) into an inmate (ideal subject), into a disciplined subject, into a mechanical subject.[1] In the end, this is not just an ideological aim but an economic one (even if it is atypically so): the production of subjects for an industrial society. In other words, the production of *proletarians* by the enforced training of prisoners in factory discipline.

The object and the form of this process of 'anthropological mutation' (from criminal to proletarian) are then subject to the iron and mechanical laws of Riccardian economy. In this way, a close link is forged between the 'logic of the free market' and 'institutional logic'. In the long run, in fact, a *Malthusian penitentiary* is realised when certain constants obtain; to be precise:

1. If the supply of labour on the free market exceeds demand – causing high unemployment and a consequent lowering of wages – 'levels of subsistence' inside institutions tend to be lowered automatically: that is, prisons revert to being places for the destruction of the workforce. Thus prisons, in harmony with the laws of demand and supply, play their part in lowering the curve of the latter.

2. Conversely: given a restricted labour supply and consequent growth in wage levels, prison is not simply a means of destruction but also a place where the labour force is usefully employed and then recycled onto the free market after a process of requalification (read: re-education).

In this way prison contributes towards raising the supply curve, thereby regulating the wage spiral. Thus what occurs in the world of production is reflected in the world of institutions: internal mechanisms, *penitentiary practices* vacillate between a *negative imperative* (the 'destructive' prison with deterrent aims) and a *positive imperative* ('productive' prison with essentially re-educative aims). The various contingent penitentiary initiatives lie between these two extremes (taken as the ideal and abstract points of a process).

The penitentiary, therefore, is like a factory producing proletarians, not commodities:

> We should rather assume what has, in fact, been assumed in connection with children's and women's institutions, that prisons are an educational investment and that they are to be conducted as such. The cost of their maintenance should be regarded in the same light as expenditure for schools and for the support and subsidy of universities.[2]

This is a convenient point from which to begin an essentially different analysis from the historic-economic account outlined in the Chap. 4. Here our interest is focused on a study of the institutional mechanisms through which the transformation of the 'criminal- prisoner' into 'proletarian' is carried out.

The Dual Identity: 'Criminal-Prisoner' and 'Propertyless-Prisoner'

A constant and almost monotonous feature of research – today richly documented in archives and libraries – is comprised in the often well-compiled, sometimes pedantic but always precise accounts of inspections, visits and reports on American penitentiaries in the first half of the nineteenth century.

Prisons thus become botanical and zoological gardens with their well-ordered range of 'criminal species'; in the 'pilgrimages' to these sanctuaries of bourgeois rationality it was possible to make special observations on a social monstrosity, observations which in turn became a 'scientific' necessity for new policies of social control.

There was a great assortment of visitors from all parts of the globe (eccentric foreigners, representatives of European governments concerned with prison reform, penitentiary experts, reformers, Utopians, etc.) but they were all intent on one aim: *observation and knowledge of the criminal.* The problem showed no sign of going away, it was not to be underestimated: a knowledge of delinquency was clearly seen as a necessary condition of the resolution of a social problem with which this epoch had become preoccupied: the struggle against rising criminality.

So far as the American situation in the first part of the nineteenth century is concerned, a ready explanation is available: this period, as we have already been able to show, saw a marked and violent process of capitalist accumulation accompanied by the inevitable phenomenon of social disintegration.[3] If anything, our interest should centre on the originality of current political-social thought in terms of the way it located criminal causes of deviancy; without doubt, we must stress above all its ability to avoid the 'repressive illusion', the obsession that penal violence pure and simple can contain what was essentially an objective social process. Reform of the penal code and departure from the principles of the old English laws, the abolition of the death penalty and of many corporal punishments, the creation of prison as the main instrument of social control as a whole are concrete testimonies of this new way of relating to criminality.

But its originality does not stop here: in the Jacksonian period, the conception of the criminal sought to give deviancy an etiological explanation, an explanation which was not just individualistic-religious but – if only in some cases – also gave a social explanation to the problem. The question of violent urbanisation, the breakdown of the 'healthy' colonial family and the phenomenon of abandoned youth on the one hand and, on the other, initiatives for a moral regeneration of society (particularly in the large towns), a new institutional regime (from poorhouse to workhouse) for the 'reeducation' and 're-integration' of the weakest sections of society were the main features – both on a conscious and on a reformist level – of this original 'revolution'.[4] But in this new system of control, prison also acquired (besides the functions we have examined) an 'instrumental', 'subordinate' role in terms of a need which arose at this time: *consciousness of the criminal.* This is not a peripheral observation: *criminology* – as a science of criminality – is, above all, in its origins, *consciousness of the criminal.* To be more precise, interpreting Foucault,[5] criminology concerns consciousness of the criminal and not consciousness of the 'transgressor of laws'.

Interest in the criminal is thus confined to interest in the deviant who can be studied, analysed, classified, manipulated and transformed over and above and divorced from the social reality from which he came and to which he will return to live. *Thus the criminal is transformed into an institutionalised deviant:* and, in the last analysis, *into a prisoner.*

From this viewpoint, it is already possible to grasp the ambiguity underlying the whole of positivist interest in criminal phenomena – the close identification between criminal and prisoner. The uncritical identification of these two terms is based on a particular form of scientistic ideology; an ideology which confuses the aggression and alienation of the 'institutional man' with intrinsic wickedness. It is an ideology which classifies and types different forms of criminality either in terms of survival in the penitentiary or (at a second stage) of adjustment to imposed models, to institutional violence. But in order for this 'dismal science' to grow and to present itself as a 'positive science', as the 'science of society' close to the heart of the enlightened bourgeoisie, the modern prison, the 'Panoptic prison' had to demonstrate an inherent tendency to transform itself into a laboratory, a scientific workshop, in which, after close observation of the phenomenon, one could dare to try out the great experiment: *transformation of man.*

Foucault clearly grasps the significance of *panoptisme,*[6] of that ideological movement which, in concrete and organic terms, is essentially realised in the invention of the disciplinary institution of nineteenth-century North America. Prison, like any other 'total institution' structured on the 'Panoptic model', is · in fact an exceptional machine, capable of splitting the 'see-being-seen' dyad.[7] It is a device which permits a small number of unseen people to observe, to scrutinise and continually to analyse a collective which is eternally exposed. Thus an essential condition is realised. A small number of people are transformed into *scientists;*

the many are transformed into *objects*, *guinea pigs*; and prison is transformed into a *laboratory*.

Exposure to scientific curiosity is absolute: every gesture, every sign of discomfort, of pain, of impatience, every intimacy comes thus to be described, classified, compared, analysed and studied. The inmate progressively internalises the consciousness of his permanent visibility, of his expropriated exposure. On this conscious level, his salvation – or his complete alienation as something 'different', 'deviant' – depends solely on self-control, on the discipline he imposes on his body, on his capacity to assume in his behavioural patterns the appearance of being 'subject to power'. The only alternative is in fact 'destruction' – insanity. Thus, the observed inmate himself comes to be the instrument of his own subjection, of his own transformation into something different.[8]

Inspection, transformed into a principle and interiorised, changes the disciplinary aspect into a power exercise *tout court*. But against what ideal does disciplinary power, institutional power, measure its ability to transform the criminal object?

The design hypothesis emerging here in its transparent rationality is all-embracing; in fact its capacity to resolve, in general terms, the thematic of social control of the *classes dangereuses* is exhaustive. There is in fact only one 'model', one paradigm. However, the fields of application, the areas, and the objects of its intervention are diverse. Whether it is realised in a prison of the Philadelphian type, whether it is concretised in institutions of assistance (for/against stray minors,[9] for/against abandoned children,[10] etc.), whether it expands the hegemonic project which inspires new forms of military discipline[11] and scholastic reform as well as the architecture and urban geography of working-class districts, its real function is constantly to reproduce *bourgeois social order* even in the most restricted social spaces. Prison – as a 'concentrated place' in which class hegemony (once exercised in the ritual forms of punitive terror) can rationally develop in a network of disciplinary relationships – becomes the institutional symbol of the new anatomy of bourgeois power, the place reserved – in symbolic terms – for the 'new order'. Thus prison appears as the model of 'ideal society'. Furthermore, the punishment of imprisonment – as a dominant system of social control – increasingly appears as the parameter of a radical change in the exercise of power.

In fact, elimination of the 'other', physical elimination of the transgressor (since he is 'outside the game' he is destructable), the politics of control by means of terror are transformed – and prisons are the fulcrum of this change – into preventive politics, thus into the containment of destructiveness.[12] Hence, from the elimination of the criminal to his integration into the social fabric. The times, the methods and the forms of this 'transformation' of the criminal into the bourgeois image of how the 'propertyless' 'should be' and therefore of how the proletarian 'should be', are complex and are based on the perceived correspondence, between *the propertyless and the criminal*.[13] The central theme – an obsession – becomes then the social danger posed by a potential aggressor to property.[14]

In this light, the propertyless class is already seen – ideologically – as being the same as the criminal class and vice versa; the similarity between the two is comparable to the difference between economic and extra-economic mechanisms of social control. Prison as a coercive instrument thus has a precise objective: in reasserting bourgeois social order (the clear distinction between the world of property owners and the world of the propertyless), the criminal (propertyless) must be educated (or re-educated) into a *socially safe proletarian*, that is, the criminal must learn to accept being property- less without threatening property.

The project risks becoming utopian. But education in submission, education in the discipline of wage labour, the reduction of every individual proletarian to the 'subject of material need', satisfiable only in/ through alienated work, finds in prison – particularly in the North American variety – a historically realised model.

But leaving aside this objective dimension (education to wage labour), the punishment of imprisonment has an important ideological implication for the discussion on bourgeois hegemony. The internal organisation of prison, the 'silent' and 'labouring' prison community, with time inexorably marked out in work and worship, the total isolation of each prisoner-worker, the impossibility of any form of association between them, the discipline of work as 'total' discipline become the paradigmatic terms for that which 'should be' in the so-called free society. The 'inside' aspires to an ideal model of what it should be like 'outside'. Thus prison assumes the dimension of an *organised project for the subaltern social world*: a model to impose, spread and universalise.

The Penitentiary System: The New Model of Disciplinary Power

The walls of the 'great laboratory' – no longer a fortress inaccessible to curious strangers – are transformed into something relatively transparent: bourgeois interest is finally satisfied. A semblance of democracy accompanies the first steps of the 'penitentiary adventure': all good citizens can now personally verify the (useful and profitable) employment of public wealth (the high costs of prisons are justified in this way!); they can witness the civil-religious values which inspire the prison staff; they can see that order reigns in the 'institutional universe'; they can delight in the 'gentle' treatment given to prisoners and in their 'submissive' behaviour; they can appreciate the promising results (for example, the reduction in recidivism), and so on.

We have already emphasised that the written records of these visits to the institutions are numerous and full of interest even if they seem – with some worthy and important exceptions – more like collector's items than actual scientific studies; there is a passion, almost an obsession, with the process of collecting, registering and amassing as much as possible (often quite contradictory), rather than any systematisation of the material gathered in political-theoretical terms.[15]

We intend to reinterpret that 'lived' experience along the lines of a theoretical model of disciplinary power; we have already partially anticipated this in the preceding pages and now we will attempt a complete synthesis.

The first stage of the penitentiary – from a chronological and a functional point of view, leaving aside for the moment the inspection function (prison as an observatory of social marginality) – has a characteristic tendency progressively to reduce the criminal personality (rich in his deviant individuality) to a 'homogeneous' dimension: to being a mere subject, that is, of need.[16] The process of classification of criminals and the disciplinary norm of solitary confinement are the most fitting instruments for this operation.

Isolation in particular – in the more markedly 'extremist' and intensive form of the Philadelphian model (absolute solitary confinement) – tends, both ideologically and factually, to counterpose itself to the chaotic and promiscuous conditions in preventive prisons (jails) on the one hand, and to prevent spontaneous solidarity amongst the dispossessed of the same class on the other. Solidarity would be doubly dangerous: it would nourish a subculture (the survival of a whole series of 'alternative values', even if they are only an expression of life at the margins of society); it would provide a vehicle for the diffusion of an 'alternative' order and discipline (for example, the discipline of 'subversive' political organisation). Isolation, in terms of the long years of total separation from the 'others', the constant dialogue with one's self, progressively destroys the entire 'structure of the self'[17]: in this way, the fear of criminal contamination (in the sense of the deviant as a dangerous germ, a potential propagator of 'disobedience', evidence of a different way of playing the role of an inferior) is exorcised once and for all.

Uprooted from his universe, the inmate in solitary confinement gradually becomes aware of his weakness, of his fragility, of his absolute dependence upon the administration, that is, on the 'other'; thus he becomes aware of himself as a subject-of-need. This is what can be described as the first stage of *reformation*: transformation of the 'real subject' (criminal) into an 'ideal subject' (prisoner).

At the same time, prison discipline – with its rigid and detailed definition of the functions, competence and scope of the administration – imposes on the prisoner ('abstract being') the mechanism of a perfect social universe in miniature: a totality of hierarchic, pyramidal relations.[18]

The model of discipline which prevails in (free) production – from the hypothesis of manufacture to the reality of the factory – is now imposed on penitentiary organisation (from the Philadelphian to the Auburn prison) as an overall plan. Despite the significant differences between them (in production and thus in 'education' in 'submission to work'), both the Philadelphian and the Auburn prisons share a common theme: destruction through solitary confinement of every *parallel relation* (between prisoner-workers, between 'equals'); the emphasis, through discipline, on *vertical relations* alone (between superior–inferior, between different kinds of people).

Apart from this, the two prison models are profoundly different: their growth, their particular structure essentially depends on developments in the capitalist process of accumulation. In this context – in line with our delineation of the 'ideal model of disciplinary power' – we wish to pick out the essential features of these two prison models. One warning: the models proposed are the result of an abstraction (abstraction of/from a reality which, historically, is necessarily complex); their validity – although it is hardly necessary to say so – is therefore purely heuristic.

Solitary Confinement: The Philadelphian Prison Hypothesis

In summary, the essential characteristics of the Philadelphian system are as follows:

1. In the first place, this type of prison is a *hypothesis* in the sense that it is an architechtonic project elevated to the point of being a principle of the educative process. Or rather: architectural science is transformed, in this specific case, into a social science. Bentham's 'dream' is materialised: 'There are principles in architecture, by the observance of which great moral changes can be more easily produced among the most abandoned of our race.'[19] Further: 'The science of architecture has been exhausted in experiments to construct a reformatory prison, as if the form of a cell could regenerate a vicious beast into virtue.'[20]

   The walls of the cell become effective instruments of punishment: they force the inmate to face himself: he is forced to 'enter' his own consciousness. The old canonical penitentiary hypothesis (*ergastulum*) is thus revived in an even more intense form through the new Quaker prison technique: 'In this solitary cell, this provisional grave, the myths of the resurrection can easily come alive'.[21] In fact:

   > Each individual will necessarily be made the instrument of his own punishment; his conscience will be the avenger of society ... the progress of corruption is arrested, no additional contamination can be received or communicated ... [the convict] will be compelled to reflect on the error of his life, to listen to the reproaches of conscience, to the expostulations of religion.[22]

2. Isolation (night and day) is total (absolute solitary confinement). The architectural unicellular project permits the principle of isolation to be taken to its extreme. The danger of 'contamination'

amongst prisoners and the outside world must be prevented by all means possible: outside the four walls of the cell, the prisoner can only move according to the needs of the administration and only if he is blindfolded or hooded.

The solitary cell of the criminal is for some days full of terrible phantoms. Agitated and tormented by a thousand fears, he accuses society of injustice and cruelty, and with such a disposition of mind, it sometimes will happen that he disregards the orders and repels the consolations offered to him. The only chastisement which the regulations of the prison permit, is imprisonment in a dark cell with reduction of food. It is rare that more than two days of such discipline are required, to curb the most refractory prisoner.[23]

3. Time – passed in absolute silence, divided up only by the rituals of penitentiary life (provision of food, work, institutional visits, worship, etc.) – tends to spread out and thus becomes entirely a matter of *subjective consciousness*; quite soon the inmate loses the notion of it as an objective, physical process.

4. Institutional discipline – in this 'simplified' form of non- communal life – is transformed (reducing itself) into discipline of the body (a discipline which therefore imposes habits of physical control: self-control). In fact, physical disorder (as a reflection of moral disturbance) must transform itself (read: educate itself) into (external) *physical order*. Certain rules are laid down in connection with this education of the body: for example, the following passage is taken from the articles of the internal regulations introduced on 5 December 1840 at the Cherry Hill Penitentiary (Philadelphia):

> 1st. You must keep your person, cell and utensils clean and in order.
>
> 2nd. You must obey promptly, all directions given to you, either by the inspectors; Warden, or Overseers.
>
> 3rd. You must not make any unnecessary noise, either by singing, whistling, or in any other manner; but in all respects preserve becoming silence. You must not try to communicate with your fellow-prisoners in the adjoining cells, either from your own apartment, or during the time you are exercising in your yard.

4th. All surplus food must be placed in the vessel provided for that purpose; and all wastage of materials, or other dirt, must be carefully collected and handed out of the cell, when called for by the Overseer.

5th. You must apply yourself industriously, at whatever employment is assigned you; and when your task is finished, it is recommended that your time be devoted to the proper improvement of your mind, either in reading the books provided for the purpose, or in case you cannot read, in learning to do so.

6th. Should you have any complaint to make against the Overseer having charge of you, make it to the Warden or Inspector-if against the Warden, to the Inspector.

7th. Be at all times in your intercourse with the officers of the penitentiary, respectful and courteous, and never suffer yourself to be led astray from your duties, by angry or revengeful feelings.

8th. Observe the Sabbath; though you are separated from the world, the day is not the less holy.[24]

Analytical reason – which tends to fragment the 'different' in order to 'reassemble' it (like a puzzle) in the image of 'civilised being' – is the inspiration behind this disciplinary process: the 'man of disorder', the 'savage man' must in fact be transformed into a 'disciplined' man. If 'wildness' (the natural exuberance of the rebellious, or desperate resistance to 'destruction') cannot be cured by the 'medicine' of institutional discipline alone (solitude, worship, work), then new forms of *physical violence* are introduced without delay: cold showers for the agitated, iron gags and iron gibbets for the 'uncontrollable'.[25] The technical-disciplinary inspiration which creates these 'objects' is not stimulated by the desire to 'increase' the degree of suffering or torment of the prisoner. In this sense, they are not so much instruments of torture as means of mechanically forcing the inmate to 'mould' his own body and spirit to the disciplinary regime: if he screams, the iron gags will educate him into silence by mechanically keeping him quiet; if he moves, the iron gibbets will teach him to control his body, mechanically immobilising him in armature and tying him to a ball.[26] They are the same instruments with which certain animals are 'tamed' and with which savages are 'civilised'; in fact, they are the instruments of the new bourgeois pedagogic science:

Of the different means which I made use of, the effect of heat appeared to me to accomplish in the most effectual manner the object I had in view … I thought it necessary to put him in the hot bath for 2 or 3 hours every day, during which, water at the same temperature as that of the bath was frequently dashed on his head … being convinced that in such a case [heat and frequent baths] the loss of muscular force is advantageous to the nervous sensibility … After some time our young savage appeared evidently sensible to the action of cold … The same cause led him soon to appreciate the utility of that clothing to which before he barely submitted. As soon as he appeared to perceive the advantage of clothes, there was but a single step necessary to oblige him to dress himself. This end was obtained in a few days, by leaving him every morning exposed to the cold within the reach of his clothes until he found out the method of putting them on himself.[27]

On the other hand, *reformation* means 'education in subjection' submissively accepting one's own inferiority, 'being subject of need'.

5. Religion (or rather, religious instruction) becomes the favoured instrument in the rhetoric of subjection: the Christian ethic (in its Protestant form) is used in this penitentiary hypothesis as the 'ethic of/for the masses'. 'Bible' is the magic, recurrent word in this universe. To show tangible signs of repentance (that is, to have made the long journey to spiritual salvation) is tantamount to giving sure proof of reformation (of progress in the 're-educative' process). In this light, religious practice is essentially administrative practice: the chaplain is a diligent book-keeper who must render his account to the administration. The following notes in the diary of a certain Lacombe (1845–50), the chaplain at Cherry Hill, illustrate this:

> No. 876. John Nugent, barber. Understands pretty well what is required in order to attain salvation, but seems not to feel; June 1839 professed conversion; have found it insincere as I supposed; pretends he only meant to try me. Incurable. No. 874. Hiram Kelsey. A sort of wild man of the woods, has lived a semi-savage life in western wilds, no sense of religion. No. 878. James Loller, 33, Virginian mulatto; very taciturn, no disposition to converse upon religious subjects, of course indifferent to them.

> No. 920. George Thomas. Does not read the scriptures; has no
> wish to repent. Says he is a free man, obviously deranged. Tell me 'go
> talk to the convicts about such damned stuff' (a dangerous fellow).[28]

6. Work is at a *premium*: in fact it is denied to those who refuse to cooperate with the 'educative process'. Judge Charles Coxe writes in his first report to the Legislative Commission on the subject of convict labour at Cherry Hill:

> Where a convict arrives he is placed in his cell and left alone, without
> work and without any books ... But few hours elapse before he petitions
> for something to do ... If a prisoner had a trade that can be pursued in
> his cell, he is put to work as a favor, as a reward for good behaviour ...
> Thus work ... [is] regarded and received as favor, and [is] withheld as
> punishment.[29]

In this situation, work is the only possible alternative to inertia, to enforced idleness; in reality, it appears to be and is the only salvation from certain madness: 'Labour seems to me absolutely necessary for existence; I believe I should die without it.'[30] Another prisoner interviewed at the same time commented: 'It would be impossible to live here without labour. Sunday is a very long day, I assure you.'[31] In this kind of prison, shoes, boots, wicker chairs were made, spinning was carried out, cigars were rolled and uniforms cut and sewn, etc.,[32] all forms of labour which required time, purely manual ability and the minimum of tools. They are the only kinds of work which can be done by just one worker, in a confined space with cheap tools; every operation must be carried out manually with an expenditure of energy disproportionate to the result.

This "enforced inducement to work" was not oriented around economic goals: in fact, prisons could never be self-sufficient by means of this (non-productive) work, nor could the prisoner ever 'pay' for his punishment – and the supporters of the Philadelphian system were fully aware of this. (Penitentiary labour would always be a liability: it was not a *paying system of prison discipline*.)[33] For work to be productive, it was held, it would be necessary to bring in machines (labour-saving machinery) and produce goods competitive with those produced on the 'free' market; but this is exactly what was not wanted:

The state has no right to interfere with [labouring man] in his work, nor to run all sorts of improved machinery against him. Let the men outside use the machinery and let the man inside use his hands.[34]

Originally, for an extremely brief period, the model which the theorists of the Philadelphian system aspired to as being ideal for the re-educated prisoner was undoubtedly based on the stereotype of the untiring, obliging, faithful, silent worker of the *craft workshop* (tailor's, shoemaker's, chair-mender's, etc.). But in the second phase, in the face of the industrialisation of the world of 'free' production, no one could delude themselves that 'the object of prison discipline is to induce him not merely to form good resolutions for the future but to lead a good life, to support himself by honest industry'[35]: by now the *factory* prevailed in the world outside, that is, communal work was the rule of the day, together with labour-saving machinery and mechanical labour. Prison labour of the Philadelphian type – in this second stage, when manufacture and craft production is replaced by industrialised work-lost any 'objective' function of education in subordinate and productive work (in work, that is, of/for the factory), retaining and emphasising only some ideological features of alienated work dear to the bourgeoisie. Or rather: even if the Philadelphian system was 'defeated' by the gradual rise of the Auburn system, the Philadelphian model, and in particular the regime of work which could be undertaken in a prison based on solitary confinement, presented an organised plan for the whole of the subaltern social universe, the 'abstract idea' (ideological in this sense only) of how class relations and production on the free market *should* be organised. Prison labour in this system thus came to have the character of a 'businessman's dream' (*capital as anarchy*), much more than that of a 'rational plan' for the whole of the system (*capital as rationality*). In fact:

(a) Solitary confinement of the prisoner-worker highlights the bourgeois desire for an isolated worker, that is, an unorganised worker.

(b) The discipline, together with the lack of competition, offers the businessman maximum use of the workforce; a workforce disciplined and totally isolated from activities in the free market is an 'unproblematic' factor in production.

(c) Reformation of the inmate has – as the parameter of its value – both the amount of goods produced in a certain time as well as the 'external forms' of subjection to authority; the idea develops of paying the worker by the 'piece' rather than 'by the day'.

(d) The absolute dependence (more existential than real) of the 'property-less', 'criminal', 'prisoner' on the 'propertied' entrepreneur becomes manifest; whilst in the world of 'free production' the dependence-subjection of the worker on/to capital is *real*, through the process of wage labour.

The Silent System: The Auburn Prison Hypothesis

With respect to the Auburn prison hypothesis, we will present a schema limited to an analysis of the elements and characteristics which distinguish this system from the Philadelphia model.

1. Convict labour in the Auburn system departs, if only for an instant, from both its *ideological* role (work as the only way of satisfying the material needs of the propertyless) and its (sole) *pedagogic* role (forced labour as an educative model of/for alienated work) in order to acquire a more economistic definition: *convict labour as a productive activity for private exploitation.* The project fails. In fact, both the pressure of strong trade union opposition (penitentiary products – the fruit of unpaid labour – were placed on the market at prices with which so-called free enterprises could not compete, with the effect of restraining wages) and the difficulty of completely industrialising prisons, as we have already seen,[36] soon stopped prisons from becoming factories. But this 'productivist illusion', even if it is momentary and in part a failure, impresses on the new penitentiary hypothesis certain original structural characteristics. The peculiar characteristics analysed in what follows can be, in fact, directly reduced to this new 'dimension of labour'.

2. The regime of *day-association* and *night-separation* is thus the cornerstone on which the whole Auburn system is based. It is a decided compromise. On the one hand, the basic pedagogic, re- educative features of the Philadelphian system still prevail (the desire to avoid any

interaction amongst the prisoners in order to prevent the spread of the 'contagion of delinquency'). On the other hand – and in even more urgent terms – there is a new 'reforming obsession'. Productive work (that is, prison as a productive concern), *night-separation* and the *silent system*, therefore, are still geared to the first aim. The principle of *day-association* (necessary for the introduction in prison of communal work and labour-saving machinery) is geared to the second aim. The compromise is therefore achieved: *day-association* for *maximum industrial production*; *night-separation* and the *silent system* for *maximum prevention of contamination*:

> Let those prisoners who are not in solitary confinement … [be] allowed to work, under a discipline so rigid as to prevent all conversation with each other, and be compelled to perform as much labour as their health and constitutions will permit.[37]

Thus the prisoners must be employed in some kind of productive work: *common hard labour* is considered to be the most suitable to this end. Hard labour becomes the new 'slogan' in the prison world.

3. Military organisation has a relevance to this kind of prison which is partly obscured in the case of the Philadelphian cellular prison. The reason is simple: the new institution must organise a certain amount of *collective activity*. To this end, even the furniture in the cell emphasises the obsession with imposing a formal, aesthetic uniformity on the inmates: a camp-bed, a bucket, a few tin tools issued to everyone, were the only objects provided by the administration; the prisoners had to wear a uniform and their heads were shaven.[38] The penitentiary administration tended to be structured along military-hierarchical lines; many of the warders had served in the navy or the army and some of them drew on this experience in their attitudes to discipline and their careers. They wore a uniform, they assembled at specific times and changed guard-just like sentries.[39]

Disciplinary standards demanded that the prison staff behave in a gentlemanly manner, as if they were officers. In fact their relationships with the inmates had to be marked by that detachment characteristic of relationships between officers and men. On this point, the regulations at Sing-Sing read as follows:

> They [wardens] were to require from the convicts the greatest deference; and never suffer them to approach but in respectful manner; they are not to allow them the least degree of familiarity, nor exercise any towards them; they should be extremely careful to *command* as well as to compel their respect.[40]

In this kind of penitentiary, discipline of the body was essentially realised through regimented activity: the inmates could not walk normally, they had to form up in close order or in single file, facing the shoulders of the man in front, their heads slightly inclined to the right and their chained feet moving in step.[41] Hours were the same as in the armed services: at the sound of a bell, the prison warders opened the doors of the cells the inmates entered the corridor and, having been chained together, marched into the garden; they emptied their slops and marched to the workshop in single file; there, seated on long benches, they worked in absolute silence until the second bell – the bell for breakfast; in groups and still in single file, they entered the canteen for their food ration (the rules did not permit the 'line to be broken'); they then marched to their cells; at the sound of a third bell, they returned – still in file – to their workshops; and so on.[42]

4. Discipline was ritualised in the rhetoric of *corporal punishment*. In this respect too we can understand the 'necessity' for prisoners to associate with each other at least part of the time; this is connected with governing a group of people by force. It was accurately observed that:

> Only relax the reins of discipline … and a chaplain's labors would be of no more use here than with a drunken mob.[43]
> I consider the chastisement by the whip the most efficient, and at the same time, the most humane which exists; it never injures health, and obliges the prisoners to lead a life essentially healthy. Solitary confinement, on the contrary, is often insufficient, and always dangerous. I have seen many prisoners in my life whom it was impossible to subdue in this manner, and who only left the solitary cell to go to the hospital.

> I consider it impossible to govern a large prison without a whip. Those
> who know human nature from books only, may say the contrary.[44]

The allegedly 'humane' punishment of flogging, as opposed to solitary
confinement for example, did not satisfy Beaumont and Tocqueville
(supporters of the Philadelphian system, among other things,) who made
the following acute observation about it:

> For various reasons this punishment is preferred to all others. It effects the
> immediate submission of the delinquent; his labour is not interrupted for
> one single minute.[45]

Moreover, flogging causes suffering (and is thus feared) without damaging the offender's physical ability (to work) beyond repair; unlike solitary
confinement (accompanied by a reduction in food, deprivation of light
and the physical impossibility of lying down) this form of discipline does
not 'destroy' the workforce.

The power to punish was totally discretionary: in fact, there was no
fixed regulation laying down when the sanction could or should be
applied, nor was there a disciplinary body which decided on this question. Disciplinary power was the exercise of power *tout court*:

> The right of the keepers over the persons of the prisoners, is that of a father
> over his children, of the teacher over his pupils, of the master over his
> apprentice; and of a sea-captain over his crew.[46]

The imposition of arbitrary power had a specific aim. R. Wiltse, the dep-
uty governor of Sing-Sing, explicitly stated:

> Convicts must be made to know that *here* they must submit to every regu-
> lation, and obey every command of their keepers.[47]

5. The rule of continuous silence is the only means of preventing both
   communication and the process of contamination and osmosis otherwise inevitable amongst inmates in a *congregate prison:*

> This union [of convicts] is strictly material, or; to speak more exactly, their bodies are together, but their souls are separated, and it is not the solitude of the body which is important, but that of the mind.[48]

The suppression of every form of subjective interaction by means of 'continuous silence' becomes, then, an essential instrument of power: that is to say, it was necessary in order that the few could govern the many. Beaumont and Tocqueville's observations on this are to the point:

> So that nine hundred criminals, watched by thirty keepers, work free in the midst of an open field, without a chain fettering their feet or hands. It is evident that the life of the keepers would be at the mercy of the prisoners, if material force were sufficient for the latter; but they want moral force. And why are these nine hundred collected malefactors less strong than the thirty individuals who command them? Because the keepers communicate freely with each other, act in concert, and have all the power of association; whilst the convicts, separated from each other by silence, have, in spite of their numerical force, all the weakness of isolation.[49]

6. The rule of silence in an institution based on communal life immediately poses the problem of obedience to regulations; the range of possible infractions tended to grow in direct proportion to new disciplinary needs. In the Philadelphian prison – the very organisation of which drastically reduced the number of disciplinary regulations simply through the physical restrictions it placed on the inmates – there was little scope for infractions of discipline. In a prison based on communal life, the fact of association necessitates an infinity of behavioural norms which must be respected. In fact:

> In observing silence, they are incessantly tempted to violate its law. They have some merit in obeying because their obedience is no actual *necessity*. It is thus that Auburn discipline gives to the prisoners the habits of society which they do not obtain in the prisons of Philadelphia.[50]

The inmate's obedience to administrative control over his body inevitably turns him into an *automaton*, a programmed, hard working machine, no longer just 'disciplined in abstraction' (as in the Philadelphian prison), but perfectly 'synchronised' in collective, dissociative activity:

> Convicts are seated in single file, at narrow tables with their backs toward the center, so that there can be no interchange of signs. If one has more food than he wants, he raises his left hand, and if another has less, he raises his right hand and the warden changes it. When they have done eating, at the ringing of a bell of the softest sound, they rise from the table, form in solid columns and return under the eyes of the turnkeys to the workshops … There is the most perfect attention to business from sunrise till night interrupted only by the time necessary to dine and never by the fact that the whole body of prisoners have done their tasks and the time is now their own and they can do as they please.[51]

The Product of the Penitentiary Machine: The Proletarian

The first stage of the long journey which integrates the criminal (*real subject*) into the bourgeois hegemonic world forcibly deprives the prisoner of his inter-subjective relationships, thus reducing him to 'a pure and abstract existence of dependence'. That is to say:

> … the 'real' subject, integrated into his social reality which is spontaneously heterogenous compared with the 'juridical' and its rules … is torn out of the specific concreteness of that 'outside' on which his dangerous aggressiveness is based, and is reduced to that 'juridical' notion of the subject, his 'primitive condition' existing 'before' the concrete rules of society, of which the 'outside' subject was the shadow or the negative.[52]

The cellular model represents the most suitable means to this end, the best way of reducing the prisoner to an *abstract subject*: 'a man is abstracted from these emotions of friendship which society inspires …; by confinement he is abstracted from all external impressions.'[53]

Abstracted from the real dimensions of his existence, reduced to a subject completely divorced from the social process, the prisoner feels alone in the face of material need. In this he is no different from the bourgeois except in one essential: while the latter can satisfy his needs through and with property, the prisoner is prevented from doing so (he is totally dependent on the administration for his existence and therefore for the satisfaction of his material needs). This (existential-political) state of dissatisfaction is arrived at through a manipulative process (read: 'progressive changes that occur in the beliefs that he has concerning himself')[54] which can be described as the *moral career of the inmate*. But once reduced to abstract subject, once his diversity is 'annulled' (to the point of extreme loss which accompanies the solitude of the individual divorced from the social), once faced by those material needs which cannot be satisfied independently and thereby rendered completely dependent on the sovereignty of the administration, ultimately the product of the disciplinary machine has only one possible alternative to his own destruction, to madness: the moral form of subjection, that is the moral form of the status of proletarian. Better still: the moral form of the proletarian is here laid down as the only condition of existence in the sense of being the only way the propertyless can survive. Therefore, at the moment of destruction (re-education of the 'different' to 'negative homogeneity') reconstruction from 'abstract concept' to 'socio-economically real' figure begins, carrying out the hegemonic task of the bourgeoisie: the propertyless is the same as the criminal – the criminal is the same as the prisoner – the prisoner is the same as the proletarian. In other words, the propertyless-prisoner *must exist* only as a proletarian, as someone who had accepted the state of subordination, who is only acknowledged as someone who accepts the discipline of wages. The practice of this *disciplined chaos* which is the prison is thus general towards: education in expropriated labour; education in wage labour as the only means of satisfying one's own needs; education in acceptance of not being a proprietor.

The two moments in which penitentiary practice is realised – the reduction, on the one hand, of the prisoner to 'pure subject of need' and the subsequent education of the 'subject of need' to proletarian – are analysed in what follows, within the specific context of North American prisons in the first half of the nineteenth century.

Appendix 1: Subordination of the Institutionalised Being (Inquiry at the Philadelphia Penitentiary, October 1831)

Gustave de Beaumont and Alexis de Tocqueville visited the Philadelphia penitentiary in October 1831. At this time the principle of solitary confinement was being seriously challenged by the silent system of Auburn. The impressions of this visit and detailed notes on prison treatment were completed and combined with written records of interviews with staff and inmates; all this was then carefully arranged in the form of appendices to their work on the American penitentiary system of 1832.[55]

Through the attentive eyes of these explorers, through their lucid and analytical writing, we can enter the labyrinth of social abnormality in early nineteenth century America. However, a few points must be classified before we quote certain parts of the enquiry:

1. We have considered it significant for the discussion we have conducted up to now to use this material because life in the Philadelphia prison – the nearest to the 'model' of the cellular penitentiary – embodies, in paradigmatic terms, the extreme destruction and reduction of the inmate to 'subject of need', to 'pure and abstract needful existence'.

2. It appears from this inquiry that the inmate is already an 'institutionalised subject' in the sense that the manipulative mechanisms have already turned the inmate into 'virtual being'. What emerges therefore is a monstruous phantom a new animal, once savage, now tame.

3. In fact, the softening-up or the 'programming' (the so-called admission procedure) following which the inmate is categorised as an institutional object, as an 'object for the process of manipulation' have already made their effectiveness plain. The law of 23 April 1826, which sets out the disciplinary norms for the Eastern Penitentiary of Philadelphia, prescribes in Article 5 that the new prisoner be:

> Examined...in order to become acquainted with his or her person and countenance, and his or her name, height, eye, place of nativity, trade, complexion, color of hair and eyes, length of feet, to be accurately mea-

sured and that these shall be entered in a book provided for that purposes together with such other natural or accidental marks, or peculiarity of feature or appearance, as may serve to identify him or her, and if the convict can write, his or her signature shall be written under the said description of his or her person.[56]

4. Therefore, once the inmate is 'relieved' of his belongings (necessary for his identity), the administration diligently seeks to turn them into 'disinfected objects' in order that they cannot be identified as 'personal'. After 'registration':

> A physician verifies the state of his health. He is washed; his hair is cut, and a new dress, according to the uniform of the prison is given to him. In Philadelphia he is conducted to his solitary cell, which he never leaves; there he works, eats and rests...At Auburn...the prisoner is first plunged into the same solitude but it is only for a few days, after which he leaves it, in order to occupy himself in the workshops.[57]

5. The 'total expropriation' of the prisoner (being seen without seeing) gradually breaks down the 'boundary that the individual places between his being and the environment',[58] and in this way, 'the embodiment of self' is profaned.

6. These standardised processes, by means of which the inmate's 'self' is mortified, induce the manipulated subject to assume – by way of defence – the 'practice of simulation': or better: the 'external reproduction' of behaviour deemed ideal by the administration.[59] On this point, de Beaumont and de Tocqueville acutely observe:

> We have no doubt, but that the habits of order to which the person is subjected for several years, influence very considerably his moral conduct after his return to society. The necessity of labour which overcomes his disposition to idleness; the obligation of silence which makes him reflect; the isolation which places him alone in presence of his crime and suffering; the religious instruction which enlightens and comforts him; the obedience of every moment to inflexible rules; the regularity of a uniform life, in a word, all the circumstances of belonging to this severe system, are calculated to produce a deep impression upon his mind.

Perhaps, leaving the prison he is not an honest man; but he has contracted honest habits.[60]

In the extracts we have selected[61] madness and simulation, bewilderment and hypocrisy abound; a hotchpotch of attitudes which, though antagonistic, describe a state of profound degradation and subordination on the part of the 'institutionalised being'.

Inmate No. A This prisoner knows how to read and write; has been convicted of murder; says his health, without being bad, is not so good as when he was free; denies strongly having committed the crime, for which he was convicted; confesses to having been a drunkard, turbulent and irreligious. But now, he adds, his mind is changed; he finds a king of pleasure in solitude, and is only tormented by the desire to see once more his family, and to give a moral and Christian education to his children – a thing which he had never thought of when free.

Q.   Do you believe you could live here without labour?
A.   Labour seems to me absolutely necessary for existence. I believe I should die without it.
Q.   Do you often see the wardens?
A.   About six times a day.
Q.   Is it a consolation to see them?
A.   Yes, Sir; it is with joy I see their figures. This summer, a cricket entered my yard; it looked to me like a companion. If a butterfly, or any other animal enters my cell, I never do it any harm.

Inmate No. B A young man; confesses to being a criminal; sheds tears during our whole conversation, particularly when he is reminded of his family. "Happily," he says, "nobody can see me here;" he hopes then to return into society without being stamped with shame, and not to be rejected by it.

Q.   Do you find it difficult to endure solitude?
A.   Ah! Sir, it is the most horrid punishment that can be imagined!
Q.   Does your health suffer by it?
A.   No: it is very good; but my soul is very sick.

Q.   Of what do you think most?

A.   Of religion; religious ideas are my greatest consolation.

Q.   Do you see now and then a minister?

A.   Yes, every Sunday.

Q.   Do you like to converse with him?

A.   It is a great happiness to be allowed to talk to him. Last Sunday, he was a whole hour with me; he promised to bring me tomorrow news from my father and mother. I hope they are alive; for a whole year, I have not heard of them.

Q.   Do you think labour an alleviation of your situation?

A.   It would be impossible to live here without labour. Sunday is a very long day, I assure you.

Q.   Do you believe your little yard might be dispensed with, without injury to your health?

A.   Yes, by establishing in a cell a continued current of air.

Q.   What idea have you formed of the utility of the system to which you are subject?

A.   If there is any system which can make men reflect and reform, it is this.

Inmate No. C Was convicted for horse-stealing; says he is innocent. Nobody, he says, can imagine the horrid punishment of continued solitude. Asked how he passes his time; he says there are but two means – labour, and the Bible. The Bible is his greatest consolation. He seems to be strongly actuated by religious ideas; his conversation is animated; he cannot speak long without being agitated and shedding tears. (We have made the same remark of all whom we have seen so far.) He is a German by birth; lost his father early, and has been badly educated. Has been above a year in the prison. Health good.

Inmate No. D A negro of twenty years of age; has received no education, and has no family; was sentenced for burglary; has been fourteen months in the penitentiary; health excellent; labour and visits of the chaplain are his only pleasure. This young man, who seems to have a heavy mind, hardly knew the letters of the alphabet previously to his entering the penitentiary; he has, however by his own exertions, attained to reading fluently his Bible.

Inmate No. E A negro of twenty-four years, convicted of theft a second time; he seems full of intelligence.

Q. You have been a prisoner of Walnut Street. What difference is there between that prison, and this penitentiary?

A. The prisoners were a great deal less unhappy in Walnut Street than here because they could freely communicate with each other.

Q. You seem to work with pleasure: was it the same with you in Walnut Street?

A. No; there labour was a burden, which we tried to escape in all possible ways; here it is a great consolation.

Q. Do you read the Bible sometimes?

A. Yes, very often.

Q. Did you do the same in Walnut Street?

A. No; I never found pleasure in reading the Bible or hearing religious discourses but here.

This prisoner has been here six months; health excellent.

Inmate No. F Convicted of an attempt to commit murder; fifty-two years of age; has seven children; has received a good education; was a prisoner in Walnut Street; makes a frightful picture of the vices of that prison; but believes most of the convicts would prefer to return to Walnut Street, than to enter the penitentiary; they shun solitude so much.

Asked his opinion respecting the system of imprisonment; he says that it cannot fail to make a deep impression on the souls of the prisoners.

Inmate No. G A negro of thirty-four has been convicted for theft once before; eighteen months here; health pretty good.

Q. Do you find the discipline to which you are subject as severe as it is represented?

A. No: but that depends upon the disposition of the prisoner. If he takes solitary confinement bad, he falls into irritation and despair; if, on the contrary, he immediately sees the advantages which he can derive from it, it does not appear insupportable.

Q. You have been imprisoned already in Walnut Street?

A. Yes, Sir; and I cannot imagine a greater den of vice and crime. It requires but a few days, for a person not very guilty to become a consummate criminal.

Q. Do you think that the penitentiary is superior to the old prison?

A. That is as if you were to ask me, whether the sun was finer than the moon?

Inmate No. H Age thirty-eight; convicted of theft; has been here eight months. Health good. Became a shoemaker in the prison, and makes six pairs of shoes a week.

This individual seems to have naturally a grave and meditative mind. Solitude in prison has singularly increased this disposition. His reflections are the results of a very elevated order of ideas. He seems to be occupied only with philosophical and Christian thoughts.

Inmate No. I This prisoner, the first who was sent to the penitentiary, is a negro. Has been here more than two years. His health is excellent.

This man works with ardour; he makes ten pairs of shoes a week. His mind seems very tranquil; his disposition excellent. He considers his being brought to the penitentiary as a signal benefit of Providence. His thoughts are in general religious. He read to us in the gospel the parable of the good shepherd, the meaning of which touched him deeply – one who was born of a degraded and depressed race, and had never experienced anything but indifference and harshness.

Inmate No. J A well-educated man, thirty-two years old. He was a physician.

Solitary confinement seems to have made a profound impression upon this young man. He speaks of the first time of his imprisonment with horror; the remembrance makes him weep. During two months, he says, he was in despair; but time has alleviated his situation. At present, he is resigned to his fate, however austere it may be. He was allowed to do nothing; but idleness is so horrid, that he nevertheless always works. As he knew no mechanic art, he occupies himself with cutting leather for the shoemakers in the prison. His greatest grief is not to be allowed to communicate with his family. He ended the conversation by saying: 'solitary confinement is very painful, but I nevertheless consider it as an institution eminently useful for society.'

Inmate No. K Aged forty. Imprisoned for robbery on the highway with arms in his hand; seems very intelligent; told us his story in the following terms:

> I was fourteen or fifteen years old when I arrived in Philadelphia. I am the son of a poor farmer in the west, and I came in search of employment. I had no acquaintance, and found no work; and the first night I was obliged to lie down on the deck of a vessel, having no other place of rest. Here I was discovered the next morning; the constable arrested me, and the mayor sentenced me to one month's imprisonment with a number of malefactors of all ages. I lost the honest principles which my father had given me; and on leaving the prison, one of my first acts was to join several young delinquents of my own age and to assist them in various thefts. I was arrested, tried and acquitted. Now I thought myself safe from justice, and, confident in my skill, I committed other offences, which brought me again before the court. I was sentenced to an imprisonment of nine years in Walnut Street prison.

Q.   Did not this punishment produce in you a feeling of the necessity of correcting yourself?

A.   Yes Sir; yet the Walnut Street prison has never produced in me any regret at my criminal actions. I confess that I never could repent them there, or that I ever had the idea of doing it during my stay in that place. But I soon remarked that the same persons reappeared there, and that, however great the finesse, or strength of courage of the thieves was, they always ended by being taken; this made me think seriously of my life, and I firmly resolved to quit for ever so dangerous a way of living, as soon as I should leave the prison. This resolution taken, I conducted myself better, and after seven years' imprisonment, I was pardoned. I had learnt tailoring in prison, and I soon found a favourable employment. I married, and began to gain easily my sustenance; but Philadelphia was full of people who had known me in prison; I always feared being betrayed by them. One day, indeed, two of my former fellow prisoners came into my master's shop and asked to speak to me; I at first feigned not to know them but they soon obliged me to confess who I was. They then asked me to lend them a considerable sum; and on my refusal, they threatened to discover the history of my life to my employer. I now promised to satisfy them and told them to return the next day. As soon as they had gone, I left the shop also, and embarked immediately with my wife for Baltimore. In this city, I found easy employment, and lived for a long time comfortably enough; when one day my master received a letter from one of the constables in Philadelphia, which informed him that one of his journeymen was a former prisoner of Walnut Street. I do not know what could have induced this man to such a step. I owe to him my being now here. As soon as my employer had read the letter, he sent me indignantly away. I went to all the other tailors in Baltimore, but they were informed of what had happened, and refused me. Misery obliged me to seek labour on the rail road, then making between Baltimore and Ohio. Grief and fatigue threw me after some time into a violent fever. My sickness lasted a long time, and my money was at an end. Hardly recovered, I went to Philadelphia, where the fever again attacked me. When I was convalescent, and found myself without resources, without bread for my family; when I thought of all the obstacles which I found in my attempts to gain honestly my livelihood, and of all the unjust persecutions which I suffered, I fell into a state of inexpressible exasperation. I said to myself: Well then! Since I am forced to do it. I will become a thief again; and if there is a single dollar left in the United States, and if it were in the pocket of the President, I will have it. I called my wife, ordered her to sell all the clothes which were not indispensably necessary, and to buy with the money a pistol. Provided with this, and when I was yet too feeble to walk without crutches, I went to the environs of the city; I stopped the first passenger, and forced him to give me his pocketbook. But I was arrested the same evening. I had been followed by the persons whom I had robbed, and, my feebleness having obliged

me to stop in the neighbourhood, there was no great pains necessary to seize me. I confessed my crime without difficulty and I was
sent here.

Q. What are your present resolutions for the future?

A. I do not feel disposed, I tell you freely, to reproach myself with what
I have done, nor to become what is called a good Christian: but I
am determined never to steal again, and I see the possibility of succeeding. If I leave in nine years this prison, no one will know me
again in this world; no one will have known me in prison; I shall
have made no dangerous acquaintance. I shall be then at liberty to
gain my livelihood in peace. This is the great advantage which I find
in this penitentiary and the reason why I prefer a hundred times
being here to being sent again to the Walnut Street prison, in spite
of the severity of the discipline which is kept up in this
penitentiary.

Has been in prison a year; health very good.

Inmates Nos. L and M These two individuals are insane. The warden of
the prison has assured us that they arrived in this state at the prison. Their
insanity is very tranquil. Nothing appears in their incoherent speeches
which would justify a suspicion that their unhappy disorder is attribut-
able to the penitentiary.

Inmate No. N Was a physician; has the charge of the pharmacy of the
penitentiary. He converses intelligently and speaks of the various systems
of imprisonment, with a freedom of thought which his situation makes
very extraordinary. The discipline of this penitentiary appeared to him,
taken in its entire operation, mild, and calculated to produce reformation. 'For a well-educated man', he says, 'it is better to live in absolute
solitude than to be thrown together with wretches of all kinds. For all
isolation favours reflection and is conducive to reformation.'

Q. But have you not observed that solitary confinement is injurious to
health? In your quality of prisoner and physician, you are more able
to answer this question than anybody else.

A.   I have not observed, that, on the whole, there are here more diseases than in society. I do not believe that people here feel worse as to health.

Inmate No. O Age thirty-eight years; has been but three weeks in the penitentiary, and seems to be plunged in despair. 'Solitude will kill me', he says, 'I shall never be able to endure my sentence until its expiration. I shall be dead before that time arrives.'

Q.   Do you not find some consolation in your labour?
A.   Yes, Sir; solitude without labour is still a thousand times more horrible; but labour does not prevent me from thinking, and being very unhappy. Here, I assure you, my soul is sick.

This unfortunate man sobbed when speaking of his wife and children, whom he never hoped to see again. When we entered his cell, we found him weeping and labouring at the same time.

Inmate No. P Age twenty-five; he belongs to the most comfortably situated classes of society. He expresses himself with warmth and facility. He has been convicted of fraudulent bankruptcy.

This young man shows a great pleasure in seeing us. It is easily seen that solitude is for him a terrible torment. The necessity of intellectual intercourse with others seems to torment him much more than those of his fellow prisoners who have received a less careful education. He hastens to give us his history; he speaks of his crime, of his standing in society, of his friends, and particularly of his parents; his feelings towards his family were extraordinarily developed. He cannot think of his relations without melting into tears; he takes from under his bed some letters which his family has succeeded in sending to him. These letters are almost in pieces, in consequence of being read so often; he reads them still, comments upon them, and is touched by the least expression of interest which they contain.

Q.   I see that the punishment inflicted upon you seems extremely hard. Do you believe it conducive to reformation?

A. Yes, Sir; I believe that this whole system of imprisonment is better than any other. It would be more painful to me to be confounded with wretches of all kinds, than to live alone here. Moreover, it is impossible that such a punishment should not make the convict reflect deeply.

Q. But do you not believe that its influence may injure the reason?

A. I believe that the danger of which you speak must exist sometimes. I remember, for my part that during the first months of my solitude, I was often visited by strange visions. During several nights in succession, I saw, among other things, an eagle perching at the foot of my bed. But at present I work, and am accustomed to this kind of life; I am not any longer troubled with ideas of this kind.

One year in prison. Health good.

Appendix 2: The Administration of the 'Silent System' (Conversations with G. Barrett, B. C. Smith and E. Lynds)

De Beaumont and de Tocqueville, in their pilgrimage to the North American prison world in the early part of the nineteenth century, visited prisons based on the Auburn silent system. This time, they spoke with the governors, the chief warders and the staff in general; they furnished ample documentation in their report to the French government.

It is interesting to observe from a reading of this rich source how both the *actual situation* and the *ideology* of the penitentiary system emerge with great clarity. We should not forget that in 1830 the dispute over solitary confinement and the silent system divided public opinion, academic polemicists and, of course, the political administrations of the various states without there being any sign as to which of the two systems would eventually triumph. Obviously, the bodies with a direct interest tended to stress the positive aspects of their choice to these illustrious foreign 'visitors' and criticised what occurred in the 'opposing' camps.

Notwithstanding the patently partisan tone of contacts with the prison administration, both direct and by letter, it seems to us that there are two tendencies here which are only apparently contradictory. The first and most obviously ideological, championed by the chief warders, highlights the 'wickedness' of the criminal and the 'moral strength' of punitive process capable of transforming a 'bestial universe' into an army of pious and religious men; the second, decidedly more crude and pragmatic, saw prison as a 'private and productive concern' ruled exclusively by symbols of managerial authority; the cold calculation of the 'manager-entrepreneur', contempt for the mass of the 'convict labourers', economic ruthlessness and deep pessimism about the 'moral regeneration' of the inmate.

Although both these perspectives were undoubtedly presented to the two foreigners in the hope of soliciting their admiration and agreement, we can still see elements of truth in them. In particular, the interviewees inevitably exalted the implacable severity of the discipline imposed when they were asked to give evidence of the difficulties encountered by the administration.

Letter of Mr. Barrett, Chaplain of the Penitentiary of Wethersfield.

Wethersfield.
October 7th, 1831.

To Messrs. de Beaumont and de Tocqueville:
Gentlemen:

The population of Connecticut amounts to about 280,000 souls. During thirty-six years, the old shafts near Timesbury and called Newgate, served as a state prison. The new prison has been inhabited only for about four years.

During the forty years preceding the month of July, 1831, the number of individuals sent to these two prisons amounted to 976. Their crimes were of the following classes; 435 had committed burglary; 139 horse stealing; 78 passing counterfeit money; 41 assault and battery; 47 attempt to commit rape; 3 attempt at poisoning; 1 murder (the punishment had been commuted); 11 robbery on the highway; 1 robbing the mail; 1 bestiality; 60 forgery; 25 misdemeanors; 15 had been committed for attempting to deliver prisoners; 34 for arson; 9 for manslaughter; 4 for rape (the punishment had been commuted); 2 for cheating; 5 for bigamy; 23 for adultery; 16 for breaking fences; 3 for attempts at escape; 9 for theft, to the injury of the prison; 4 for incest; 3 for perjury; and 5 for crimes not known.

There are, in Connecticut, about 3 coloured people to 100 white. In the prison, the proportion of the negroes is about 33 to 100.

Of 182 convicts whom I have examined, there were 76 who did not know how to write, and 30 who had not learned to read.

Sixty had been deprived of their parents before their tenth year; and 36 others had lost them before their fifteenth year.

Of 182, 116 were natives of Connecticut.

Ninety were from twenty to thirty years old, and 18 were sentenced for life.

The prison contains at present 18 women. Some are employed in the kitchen, and in washing for the prisoners; others in sewing shoes.

For a pair of shoes they receive 4 cents; a woman can finish from 6 to 10 pair a day. During night they are in separate cells.

Morning and evening, prayers are said in the presence of the prisoners; passages of the Bible are read and explained to them. The convicts show themselves attentive and collected on these occasions. Every one finds in his cell a Bible furnished by the state, and in which he may read when he likes. Generally they are disposed to this kind of reading. The other day, passing by their cells, I observed 23 prisoners out of 25, who were seriously occupied in reading.

On Sunday, a sermon is preached in their presence, which they never fail to hear with great attention. They often make, afterwards, curious questions respecting the meaning of what they have heard.

When the principles of the Holy Scriptures are impressed on the heart of a convict, it certainly may be believed that his reform is complete: we have reason to believe that this result has been sometimes obtained. I should think that fifteen or twenty of the actual number of prisoners are so affected in this case. It is, however, impossible, so far, to establish this point in a positive way. It is necessary to wait until the state of liberty, and resistance to temptations, finally prove their reformation.

None of the convicts refuse at least religious instruction; and I have not yet found a single one who has shown the least want of respect, when I have come to visit him in his cell.

I have observed that ignorance, neglect on the part of parents, and intemperance, formed, in general, the three great causes to which crime must be attributed.

The majority of convicts show themselves anxious to be instructed. There were some who arrived without knowing a letter, and learned to read within two months. Yet they could make use of the Bible only, and received no other lessons than those which could be given through the grates of their cell.

The result to be expected from a prison depends much upon the character of the keepers. They ought to have moral habits, to speak little, and to be ready to see everything.

If the keepers are what they ought to be; if the convicts, separated during night, labour during day in silence; if continued surveillance is joined with frequent moral and religious instruction, a prison may become a place of reformation for the convicts, and a source of revenue to the state.

I am, respectfully &c.

G. BARRETT, Chaplain of the Prison.

The Opinion of the Chaplain of Auburn Prison, the Rev. Mr. B. C. SMITH.

The fact which, of all others, is the most striking to a person conversant with the religious history of convicts, is that of their great and general *ignorance of the Bible ... Without mentioning particular instances of ignorance, which would scarcely be credited, it is sufficient to remark, that many, upon being questioned, have betrayed their inability to name any one of the books or part of which the Bible is composed ....*

Another fact, little less remarkable, respecting this class of men, is their general ignorance of letters ... and *prevalence of intemperance* among this class of men ... The number of convicts now in this prison is 683; of these, 385 were under the influence of ardent spirits at the time they committed their crimes; and of the number, 219 have acknowledged that either one or both of their parents, or their masters, were more or less intemperate ....

Is not the *proportion of unmarried convicts* also worthy of remark? It would be an interesting subject of inquiry, and perhaps lead to some important conclusions, to ascertain and compare this proportion between married and unmarried adults in the community at large. I have not the means at hand of ascertaining the proportion of marriages among the latter, but give that of the former in this prison, to enable, any one, who may be curious enough, to prosecute to inquiry.

Conversation with Mr. Elam Lynds.

I have passed ten years of my life in the administration of prisons, he said to us; I have been for a long time a witness of the abuses which predominated in the old system; they were very great. Prisons then caused great expense, and the prisoners lost all the morality which they yet had left. I believe that this system would have led us back to the barbarous laws of the ancient codes. The majority at least began to be disgusted with all philanthropic ideas, the impracticability of which seemed to be proved by experience. It was under these circumstances that I undertook the reform of Auburn. At first I met with great difficulties with the legislature, and even with public opinion: much noise was made about tyranny; nothing short of success was requisite for my justification.

Q. Do you believe that the discipline established by you might succeed in any other country than in the United States?

A. I am convinced that it would succeed wherever the method is adopted which I have followed. As far as I can judge, I even believe that in France there would be more chances of success than with us. I understand the prisons in France stand under the immediate direction of government, which is able to lend a solid and durable support to its agents: here we are the slaves of a public opinion which constantly changes. But, according to my experience, it is necessary that the director of a prison, particularly if he establish a new discipline, should be invested with an absolute and certain power; it is impossible to calculate on this in a democratic republic like ours. With us, he is obliged to labour at once to captivate public opinion, and to carry through his undertaking – two things which are often irreconcilable. My principle has always been, that in order to reform a prison, it is well to concentrate within the same individual, all power and all responsibility. When the inspectors wished to oblige me to act according to their views, I told them: you are at liberty to send me away; I am dependent upon you; but as long as you retain me, I shall follow my plan; it is for you to choose.

Q.   We have heard it said to Americans, and we are inclined to believe it, that the success of the penitentiary system must be partly attributed to the habit, so general in this country, of obeying scrupulously the laws.

A.   I do not believe it. In Sing-Sing, the fourth part of the prisoners is composed of foreigners by birth. I have subdued them all, as well as the Americans. Those whom it was most difficult to curb, were the Spaniards of South America – a race which has more of the ferocious animal, and of the savage, than of the civilized man.

Q.   What is then the secret of this discipline so powerful, which you have established in Sing-Sing, and of which we have admired the effects?

A.   It would be pretty difficult to explain it entirely; it is the result of a series of efforts and daily cares, of which it would be necessary to be an eye-witness. General rules cannot be indicated. The point is, to maintain uninterrupted silence and uninterrupted labour; to obtain this, it is equally necessary to watch incessantly the keepers, as well as the prisoners; to be at once inflexible and just.

Q.   Do you believe that bodily chastisement might be dispensed with?

A.   I am convinced of the contrary. I consider the chastisement by the whip, the most efficient, and, at the same time, the most humane which exists; it never injures health, and obliges the prisoners to lead a life essentially healthy. Solitary confinement, on the contrary, is often insufficient, and always dangerous. I have seen many prisoners in my life, whom it was impossible to subdue in this manner, and who only left the solitary cell to go to the hospital. I consider it impossible to govern a large prison without a whip. Those who know human nature from books only, may say the contrary.

Q.   Don't you believe it imprudent at Sing-Sing, for the prisoners to work in an open field?

A.   For my part, I should always prefer to direct a prison in which such a state of things existed, than the contrary. It is impossible to obtain the same vigilance, and continual care from the guardians, in a prison surrounded by walls. Moreover, if you have once completely curbed the prisoner under the yoke of discipline, you may, without danger, employ him in the labour which you think best. It is in this manner, that, the state may make use of the criminals in a thousand ways, if it has once improved the discipline of its prisons.

Q. Do you believe it absolutely impossible to establish sound discipline in a prison, in which the system of cells does not exist?

A. I believe that it would be possible to maintain considerable order in such a prison, and to make labour productive: but it would be quite impossible to prevent a number of abuses, the consequences of which would be very serious.

Q. Do you believe that it would be possible to establish cells in an old prison?

A. This depends entirely upon the state of those prisons. I have no doubt, that, in many old prisons, the system of cells might be introduced without great difficulties. It is always easy, and not expensive, to erect wooden cells; but they have the inconvenience of retaining a bad smell, and consequently of becoming sometimes unhealthy.

Q. Do you really believe in the reform of a great number of prisoners?

A. We must understand each other; I do not believe in a *complete* reform, except with young delinquents. Nothing, in my opinion, is rarer than to see a convict of mature age become a religious and virtuous man. I do not put great faith in the sanctity of those who leave the prison; I do not believe that the counsels of the chaplain, or the meditations of the prisoner, make a good Christian of him. But my opinion is, that a great number of old convicts do not commit new crimes, and that they even become useful citizens, having learned in prison a useful art, and contracted habits of constant labour. This is the only reform which I ever have expected to produce, and I believe it is the only one which society has a right to expect.

Q. What do you believe proves the conduct of the prisoner in the prison, as to his future reformation?

A. Nothing. If it were necessary to mention a prognostic, I would even say that the prisoner who conducts himself well, will probably return to his former habits, when set free. I have always observed, that the worst subjects made excellent prisoners. They have generally more skill and intelligence than the others; they perceive much more quickly, and much more thoroughly, that the only way to render their situation less oppressive, is to avoid painful and repeated punishments, which would be the infallible consequence of insubordination; they therefore behave well, without being the better for it. The result of this observation is, that a pardon never ought to be granted, merely on account of the good conduct of a prisoner. In that way, hypocrites only are made.

Q. The system, however, which you attack, is that of all theorists?

A. In this, as in many other points, they deceive themselves, because they have little knowledge of those of whom they speak. If Mr. Livingston, for instance, should be ordered to apply his theories of penitentiaries to people born like himself, in a class of society in which much intelligence and moral sensibility existed, I believe that he would arrive at excellent results; but prisons, on the contrary, are filled with coarse beings, who have had no education, and who perceive with difficulty ideas, and often even sensations. It is this point which he always forgets.

Q. What is your opinion of the system of contract?

A. I believe it is very useful to let the labour of prisoners by contract, provided that the chief officer of the prison remains perfect master of their persons and time. When I was at the head of the Auburn prison, I had made, with different contractors, contracts which even prohibited them from entering the penitentiary. Their presence in the workshop cannot be but very injurious to discipline.

Q. Wages for the labour of a prisoner, are very low in France.

A. It would rise in the same degree as discipline would improve. Experience has taught us this. Formerly, the prisons were a heavy charge to the state of New York; now they are a source of revenue. The well-disciplined prisoner works more; he works better, and never spoils the materials, as it sometimes happened in the ancient prisons.

Q. Which is, in your opinion, the quality most desirable in a person destined to be a director of prisons?

A. The practical art of conducting men. Above all, he must be thoroughly convinced, as I have always been, that a dishonest man is ever a coward. This conviction, which the prisoners will soon perceive, gives him an irresistible ascendency, and will make a number of things very easy, which, at first glance, may appear hazardous.

During all this conversation, which lasted several hours, Mr. Elam Lynds constantly returned to this point – that it was necessary to begin with curbing the spirit of the prisoner, and convincing him of his weakness. This point attained, every thing becomes easy, whatever may be the construction of the prison, or the place of labour.

Notes

1. M. Foucault, *Surveiller et punir. Naissance de la prison* (Paris, 1975) p. 246.
2. P. Klein, *Prison Methods in New York State* (New York, 1920) p. 281.
3. See pp. 108 ff.
4. See pp. 117 ff.
5. Foucault, *Surveiller et punir*, p. 254.
6. Ibid., ch. 3, pp. 197–229.
7. Ibid., p. 203.
8. M. Horkheimer, T. W. Adorno, *Dialectic of Enlightenment* (New York, 1972) pp. 226–8.
9. See note 93, Chap. 4.
10. See note 94, Chap. 4.
11. Foucault, *Surveiller et punir*, p. 212.
12. P. Costa, *Il progetto giuridico, Ricerche sulla giurisprudenza del liberalismo classico*, vol. I: *Da Hobbes à Bentham* (Milano, 1974) p. 364.
13. Costa, *Il progetto giuridico*, p. 358.
14. Ibid., pp. 334 ff.
15. Besides B. de Beaumont, A. de Tocqueville, *On the Penitentiary System in the United States and Its Application in France* (translated from the French, with introduction, notes and comment by F. Lieber) (Philadelphia, 1833) (New Edition, Southern Illinois Press, 1964) which is still the most reliable source on the US penitentiary. Also of interest are the enquiries conducted in the various States by Reform Societies, amongst which: Philadelphia Association for Alleviating the Miseries of Public Prisons, *Extracts and Remarks On the Subject of Punishment and Reformation of Criminals* (Philadelphia, 1790); R. Sullivan et al., *Report of the Massachusetts Committee, to Inquire into the Mode of Governing the Penitentiary of Pennsylvania* (Boston, 1817); idem, *The Report of the Committee [...] in the Connecticut State Prison* (Hartford, 1833).

16. Costa, *Il progetto giuridico*, p. 373.
17. E. Goffman, *Asylums, Essays on the Social Situation of Mental Patients and Other Inmates* (Harmondsworth: Penguin, 1968) pp. 24 ff.
18. Foucault, *Surveiller et punir*, pp. 240 ff.
19. BPDS (Boston Prison Discipline Society), *Fourth Annual Report*, p. 54.
20. J. Reynolds, *Recollections of Windsor Prison* (Boston, 1834) p. 209.
21. Foucault, *Surveiller et punir*, p. 242.
22. G. W. Smith, *A Defence on the System of Solitary Confinement of Prisoners* (Philadelphia, 1833) p. 75.
23. Beaumont and Tocqueville, *On the Penitentiary System in the United States*, pp. 39–40.
24. In N. K. Teeters, J. D. Shearer, *The Prison at Philadelphia: Cherry Hill. The Separate System of Penal Discipline: 1829–1913* (New York, 1957) pp. 137–8.
25. T. Sellin, 'The Philadelphia Gibbet Iron', *The Journal of Criminal Law and Criminology*, vol. 46 (1932) pp. 11–25.
26. Ibid., p. 20.
27. J. Itard, *The Wild Boy of Aveyron* (London, 1972) pp. 106–7.
28. In Teeters and Shearer, *The Prison at Philadelphia: Cherry Hill*, pp. 154–5.
29. In *First Annual Report*, 1830, p. 9.
30. Beaumont and Tocqueville, *On the Penitentiary System in the United States*, pp. 187 ff. (also see Appendix 1).
31. Ibid., p. 188.
32. Teeters and Shearer, *The Prison at Philadelphia: Cherry Hill*, pp. 141 ff. On the method and type of labour in the Philadelphian prison also see: R. Vaux, *A Brief Sketch of Origin and History of the State Penitentiary for the Eastern District of Philadelphia* (Philadelphia, 1872) pp. 87 ff.
33. J. R. Chandler, *Journal of Prison Discipline and Philanthropy*, no. 14 (1875) p. 63.
34. W. Cassidey, *On Prisons and Convicts* (Philadelphia, 1897) p. 30.
35. F. Gray, *Prison Discipline in America* (Boston, 1847) p. 70.
36. See pp. 130 ff.
37. In O. F. Lewis, *The Development of American Prisons and Prison Customs: 1776–1845* (New York, 1922) p. 86.
38. Rothman, *The Discovery of the Asylum*, p. 106.
39. Ibid.
40. In Government, *Discipline of the New York State Prison* (1834) p. 16.

41. S. G. Howe, *An Essay on Separate and Congregate Systems of Prison Discipline* (Boston, 1846) p. 55.
42. Ibid.
43. Board of Inspectors of Iowa Penitentiary, *Reports for the Two Years ending October, 1, 1859* (Des Moines, Iowa, 1859) p. 10.
44. Beaumont and Tocqueville, *On the Penitentiary System in the United States*, p. 201.
45. Ibid., p. 41.
46. From report of G. Powers (1827, p. II) related by Beaumont and Tocqueville in *On the Penitentiary System in the United States*, p. 44.
47. Reported in Rothman's *The Discovery of the Asylum*, p. 101.
48. Beaumont and Tocqueville, *On the Penitentiary System of the United States*, p. 24.
49. Ibid., p. 26.
50. Ibid., p. 25.
51. BPDS (Boston Prison Discipline Society), *Annual Report, 1826*, p. 36.
52. Costa, *Il progetto giuridico*, p. 373.
53. J. Bentham, *Principles of Penal Law in The Works of J. Bentham*, ed. J. Bowring (New York, 1962) vol. I, p. 425.
54. Goffman, *Asylums*, p. 24.
55. As we have already specified, all references are from the English translation by F. Lieber (1833), of Beaumont and Tocqueville, *On the Penitentiary System in the United States and Its Application in France*, and specifically from appendix No. 10: 'Inquiry into the Penitentiary of Philadelphia, October', pp. 187–98.
56. In Teeters and Shearer, *The Prison of Philadelphia: Cherry Hill*, p. 135.
57. Beaumont and Tocqueville, *On the Penitentiary System in the United States*, p. 31.
58. Goffman, *Asylums*, p. 32.
59. Ibid., p. 63.
60. Beaumont and Tocqueville, *On the Penitentiary System in the United States*, p. 90.
61. Ibid., pp. 187–98.

Conclusions: Contractual Reason and Disciplinary Necessity at the Basis of Punishment by Deprivation of Liberty

Massimo Pavarini

The luminaries who invented liberty also invented discipline.
(M. Foucault, Surveiller et punir. Naissance de la prison, Paris, 1975, p. 247)

The concept of the penitentiary as 'disciplinary apparatus' emerges almost overwhelmingly from the analysis conducted here of the organisational structure of American prisons in the first half of the nineteenth century.

In synthetic terms, we can easily grasp the theoretical kernel of the problem examined here in the following contradiction (it is irrelevant here to qualify this as 'apparent' or 'real'). The hypothesis of a prison as an instrument of the *reformation* of the inmate into a state of submission by means of discipline (the non-'ideological' interpretation of the concept of *re-education*) is historically present in, concomitant with, and essentially interpenetrates with the struggle for codified law, with the struggle for codified punishments and therefore, in the final analysis, for punishment as *retribution* (read: prison punishment as deprivation of a *quantum* of liberty determined abstractly and proportionately in advance).

This aspect – which we will for the moment call antinomic – is readily revealed in the juridical-penal thought of classical liberalism. Bentham,

© The Author(s) 2018
D. Melossi, M. Pavarini, *The Prison and the Factory (40ᵗʰ Anniversary Edition)*,
Palgrave Studies in Prisons and Penology, DOI 10.1057/978-1-137-56590-7_6

for example, while projecting an architectural and paradigmatic model of corrective-disciplinary power for the whole of the bourgeois world,[1] in his work *An Introduction to the Principles of Morals and Legislation*, can at the same time be seen to adhere to that overall reform in penal legislation which puts the 'principle of legality' at the basis of criminal justice.[2] In the same way, although Beccaria himself argues that proportionality between crime and punishment is necessary (thus assuming the principle of retribution as a logical-political necessity),[3] in the third edition of his book (Livorno, 1765) he provides the publishers with a draft frontispiece depicting Justice in the guise of Minerva who, on the one hand, makes a horrified gesture at an executioner who is presenting her with a bunch of mutilated heads, and who, on the other hand, turns approvingly towards certain instruments of labour (hoes, hammers, saws, etc.) as being means of penitentiary education.[4] Again, returning to the North American situation, while Rush, Bradford, Lownes and most of the Quaker philanthropists belonging to the Philadelphia Society for Alleviating the Miseries of Public Prisons struggled for the reform of penal codes, for the abolition of the cruel and bloody laws of the colonial period for the application of enlightenment principles in the legislation of the young American republic, they also sought to transform Walnut Street jail into the first example of cellular penitentiary in history.[5]

An attempt was made to resolve the contradictory nature of certain aspects of the political-juridical debate by giving 'retribution' (proportionality between crime and punishment) and, more generally, 'the principle of codified law' validity as rationalised instances of repressive terror:

> The reasoning of many reformers – it has been said – was simple: penal laws operate, are effective, achieve the aim of prevention and of social control only if [and to the extent that] they impose specified terror rather than the indiscriminate use of terror as such.[6]

The theme of 'codified repression' (as against its indiscriminate application) – in sum, the theme of 'retribution' (as against irrational and politically unreasonable disproportionalities between crime and punishment) – thus came to be interpreted as the purely rationalising will of the juridical penal system, in which rationalisation should be rigorously defined as the need to transform penal law into an instrument – by now conscious – of bourgeois social control, in the sense that 'the invoked rationality of penal law coincided with the necessity of an instrumental character functional to its logic'.[7]

The retributive aspect of punishment – to return to our specific theme – would in this way retain a 'subordinate' position to that hegemonic need which would in turn come to be realised in the disciplinary model of the penitentiary (limited, obviously, to social control or criminal deviancy).The 'contradiction' revealed between *reformation* and *retribution* would therefore become 'apparent' once the latter was instrumentally subordinated to the former.

This interpretation is unsatisfactory in that we do not consider the retributive imperative of punishment (read: rationale) in bourgeois juridical thought to be 'instrumental' and therefore 'ideological'. The interpretation that is more convincing theoretically is the one that grasps the proportionality between crime and punishment as a reflection, on a juridical-penal level, of a form of social relations based on the 'exchange of equivalents', that is, on 'exchange value'.

The uniform nature of 'crime-value' and 'punishment-value', and therefore the logical possibility of comparing the two, together with the essentially 'contractual' nature of punishment, are already the heritage of classic bourgeois speculation. The notion of 'equivalence' as a juridical idea already finds its matrix in the Hegelian 'notion of commodities'.[8] In this light, 'crime' itself must be interpreted as a 'particular variant of exchange' in which the contractual relationship is established *post factum*, after the injury to the norm; the proportionality, therefore, between crime and punishment is necessarily retribution (*Wiedervergeltung*), that is, it is the proportion of exchange.

As has already been shown,[9] Marx himself, later developed the Hegelian thesis as to the 'real' and 'non-ideological' nature of the concept of retribution. He demonstrated how this is capable of reaching its maximum level of differentiation, to the point of objectively realising itself, at the stage of the economic process in which the 'form of equivalent' and the 'principle of exchange' become dominant, that is, in capitalistic society. However, the 'concept of retribution' in this its original formulation, eludes a later process of historicisation: retribution by equivalents from every abstract typology of sanctions (from fines to corporal punishment to capital punishment itself) has yet to find its concrete specificity in prison punishment, that is, in punishment consisting of the deprivation of liberty.

It is only with Pashukanis that the contractual-bilateral thesis of prison punishment reaches its highest point of theoretical elaboration[10]; and it is essential for the validity of the thesis itself that it should only attain its fullest expression in the hypothesis of prison punishment, in punishment by deprivation of liberty.

The idea of the deprivation of an abstractly determined quantum of liberty, as the dominant form of penal sanction can in fact only be realised with the advent of the capitalist system of production, that is, in that economic process which reduces all forms of social wealth to that most simple and abstract form of human labour measured by time.[11]

Punishment in prison – as the deprivation of a *quantum* of liberty – becomes punishment *par excellence* in a society producing commodities; *the idea of retribution by equivalent* thus finds in prison punishment its most complete realisation precisely in so far as (temporary) loss of liberty represents the most simple and absolute form of 'exchange value' (read: value of wage labour).

Having traced prison back – in terms of punishment as deprivation of liberty – to its original *contractual matrix* we can now make sense of certain essential features of the phenomenology of bourgeois legal sanctions; to be precise:

1. Prison as a repressive instrument for the modulation of punishment (days, months, years) can fully satisfy the new need for a different (rigorous) hierarchy of values to be protected by law.
2. The model of the contract (in particular the contract of labour, as we will see) further accentuates the adaptability of the punishment. Retributive punishment is like wages: every circumstance intrinsic to the relationship must be evaluated, every particular intrinsic to the crime must be considered. Prison punishment realises the circumstantiated crime on the level of sanction.

3. The rationalistic stance, the obsession for classification (in which the desire to set out 'differences' is exhausted) finds in the prison sentence the best means for rationalising the repressive system of social control.

4. Prison aspires to a (formally) democratic model of punishment. Having reduced every value to the most simple form of wage labour, punishment by deprivation of liberty is offered to society in our egalitarian and democratic guise. Prison punishment thus becomes the general juridical form of a system of egalitarian rights (in principle). These elements, which derive from the bilateral nature of punishment and which are essential to a comprehension of bourgeois punishment, must then be 're-interpreted' in the light of the real function of the penitentiary apparatus: *reformation* through discipline. The contradiction previously stressed between retribution and reformation can now be reformulated within the following 'antithetical couples':

 I. *moment of right* (in the punishment as retribution); *moment of discipline* (in the punishment as execution)

 II. *formal equality* (in punishment as retribution), *inequality, inferiority, substantial subordination* (in the punishment as execution)

 III. *juridical codification* (in punishment as retribution); *actual arbitrariness* (in the punishment as execution).

The central contradiction of the bourgeois universe is reflected in the microcosm of prison: the general juridical form which ensures a system of egalitarian rights is neutralised by a close-knit web of inegalitarian power-structures which reproduce those politico-socio-economic disjunctures which negate the relations formally cemented by the (contractual) nature of right. We thus witness the simultaneous existence of a *right* and of a *non-* or *counter-right*, or indeed of *contractual reason* and of *disciplinary necessity*. The contradiction at this level of interpretation is 'objective' and in fact reflects the insoluble problem inherent in the capitalist mode of production itself between the sphere of distribution or circulation and the sphere of production or extraction of surplus value.[12]

The *contract* can therefore safely be assumed to be *a basic ideal* of bourgeois political power, provided that the disciplinary principle which sustains the technical apparatus of coercion is recognised as its coessential. If the punishment as deprivation of liberty is structured, then, on the model of 'exchange' (in terms of retribution by equivalent), its execution (read: penitentiary) is modelled on the hypothesis of manufacture, of the 'factory' (in terms of discipline and subordination).

In this light, the paradignmatic model to which the relationship between 'contractual reason' and 'disciplinary necessity' of punishment seems to refer, can be none other than that which prevails in 'labour relations' between 'contract of labour' and 'labour sub-ordination'. In fact:

1. If the contract of labour formally presupposes employer and employee, as free subjects on equal terms, the actual work relationship necessitates the sub-ordination of the worker to the employer. Similarly with the punitive relationship: 'punishment as retribution' presupposes a free man; prison commands a 'slave'.
2. Further, the maximum discretionary power of the employer in his employment of the labour power of his employee coincides historically with the same 'adaptability of the body' of the latter in a manner which is similar to what occurs in the disciplinary relationship in the execution of punishment.
3. Just as a labour contract between equals (horizontal relationship) creates a 'superior' and an 'inferior' so the punishment-retribution creates (or is) the penitentiary sentence, that is, an apparatus of 'vertical relations'.
4. 'Subordination within work' is the exercise of a power conferred by the 'contract'. The 'subordination of the prisoner' is the exercise of power conferred by the 'punishment-retribution'.
5. In the work relationship, the subordination of the employees is (also) 'alienation from/by the means of production'. In the penitentiary relationship the subordination of the prisoner is 'expropriation (also) from/of his own body'.
6. The contractual freedom of the proletarian finds in the 'performance of work with a passive content' (loss of liberty for a *quantum* of time)

its own object. This loss of liberty and autonomy corresponds to the disciplinary power of the employer. In an analogous way in prison punishment: the object of the punishment is the 'deprivation of time' (*quantum* of liberty) which must in the process of execution be lived as subjection.

7. The performance of subordinated work (*labour, travail,* etc.) is painful effort – suffering, 'punishment'-for the worker. The prison sentence, as the content of retribution modelled on the factory, is essentially work.

8. If subordinated work is thus compulsion, prison punishment is the 'highest level' (the terminal and ideal point) of compulsion. Here we have the main ideological function of the penitentiary: the emerging hypothesis of prison as a world in which the material situation of the subjected (prisoner) is always and in every way 'inferior' to that of the lowest worker.

9. The painfulness of subordinated work is directly proportionate to the level of subordination, that is, to the degree to which the employee loses his autonomy and independence. Punishment as a disciplinary apparatus modelled on the example of the factory represents, in terms of loss of total autonomy, the highest point of subordination and thus of suffering.

10. The disciplinary moment of the work relation coincides with the institutional moment, that is, with the entrance of the employee (contractor) into the factory, namely, into the place where the employer (the other contractor) forcibly organises the factors of production. It is the same in punitive relations: the condemned (free subject) becomes subordinated subject (prisoner) on entering the penitentiary.

11. Finally: 'for the worker the factory is like a prison' (loss of liberty and subordination); 'for the inmate the prison is like a factory' (work and discipline).

The ideological meaning of this complex reality can be summarised by the attempt to rationalise and conceptualise a dual analogy: *prisoners must be workers, workers must be prisoners*:

Thus the way, without transitional solution, is open from the organisation of the coercive prison to the organisation of a coercive labour economy. The distinction between the two is so subtle and yet it is not 'qualitative' as to make the same institutional apparatus functional for both.[13]

Notes

1. 'It [the Panopticon] will be found applicable, I think without exception, to all establishments whatsoever, in which within a space not too large to be covered or commanded by buildings, a number of persons are meant to be kept under inspection. No matter how different, or even opposite the purpose ... whether it be applied to the purposes of perpetual prisons in the room of death, or prisons for confinement before trial, or penitentiary-houses, or houses of correction, or work-house, or manufactories, or mad-houses, or hospitals, or schools' in J. Bentham, *Panopticon or the Inspection House*, in J. Bowring (ed.), *The Works of J. Bentham*, vol. IV (New York, 1962) p. 40.
2. J. Bentham, *An Introduction to the Principles of Morals and Legislation*, in J. Bowring (ed.), *The Works of J. Bentham*, vol. I, pp. 1–194.
3. 'If the infinite and obscure combinations admitted of mathematical treatment, there ought to be a corresponding scale of punishments, varying from the severest to the slightest penalty ... If pleasure and pain are the motors of sensitive beings, if the invisible lawgiver of humanity has decreed rewards and punishments as one of the motives to impel men to even their noblest endeavours, the inexact distribution of these motives, will give rise to that contradiction as little noticed as it is of common occurrence, namely, that the laws punish crimes which are entirely of their creation. If an equal penalty is attached to two crimes of unequal injury to society, the greater crime of the two, if it promise a greater advantage than the other, will have no stronger motive in restraint as of its perpetration.' C. Beccaria, *Crimes and Punishments* (London, 1880) pp. 196, 198.
4. From the Introduction by F. Venturi to C. Beccaria, *Dei Delitti e delle pene* (Torino, 1970) p. XVII.
5. See pp. 123 ff.

6. P. Costa, *Il progetto giuridico. Ricerche sulla giurisprudenza del liberalismo classico, vol. I: Da Hobbes à Bentham* (Milano, 1975) p. 267.
7. Costa, *Il progetto giuridico*, p. 366.
8. 'Value as the *inner identity* of things specifically different, has already been made use of in connection with contract, and occurs again in the civil prosecution of crime. By it the imagination is transferred from the direct attributes of the object to its universal nature. Since the essential character of crime lies in its infinitude, i.e. in the breach of its own right, mere external details vanish. Equality becomes only a general rule for determining the essential, namely, a man's real desert, not for deciding the special external penalty. Only when we limit ourselves to equality in the external details are theft and robbery unequal to fine and imprisonment. But from the standpoint of their value and their general capacity to be injuries, they can be equated. To approach as nearly as possible to this equality in value is, as has been remarked, the task of the understanding.' In G. W. F. Hegel, *Philosophy of Right*, trans. S. W. Dyde (London, 1896) para. 101, pp. 98, 99, 100.
9. D. Melossi, *The Penal Question* in '*Capital*' (see note 1 to 1981 Editors' Introduction).
10. 'Deprivation of freedom, for a period stipulated in the court sentence, is the specific form in which modern, that is to say bourgeois-capitalist, criminal law embodies the principle of equivalent recompense. This form is unconsciously yet deeply linked with the conception of man in the abstract and abstract human labour measurable in time. It is no coincidence that this form of punishment became established precisely in the nineteenth century, and was considered natural (at a time, that is, when the bourgeoisie was able to consolidate and develop to the full all its particular features).' In E. B. Pashukanis, *Law and Marxism: A* General Theory, (London, 1978) pp. 180–1.
11. Ibid., p. 181.
12. See Melossi, *The Penal Question in 'Capital'*.
13. Costa, *Il progetto giuridico*, p. 377.

Understanding Punishment Today (2017): The Prison *Without* the Factory

Massimo Pavarini

Chronicle of a Young Man's Work

More than 40 years ago, I wrote *Carcere e fabbrica* with my friend Dario Melossi.[1] This work turned out to be a scholarly undertaking, a bit unripe in several respects. It received, however, unexpected acclaim, especially at the international level, when it came out in an English edition under the title *The Prison and the Factory*.[2] Dario and I wrote the book in only a few months upon returning from a stay in England, and the initial spark for it came from a footnote we came across in Maurice Dobb's *Studies in the Development of Capitalism*.[3] In it Dobb mentioned two Frankfurt sociologists, Georg Rusche and Otto Kirchheimer, noting that in a work of 1939 they had investigated the historical connection between the development of the labor market and punitive systems.[4] We felt compelled to look for this "forgotten" book and found a copy at the library of the London School of Economics.[5] We immediately began work on an

---

Massimo Pavarini had written this chapter in Italian and had it translated into English shortly before passing away on 29 September 2015. The translation was done by Elisabeth Barili and was then revised by Filippo Valente and edited by Dario Melossi.

© The Author(s) 2018
D. Melossi, M. Pavarini, *The Prison and the Factory (40ᵗʰ Anniversary Edition)*,
Palgrave Studies in Prisons and Penology, DOI 10.1057/978-1-137-56590-7_7

257

Italian translation of it, which came out one year after the publication of *Carcere e fabbrica*.[6]

In the same period, Michel Foucault was working on *Surveiller et punir* (later translated as *Discipline and Punish*).[7] From an interview given by Foucault—as well as from a prospective program we gained access to that was listing the topics planned for discussion at the famous and exclusive Collège de France seminars—we learned that he was beginning to take an interest in the history of prisons. We were delighted to see that early on in *Surveiller et punir*, Foucault, ever-sparing in footnote and bibliographic sources, cited Rusche and Kirchheimer as a "great work" that "provides a number of essential reference points."[8] It was only by chance—beginner's luck—that Dario and I rediscovered Rusche and Kirchheimer at about the same time as Foucault, if not before.

This is the story of the genesis of a fortunate book from the mid-1970s.

The Revisionist Penology of the 1970s

The Prison and the Factory, and indeed the whole of the "radical" criminology of the 1970s, differs in several respects from the criminological literature of the same period by virtue of its emphasis and method, and ultimately its quality. But a basic element they all do share, in that they all offer a critical outlook on the social and penal control exercised *in* and *over* democracies marked by mature social institutions. More to the point, as far as the question of penology is concerned, *The Prison and the Factory* belongs to the "revisionist" movement that sees prisons and correctional culture as necessities of modernity, as articulations of that "project" of modernity which at the time was coming under theoretical scrutiny by Macpherson and then Costa.[9] In this radical literature, prisons were conceived not only as "creations" of legal thought but also, and more importantly, as tools with which to produce and preserve a specific politico-economic order, the capitalistic one—and in that emphasis lies the trait that characterizes this body of literature as revisionist in comparison with the then-dominant legal-philosophical literature, in which imprisonment, in accord with the dictates of Whig historiography, was considered as the advanced phase in the evolution of punitive systems. Though critical of the penitentiary, *The Prison and the Factory* views the historical systems of contemporary penality as geared toward inclusive social control. This body of literature is critical, but the critique is framed from within the correctional system itself, and above all it is blind to a change which it cannot see and yet is already afoot.

The Ambiguity of the Correctional Model

In its essence, the experience of resorting to punishment as a way to discipline or, better yet, "domesticate" people expresses a hegemonic project as well as a hope for liberation: As a hegemonic project, its intent is for those who have been excluded from property, the social pact, and citizenship to gain acceptance, and hence inclusion, but only on condition that they are educated and disciplined; at the same time, however, the project also expresses the hope that liberation can be achieved through the birth of class consciousness, through a faith in proletarian virtues.

The idea is, on the one hand, to educate these outcasts into a new dependence on capitalistic rationality, and, on the other, to construct a virtuous path for them to count as a historical subject, the proletariat.[10]

Into this basic ambiguity is woven the rich and contradictory fabric of correctional punishment, that is, of prisons. But, as we will see shortly, this ambiguity is mostly based on two political objectives that often did not make it past an aspirational state.

There is a decisive phase in the correctional ideology of punishment, the phase underway in the second half of the nineteenth century: It is built on the *deficiency* paradigm as key to interpreting deviance/criminality, and it accordingly projects a positivist typological image of the criminal.[11] A deviant, in other words, is one who has "less" and is thus in some way deficient: Reduce or eliminate these deficiencies, and the deviant's social threat is correspondingly reduced or eliminated. In penal policy this entails the aim of special prevention of punishment—a "medical" punishment that can attack the causes of evil. The first step in moving from a culture of illegality to one of legality—for those who are excluded because poor—is accomplished by getting them to learn how to be thrifty, a lesson to be drawn from those who make their living by working. This work culture and the subsequent inclusion of the outcasts in the labor market are necessary steps in any process of social inclusion. The content of this rhetoric is then enriched with the production model known as Fordism, in an effort to convince the "left" of the utility of this pedagogical enterprise. This is the golden age, marked by great optimism, of the policy of re-education through penitentiary pedagogy: the glorious spring of the model of correctional penal justice, which imagines a punishment capable of integrating the nonproletarian by recognizing this class as having the status of proletarian.[12]

As the project of socially including the outcasts by educating them to the wage discipline moves forward, it gets progressively watered down, morphing from a political project to a nostalgic rhetoric. In the welfare states, and at different paces, capitalistic hegemony, on the one hand, and the assimilation of the work discipline, on the other, definitely realize themselves and become a concrete reality. After this first phase, a new one begins that rests on a different paradigmatic basis. The view that ties crime to a lack of education in work culture increasingly falls out of favor, and the same goes for the idea of devoting prison reform to the task of turning out useful men, educated in the wage discipline, or to the task of developing pedagogical practices aimed at integrating the working class.

Since the first half of the twentieth century, penal reform in the West has leaned toward *decarceration*,[13] as if this was its necessary path and rightful destiny—a progressive reformist path toward freedom from the necessity of prison, a freedom to be achieved by tools such as pretrial diversion, reduced sentencing, and alternatives to imprisonment. The aim of socially integrating convicts no longer requires correctional practices through the prison system: Better to place the deviant directly in the care of the community, of society. Penality "in freedom" is granted by evaluating the trustworthiness of the convict: This is the new form of punishment for those who are deemed to have greater "social capital" than others, and hence can be regarded as participating members of society. In the welfare state, the socialization of the marginalized is by now based on a commitment to "care" for them, tackling social complexity and social problems exclusively or primarily by welfare programs.[14]

"Prison and *factory*" thus becomes a metaphor for "prison and *society*." That marks a key transition in modern history, even if both terms—*factory* and *society*—still fall under the sway of the hope that the aim of legal punishment is to bring the deviant into the fold of society.

The third phase in this "ideal" history, in Weber's terms, is the present time. It is marked by the shift from rhetoric and practice of *welfare* to what has regrettably but realistically been defined as *prison fare*. The growth of the "multitude" of outcasts—from the guaranteed-work market as well as from an entitlement system offered by an increasingly impoverished society—makes the project of social order through inclusion more and more politically unrealistic. Now we have the dismal decline of re-education ideologies and the emergence and triumph of social control based on the practice of selective neutralization, in a manner fully consistent with the language of war on the enemy within.[15]

Ergo: Does "prison without the *factory*" amount to "prison without *society*"?

Regardless of how effective metaphors may be in making vivid the point we want to put across, I would say yes.

The Splendor of Punishment That Excludes

Today we are discovering that the prison can work in driving back criminality, by emphasizing the processes of social exclusion (in truth we are not so much *discovering* this phenomenon as we are *rediscovering* it, considering that in earlier times the penal system has already been caught in the grip of a Malthusian logic, however much trustingly perceived as an economic contingency bound to be soon overcome): The prison, and the penal system in general, can be useful in governing and reducing crime only if enabled to select and neutralize those whom the social system cannot include or feels unable to include. The aim of "selective neutralization" originates within a technocratic and administrative culture of punishment: It interprets penal justice as a system that pursues efficient objectives; for example, it gauges its response to the degree of risk and implements strategies by which to control different social groups. The rhetoric that comes out is that of probability and statistical distribution applied to the population that creates social problems.[16]

Not unlike insurance technique, the language of social utility and the government of social risks gradually displace the language of individual responsibility and special prevention in criminal policy. The language of technocratic penology is therefore characterized by an emphasis on systemic and formal rationality.

The administrative government of penal control tends to be constructed around systematic goals that radically differ from the symbolic use of penality. The administrative management of penality responds only to its own internal logic, freed from extra-systemic goals.

The entire correctional arsenal undergoes a radical change of function and meaning: Treatment and therapy, as well as assistance, lose any relation to their special preventive goal. Treatment, therapy, and assistance become useful resources for guaranteeing that the criminal problem is governed to a degree compatible with the penal justice system: They prove to be useful resources in differentiating deviant populations according to their criminal risk, so as to selectively incapacitate the most dangerous elements, articulate the custodial spectrum, and economize resources. Hence, as Pietro Costa remarked in the introduction to his *Progetto giuridico*, "the whole of legal discourse is steeped in metaphor, and in the end it is itself no more than a grand metaphorical construction."[17] I can't think of any better way to capture the gist of the present penal system than through the binomial "prison and *war*." I say this not so much because the practice of widespread or massive imprisonment makes the present prison system look like a "Gulag Archipelago" (in truth, the penitentiary has always resembled more a concentration camp than a factory, and for this opinion I hope I will not be taken to task by Bentham and the vast array of technocratic reformists).

I therefore say "war," thus adding to, while modifying, the notion of punishment, in a sense of re-functionalizing punishment and the penal judicial system toward a rhetoric and a system of stated and hence explicit hostility toward those who are increasingly perceived as "others."

A New Discourse on Crime

This approach to governing criminals reflects a new discourse on crime itself and the role of the criminal justice system. Deviants are no longer, or increasingly less, an object of criminological investigation, because criminology is progressively becoming a marginal chapter in a general analysis of public policy. The concern is no longer with the overambitious, naive aim to beat back crime but simply to rationalize how systems should operate if they are to make it possible to "manage" crime on the basis of statistical and actuarial calculations.

Without any sense of paradox, this approach espouses a different way of approaching criminality, introducing what has aptly been described as "the criminality of everyday life": The deviant act is an habitual risk that can be calculated, and to some extent even avoided, and since there is nothing exceptional or pathological about it, it can be understood simply on the basis of common motivational tendencies. Criminal activity is accordingly seen as routine activity—an opportunity, if not a rational choice. On the premise that it is *opportunity that makes one a thief*, we can rationally reduce the risk of victimization simply by adopting a precautionary lifestyle or investing in a preventive technology that will reduce opportunities or make it more difficult to commit crimes.[18]

This, however, is not a task or duty pertaining only or mainly to the state and the traditional control system: It is rather a "realistic" choice, and ultimately a "duty" of civil society. The range of potential victims includes us all, for we can all potentially be singled out for protection, and in that capacity we are all invited to take up our own defense, by getting organized and adopting different lifestyles. In this sense the state progressively moves away from its monopolistic role protecting society against crime.

This shift has been described by Sandro Baratta in his distinctively lapidary style: "The transition from 'security of rights' to the 'right to security' transforms security into a 'private good.'"[19] Consider in that regard the now-dominant security policy, which almost exclusively invests in situational preventive strategies and thus ends up accustoming us to living "on our own," that is, without placing too much trust in the state prevention system in a society at high criminal risk. And, in the same light, the increasing push toward the compensatory paradigm, supporting the new mediatory strategy in criminal justice, ends up suggesting a refeudalization of social life with premodern nuances.

The consequences of this shift can significantly be appreciated on a cultural level. Criminality, and in particular mass criminality, is ceasing to be investigated from a causal perspective, and so, in the end, it ceases to be an object of knowledge *tout court*. Only on a statistical basis does it continue to be investigated, where it is measured in terms of risk variation. In this sense, it is fair to say that the "new administrative criminology" has profitably taken up the contributions of critical criminology, which is famously anti-etiologic. However, it is significant that the new criminologists, now *maîtres à penser* of actuarial criminal policy, cannot be counted as "criminologists" either academically or in terms of their professional training, for they are in the main statisticians.

Thus, it is not by rooting out the *causes* of criminality that we can defend ourselves against it, for the simple reason that criminal action is not the outgrowth of any particular, personal, or social cause. If we are to ward off criminality as a noxious reality, it will have to be by reducing the risk of victimization, on the one hand, and selectively neutralizing the "enemies," on the other.

There is no doubt that the ideology of selective neutralization, and even more so *preventive* neutralization, is often forced to frame the criminal as the "other," as irreparably "different" from us, taking out of the picture all "fellow feeling" and all understanding of this subject, as well as all formal guarantees of rights—an attitude typical of the so-called criminology of self. Depending on the occasion, the "other" can be a terrorist, a pedophile, a serial killer, a gangster, but is more often a habitual offender.

Alongside "everyday life criminology," there also develops a "criminology of the other," which sees criminals as "enemies," people who cannot be "managed" except by neutralizing them, and since the aim is to disable them, putting them in a condition where they can no longer do any harm, it ultimately doesn't even matter too much whether they are recognized as enemies. Recall the golden rule that now governs criminal policy in the USA: Three strikes and you're out, meaning three convictions and you are "put away for good" under a life sentence. Baseball, from which we get that sentencing rule, offers an apt metaphor for this war, capturing both its defensive side (covering the base) and its offensive side (attacking the strike zone).[20]

On closer inspection we will see that *both* of those criminological theses—that of "everyday criminology" and that of the "criminology of the other"—suggest a warlike approach to the question of criminology. In a state of war, when facing the threat of the enemy, we try to minimize the risk of attack, acting in passive defense, while trying to go on the offense and neutralize the enemy by launching preemptive strikes against him. Defense and attack: The more I make it difficult for the enemy to attack me, the greater will be my chances of success on the field; the more enemies I can neutralize, the fewer will I need to face—except that in a war against the domestic enemy, the enemy of criminality, you don't fight to win, as in baseball, but only to maintain a precarious position of "tactical advantage" in facing the belligerent enemy.

Ultimately, the transition from an inclusive model to an exclusive one in criminal policy is marked by increasingly denying that criminality is an "issue," a problem: There is therefore nothing problematic that needs to be studied, understood, and possibly resolved by going after its cause. In fact, there is no possible alternative to the normality of the present social disorder. Once this disorder is accepted as a matter of course, criminality figures as no more than an inevitable social cost, something to be fought by "military" means and to the extent that the political economic system as a whole will bear (a system whose scope is actually much more constrained than is commonly, and illusorily, believed). And the effectiveness of criminal policy is now only measured exclusively through war bulletins proper, detailing how many enemies have been neutralized (witness the emphasis on the incarceration rate), how many soldiers can be deployed and how much will they cost (witness the emphasis on the costs of criminal justice and the police force), which and how many social and urban territories have been liberated or been occupied by the enemy (witness the emphasis on the rate of criminality across the territory), and so on.

A unique criminology, as we said, whose status as a science no longer hinges on the deviant and the criminal but rather on the management of a permanent state of belligerence, a management often reduced to an accounting equation.

Prison and War

We now have a progressive hegemonization of the criminal question by scholars and officials entrusted with security and penal law. This cadre essentially consists of professionals in the ongoing war. And in a state of war, the military class gains political weight and public visibility. It certainly makes sense to hand the criminal question back to social scientists, while pulling back the role accorded to criminologists and the criminal justice system, but in working toward that goal we first have to put an end to the state of belligerence.

The present state of war has never been explicitly declared. To be sure, some time ago an influential politician of worldwide fame did announce a war on drugs. And his call to action was taken up by other, no less powerful leaders, stating that it was time to move "from studying criminality to fighting criminals." Others said the time had come to "understand less and punish more," but this nonsense—as I should like to call it—is something we've already heard before, and indeed it may well have been with us since politics began. But the truth is different. The truth is that we found ourselves at war without realizing it, and we did not realize it because the war we have been waging against the domestic enemy has progressively convinced us that we have no other choice in facing situations that over time have presented themselves as "emergencies."

The shift from a culture of bulimia to one of anorexia as regards the outcasts,[21] the "wretched refuse" becomes in the end inevitable as a certain point of view becomes progressively hegemonic. The point of view that has become dominant and has persuaded us—which of course does not make this the proper or "true" point of view—is that inclusion through work is no longer possible for everyone in our new globalized economy and, at the same time, that the state is no longer capable of distributing enough social wealth to those who have been pushed out of the market. To return to the previously mentioned metaphor, "prison and society" can no longer be proffered as a model for inclusive social discipline.

As a matter of fact, this point of view is very similar to what historically marked the transition from the "Old Poor Law" to the "New Poor Law," setting off the modern experience of mass deportation of prisoners. But colonial imperialism was then dominant, and the exclusion of the poor and of prostitutes and delinquents from Europe offered a new opportunity of social inclusion, even if on the other side of the globe. Unfortunately, however, there is no Australia to be colonized in the hegemonic story of postmodernism.[22]

We are therefore faced with the necessity, or at least the *perceived* necessity, of defending ourselves against outcasts, even militarily. In the same way, the masses of immigrants who press in around the borders of the First World are driven by a desire for social integration, offering labour and services which do not find a suitable market, and which will in fact never be able to find one. These masses are in the end of no use in the First World. We tell ourselves that—however many we may imprison or keep in the new large concentration camps that are sprouting up across the "civilized" Europe and the North America of habeas corpus, and however many we may keep away at gunpoint from our wealth—the numbers pale in comparison to what is "out there," in a world teeming with outcasts. That much is true. But this was also true in the past as far as coercive practices of social control are concerned. When the paradigm of integration through the work discipline was prevalent, the "prison as factory" domesticated a few tens of thousands in the lumpenproletariat, which is nothing compared to the proletarian masses of the Fordist factory. When in the splendor of the welfare state we tricked ourselves into believing that we could do without prisons and other practices of institutional sequestration because we trusted in a sufficiently disciplined and opulent civil society, the reality of social services was in effect always so marked by a lack of resources that it could only manage to take care of a negligible minority of those in need. That, then, is not the point, and it never has been. Inclusion has never materially come about through the "prison" or through "civil society," just as today exclusion does not come about through the war on crime. The prison, civil society, and war are only pedagogical expressions conforming to distinct "worldviews."

On closer inspection, penal and social-control practices and ideologies in modern and contemporary history can be seen to have always undergone a process of diffusion and expansion that ultimately traces or adheres to the dominant approach to the criminal question (and we can call it "dominant" in the sense that it has been developed in hegemonic countries).

How to treat delinquents is not a matter that in modern and contemporary times has ever been left to the twists and turns of national contingency. In fact, the principle of noninterference in internal affairs never succeeded in containing the dominant cultural attitude to criminality. In fact, the governing of the criminal question is one of the different expressions of how to understand the social order as a whole, and so is eminently the most valuable component a culture on the whole can express. It therefore should not come as a surprise that the historically hegemonic culture—here, that of Western and economically more advanced countries—tends naturally to impose itself and progressively make others accept its own point of view as to what counts universally.

In short, having more or less incarceration in the world (and I say "more or less" more "symbolically" than "materially") seems to have little to do with criminality, with the extent to which the universe of those excluded from the labor market may expand or contract, with the changing ways in which society may represent danger in the large outlying areas of the world. Or rather, there may indeed be a connection there, but in the sense that in the present historical contingency, the increasing criminality and social insecurity, the practice of exclusion imposed by the world economy, the new mobility tied to globalization, the rollback of the welfare state, and so on, act as elements enabling a new moral philosophy to be constructed and take hold, especially in the "capitals" of the world: a point of view that gradually spreads universally and dictates what is good or bad, legal or illegal, worthy of inclusion or exclusion.

Notes

1. Dario Melossi and Massimo Pavarini, *Carcere e fabbrica: Alle origini del sistema penitenziario, XVI–XIX secolo* (Bologna: il Mulino, 1977).
2. Dario Melossi and Massimo Pavarini, *The Prison and the Factory: Origins of the Penitentiary System* (London: The Macmillan Press, 1981).

3. Maurice Dobb, *Studies in the Development of Capitalism* (London: Routledge, 1946, pp. 23, 235).

4. Georg Rusche and Otto Kirchheimer, *Punishment and Social Structure* (New York: Columbia University Press, 1939).

5. To be honest, this rediscovery was due more to luck than to the sleuthing skills of two young scholars from the University of Bologna. Only one copy of the book was held at the library: It had been sitting on the shelves for years and was at serious risk of being left to the "gnawing criticism of the mice."

6. Georg Rusche and Otto Kirchheimer, *Pena e struttura sociale* (Bologna: il Mulino, 1978). New editions in English had come out in 1967, again by Columbia University Press, then reissued in 1968 by Russell & Russell, and would then come out again in 2003 (New Brunswick (NJ): Transaction Publishers). Our Italian translation was followed by a Spanish and a German one, followed by translations in French and Portuguese.

7. Michel Foucault, *Discipline and Punish: The Birth of the Prison*, trans. Alan Sheridan (New York: Vintage Books, 1977).

8. Michel Foucault, *Discipline and Punish: The Birth of the Prison*, cit., p. 24.

9. See C. B. Macpherson, *The Political Theory of Possessive Individualism: Hobbes to Locke* (Oxford: Clarendon Press, 1962), and Pietro Costa, *Il progetto giuridico: Ricerche sulla giurisprudenza del liberalismo classico* (Milan: Giuffrè, 1974).

10. On this point, see David J. Rothman, *Conscience and Convenience: The Asylum and Its Alternatives in Progressive America* (Boston: Little Brown and Co., 1980).

11. See Piers Beirne, *Inventing Criminology: Essays on the Rise of "Homo Criminalis,"* ed. Ronald A. Farrell (Albany: University State of New York Press, 1993).

12. See the recent Michele Pifferi, *L'individualizzazione della pena: Difesa sociale e crisi della legalità penale tra otto e novecento* (Milan: Giuffrè, 2013) (English transl.: Michele Pifferi, *Reinventing Punishment: A Comparative History of Criminology and Penology in the Nineteenth and Twentieth Centuries* (Oxford: Oxford University Press, 2016)).

13. See Andrew T. Scull, *Decarceration: Community Treatment and the Deviant—A Radical View* (New Jersey: Prentice Hall, 1977).

14. See David Garland, *The Culture of Social Control: Crime and Social Order in Contemporary Society* (Oxford: Oxford University Press, 2001), esp. chap. 4.

15. See, among others, Jock Young, *The Exclusive Society: Social Exclusion, Crime and Difference in Late Modernity* (London: Sage, 1997).

16. See Malcolm Feeley and Jonathan Simon, "The New Penology: Notes on the Emerging Strategy of Corrections and Implications," *Criminology* 20 (1992): 440–74; idem., "Actuarial Justice: The Emerging New Criminal Law," in *The Futures of Criminology*, ed. David Nelken, 173–201 (London: Sage, 1994).

17. Costa, *Il progetto giuridico*, cit., p. XIII (my translation).

18. See Marcus Felson, *Crime and Everyday Life* (Thousand Oaks, Cal.: Pine Forge Press, 1994) and James Q. Wilson, *Thinking About Crime*, 2nd ed. (New York: Basic Books, 1983). In Italian criminology, see Marzio Barbagli, *L'occasione e l'uomo ladro: Furti e rapine in Italia* (Bologna: il Mulino, 1995).

19. Alessandro Baratta, "Politica criminal: Entre la politica de seguridad y la politica social," in *Delito y seguridad de los habitantes*, ed. Elías Carranza, 85–95 (San Josè de Costa Rica: Siglo XXI, 1997).

20. Cf. Digby Anderson, ed., *This Will Hurt: The Restoration of Virtue and Civil Order* (London: Social Affairs Unit, 1995), and Joel Best, *Random Violence: How We Talk about New Crimes and New Victims* (Berkeley: University of California Press, 1999).

21. The underlying distinction here is between anorexic and bulimic societies. It was introduced by Jock Young in *The Exclusive Society*, cit., who draws on a similar distinction by Claude Lévi-Strauss.

22. One of the most compelling and interesting books I have come across on the criminal question is by an author who is neither a criminologist nor a historian of penal thought but is rather the most recognized critic of contemporary work on the reconstruction and history of English deportation to Australia: Robert Hughes, *The Fatal Shore: The Epic of Australia's Foundation*, masterfully translated into Italian as *La riva fatale: L'epopea della fondazione dell'Australia* (Milan: Adelphi, 1990).

Index[1]

---

[1] Note: Page numbers followed by "n" refers to notes.

© The Author(s) 2018
D. Melossi, M. Pavarini, *The Prison and the Factory (40ᵗʰ Anniversary Edition),*
Palgrave Studies in Prisons and Penology, DOI 10.1057/978-1-137-56590-7